Uncommon Kingdom

Uncommon Kingdom

The British in the 1980s

STEPHEN
HANDELMAN

Collins   Toronto

First published 1988
by Collins Publishers
100 Lesmill Road, Don Mills, Ontario

Canadian Cataloguing in Publication Data
   Handelman, Stephen
      Uncommon kingdom

Includes index.
ISBN 0-00-217752-8

1. Great Britain – Social conditions – 1945-
2. Great Britain – Economic conditions – 1945-
3. Great Britain – Politics and government – 1979-   . I. Title.

DA592.H36 1988   941.085′8   C88-093636-3

Printed and bound in Canada
by T. H. Best Company Limited

CONTENTS

To the memory of George Orwell,
who asked the right questions
to begin with

PREFACE

I began this book in a room overlooking a quiet London garden and completed it in an apartment thirteen storeys above Moscow. The sheer logistics of arriving at a finished product tested the ingenuity and patience of editors, postal services, family, and friends on three continents. I don't know of any better proof that an author is only one of the links — and not necessarily the most important one — in the process that begins as an ambitious idea and ends on someone's bookshelf.

But I have reason for additional humility. What follows in these pages would never have been possible without the British people, who generously gave their time and insight to help an outsider understand them better. Recalling their angry, cheerful, or sardonic voices as I sat hunched over my computer never failed to remind me that this book is more theirs than mine. They are responsible for neither my conclusions nor my mistakes, but if they can recognize something of what they tried to share with me, I will be satisfied that one of my aims has been achieved.

I owe a special debt to my employer, the *Toronto Star*, and in particular to Ray Timson, now executive editor, and Joe Hall, foreign editor, for allowing me a leave of absence to do the necessary research, for tolerating the painful apprenticeship of an author, and for giving me the privilege of reporting from Britain.

There are many other debts that could never be repaid, particularly to those friends in Britain and Canada who read and commented on parts of the manuscript, suggested ideas, or sometimes just kept me going. They

PREFACE

include John and Mary Bastick, Rupert Cornwall, Steve and D'Arcy Farlow, John Fraser, Carol Goar, Sandra Gwyn, Joe Hall, John Honderich, Paul Koring, Neil and Polly Landsberg, Don Miller, Gail and Brian Mooney, John and Joan Petit, Leslie Plommer, Elizabeth Tollington, Phillip Winslow, among many others. I am grateful to Adam Linford, John Gillen and the staff at the British Central Office of Information for their help in arranging some of the interviews, and similarly to John Ledlie at the Ministry of Defence. I owe special thanks to my sister, Janet Weingarden, and her husband, Mitchell, to my parents-in-law, Jack and Janet Simpson, and of course to my parents, Theodore and Phyllis.

I also couldn't have done without the "courier" services of Bill Cobbin, Lawrence Martin, Michael McIvor, and Mary and Nick Dejevsky in getting parts of the manuscript to London and to Toronto from Moscow — not to mention their interest in the project.

Joy Law, my researcher in London, saved me from some embarrassing mistakes, and her growing fascination with the subject kept me inspired. Without the help and good humour of Marion Finlay, the *Toronto Star*'s assistant bureau manager in London, this project would have taken twice as long to complete.

Nancy and Stan Colbert, agents and now friends, took the first risk in fashioning a solid idea out of a journalist's pretensions. Chuck Macli and Jan Whitford at Collins in Toronto and freelance editor Anne Holloway proved beyond any doubt that there are saints in the publishing business.

Curious strangers who bother to read authors' prefaces know the last acknowledgement is always the most emotional, since it's usually reserved for the person to whom the author owes the greatest debt. My wife Susan discovered to her astonishment she had married not only a husband but a book. She knows better than anyone what it cost — and she endured.

Stephen Handelman
Moscow, October, 1987

Introduction
THE "DEAR OLD TROLLEY"

There'll always be an England
While there's a country lane,
Wherever there's a cottage small
Beside a field of grain.

— *Music hall song of the Second
World War.*

Journalists love statistics. We pore through the strangest collections of figures, like pathologists in a lab, searching for hidden causes and hoping for sudden flashes of insight. But a survey published in Britain in 1985 startled me. The people of England, Wales, and Scotland, the survey claimed, were among the happiest on the globe.

On a "World Happiness League" table of 20 major nations, Britain came a surprising third. Supposedly happy, lifestyle-conscious North America didn't have a chance. Americans occupied a dismal seventh place and Canada came sixth. The Japanese, according to the table, were an unhappy fourth from the bottom. The only people happier than the British, it seemed, were the Irish, who came first, and the Northern Irish, who were second.[1]

Someone, I thought, was playing a tasteless joke.

When the "happiness poll" appeared, I was living in the United Kingdom as correspondent for the *Toronto Star*. For nearly five years, I had been interviewing countless Britons who were the victims of unemployment and social conflict on a scale not seen in the country since before the Second World War, and I had met many of the notable figures in Britain's political and cultural life. A number of those with whom I had spoken were angry. Some wondered how their country would survive; others were frankly complacent. I could think of few who were actually happy.

Something even stranger had happened almost a year before the survey was published. On January 23, 1985, Harold Macmillan, former prime minister of Britain, had risen from his seat in the House of Lords to deliver an unusual speech. The murmur of conversation in the crimson chamber died away, and the fidgeting stopped. The assembled peers, preparing to be entertained by "Supermac's" usual oratorical brilliance, leaned forward.

Harold Macmillan was then 90 years old, a wraithlike figure in blue pinstripes. He had achieved the dignity that comes to politicians only in the twilight of their lives. Like other ageing leaders of the British establishment, he was honourably retired to Britain's ancient upper house, where he bore the decorous title of Earl of Stockton. Although his listeners occasionally squirmed with embarrassment when they recalled how he had assured them, as prime minister in 1957, that they had "never had it so good,"[2] he could still turn a speech into a performance as gripping as any on a West End stage. On that day in 1985, their lordships were debating the future of Britain, and the earl did not disappoint his admirers.

Macmillan's voice was weak at first, barely rising above a whisper. He called on memories of an earlier time, when British power and civilization dominated the world. He was one of the few left, after all, who could still remember the Empire's days of glory. Stirring phrases drifted in and out of the great, silent hall. He stamped his cane on the floor for emphasis, and his voice grew stronger.

The British people would have to make an important choice, he said, a choice as decisive as any faced by generations stretching back through Britain's long, remarkable history. "Do we just majestically sink, go slowly down like a great ship?" he asked. "Or make a new, united, determined effort?" He paused for effect. Macmillan knew his remarks would travel beyond his parliamentary audience. The lords, after several years of debate, had allowed television cameras inside their chamber for the first time. Macmillan was aware that he was broadcasting his challenge to a younger generation of Britons who would see his performance on the evening BBC-TV news. "Let us hope," he began again, "that historians will not describe the end of this century as the decline and fall of Britain... but as the beginning of a new and glorious renaissance."

It was as if a venerable relic had jumped off the museum shelf to quarrel with its curators. Until the early 1980s, the decline of British prestige and industrial strength was virtually accepted as fact by British historians and economists. In the houses of Parliament, in the Church of England, in pubs, and in letters to the editor of *The Times*, the only debate was over how to prolong the inevitable. Britain's transformation into a quiet backwater nation of the late twentieth century was regarded as merely a matter of time.

The elderly former prime minister's challenge seemed more poignant for having come too late. The British landscape was scarred by one of the worst industrial crises in the West, and the 1980s were already proving to be one of the most traumatic decades in British history. In fewer than ten years, the country that had "invented" the industrial revolution had suffered the loss of a major part of its manufacturing base. Large sections of the nation had slid from first-world prosperity to third-world poverty. Statistics confirmed the widespread view that the welfare state had become the West's welfare case.

Between 1979 and 1986, the number of unemployed Britons climbed officially from 1.3 million to the Depression-era level of over 3 million. The unofficial figure was closer to 4 million. For the first time since the mid-nineteenth century, Britain experienced a deficit in international trade.[3] Even during the recent oil-induced recession, no other Western society had experienced such huge increases in unemployment and such massive economic dislocation.

But as I considered the happiness poll and the brave new world outlined by Macmillan, I began to wonder whether I had missed something. It would not have been the first time visitors to Britain had jumped to wrong conclusions on the basis of a selective use of evidence.

The nineteenth-century American novelist Henry James, who settled in England after a long flirtation with the country, was an enthusiastic admirer of what he saw — or thought he saw — around him. "It is difficult," he wrote in 1879, "to imagine any combination of adverse circumstances powerful enough to infringe very sensibly upon the appearance of activity and prosperity, social stability and luxury, which English life must always present to a stranger."[4] At that time, however, England was in the middle of another economic crisis. America and Germany were beginning to challenge Britain's position as the "furnace of the world." The loss of markets abroad and the first hints of industrial decline sent shudders through the colonial administrators of the Empire.[5] If James could be beguiled by the "appearance of ... stability and luxury," was it possible, more than a century later, to be equally misled by the "evidence" I had seen of decay and decline?

This book argues that it was possible. The happiness poll, if it could be believed, indicated there was more in Britain's industrial crisis than met the eyes of the casual observer, and certainly much more than was portrayed by the gloomy statistics of decline. Nor was the poll the only clue. If an observer were looking for them, signs of new life were visible throughout the derelict landscape of Britain's postindustrial society.

But few people bothered to look. Britain's condition in the 1980s lent itself easily to the opposite interpretation. Most foreign observers, and many British ones, tended to emphasize the disturbing trends that confirmed their political biases or private experiences. It was hard to deny the strength of their arguments. "I wouldn't go back there to live for any-

INTRODUCTION

thing," said one of my British-born editors before I left Canada. "It's a dead place." Britons still living on their sceptred isle could be even more stinging. Turn the pages of any British magazine or newspaper, and you were likely to find some patriot comparing the grey rigidities of his homeland to somewhere like South Africa or Eastern Europe.

I had visited Britain only once before in my life, during the year of the Queen's Jubilee in 1977, and the experience had left me with a tourist's typically awestruck impression of old-world pageantry and style. Nevertheless, I knew what my editor meant. The United Kingdom, except for occasional flashes of brilliance in pop music and the arts, no longer appeared to count in the world. It was now a country of petty preoccupations and limited opportunities.

Most Britons lived their lives accordingly. By the 1980s, Britain was already one of the world's most thoroughly leisure-oriented societies. The "startling eccentricities" James had noted a century earlier were now the hobbies of a bird-watching, games-mad, pleasure-seeking population that sometimes made Californians look like anchorites.

At home, the British spent long hours in front of their television sets or computer games. Abroad, they had become inveterate hedonists. More than two-thirds of the British adult population, some 16 million people, annually took their holidays out of the country, bundling cars, dogs, and suntan oil onto the cross-Channel ferries for two weeks in the Greek islands or on the Spanish "Costa del Dole," nicknamed for the unemployment insurance recipients said to be seen there. Britain, in the words of one observer, was already a nation in "semiretirement."

The British were armchair aficionados of sex and crime. Fleet Street tabloids, boasting the largest daily circulations in the English-language world, churned out some of the world's most titillating, and most inventive, stories for their millions of avid readers. They had some excellent material to work with. In one two-week period in early 1987, "home news" on the front pages of the national newspapers of a country that had once soberly administered the affairs of millions around the world focused on the love affair between a knighted company director and his teenage mistress, and on a trial in the Old Bailey of a middle-aged woman who "entertained" members of the British establishment with private predilections for whips and leather.

The adventurous spirit of the Empire was now subsumed in a taste for the bizarre and eccentric, like the homicidal civil servant in 1982 who lured victims into his North London home for tea and then neatly disposed of their severed remains in the local sewers, and in intensely fought campaigns to preserve "real ale" or keep ancient woods and marshlands out of the hands of developers.

The past invariably received more solicitous attention than the present.

INTRODUCTION

The British had already turned much of their heritage into a profitable business. An annual influx of some 14 million foreign visitors made tourism one of the country's few growth industries. Shakespeare's birthplace in Stratford-upon-Avon shared space with a McDonald's hamburger franchise and countless souvenir shops, and crusty auctioneers at Sotheby's were taking bids for Beatles' memorabilia. Aristocrats turned their family castles into bed-and-breakfast inns, and the grounds of their estates into safari parks. Yet even in the face of this commercialism, British institutions remained among the most archaic and secretive in the modern world. An Australian, finding himself in a British courtroom, imagined he "had been transported back in time to a wonderland of wigs and starched collars, of liveried courtiers and secret passageways ... deposited amidst an eternal, antique stage play."[6]

But the British could not always keep sole ownership of their traditions. Some of their most famous monuments had already fallen into the hands of foreigners. An Arab millionaire owned Harrod's. An American was in charge of *Burke's Peerage,* which is to British bluebloods what the *Oxford English Dictionary* is to the English language. "How shall we recognize each other?" lamented *The Times*, when it appeared that even the bowler hat, the eternal trademark of the Englishman, was losing out to hatlessness among the new breed of foreign entrepreneur in the City of London.

The British aristocracy, still the most enduring of the species, continued to exert a powerful grip on the popular fancy. Of all the props that surrounded the British in their old age, the most antiquated were the class divisions handed down from the High Victorians and the salad days of Empire. Newcomers often found themselves embarrassingly lost within the maze of the British class structure. A Scandinavian couple I knew who moved into an apartment block in the polyglot Earls Court neighbourhood of London once tried to invite their neighbours in for a get-acquainted drink. A friendly fellow tenant advised them it was the wrong thing to do. "Some of the people in the building are tradesmen, plumbers, electricians," he sniffed. "It won't get you off on the right foot." The persistence of such Victorian distinctions was hard to explain when one realized that the electrician and plumber often earned more than the "gentleman." Nevertheless, class "identity" provided a consoling sense of security in Britain that probably has no parallel in the Western world. *The Economist* magazine once conducted a poll in which it discovered that a majority of those Britons who considered themselves "working class" actually earned an income that allowed them middle-class lifestyles. However, such incongruities between form and content also suggested Britons were hiding a lot more behind their carefully constructed shelters of tradition and custom than most outsiders suspected.

In the face of their country's industrial problems many Britons enjoyed a relaxed, tolerant way of life that would be the envy of pressured North Americans. Their laid-back approach was not necessarily the product of industrial languor. Britain is one of the few modern countries where mail is delivered to private homes twice a day. And the widespread British air of contentment was not confined to those who could afford untroubled lifestyles. Young people, including both the unskilled and university graduates who were unable to find jobs, were part of a thriving "unemployment culture." Sustaining themselves with state assistance, they used their time away from formal work to produce some of the most interesting developments in British rock music and design, and they formed one of the largest and most profitable markets in the country for new films, records, and consumer goods. Intriguingly, both Macmillan's speech and the happiness poll underscored some of the earlier predictions about Britain.

The economist J.K. Galbraith observed as early as 1977 that the British were showing indications of "living out the concern for some more leisurely relationship with industrial life that other people have been discussing for 50 years or more."[7] A reporter for the *Washington Post* in the late 1970s called Britons the "first citizens of the postindustrial age," because, he said, they were clearly choosing leisure over material progress.[8] The choice was not necessarily a conscious one. The British often felt as if they were swept up in forces beyond their control. "We're like people sitting on a dear, lumbering old trolley," actor Simon Callow commented. "We just all trundle along with it, not knowing where we're going, or why we're going, and fighting sometimes amongst ourselves." Nevertheless, despite the self-mocking, "dear old trolley" tone they used to protect themselves from the prying eyes of foreigners, Britons were eagerly, and occasionally profitably, finding ways to exploit the opportunities presented by decline.

By the time Harold Macmillan rose to speak in the House of Lords, the "stage play" Britons put on for foreigners was turning into a revival. The British genius for innovation and invention was returning to the spotlight. More than half the new ideas and techniques adopted by manufacturers around the world during the decade originated in the United Kingdom.[9] British styles and fashions — punk, Sloane Ranger, Brideshead aristocrat — were news in Paris and New York. The special magnetism of British rock music returned in the outrageous shape of Boy George to capture a new generation of fans around the world. The British were asserting themselves in an astonishing variety of fields. Three of Andrew Lloyd Webber's musicals played at the same time on Broadway, a show business record. British business seemed to have a completely un-British vigour. A long-haired pop tycoon named Richard Branson, who lived on a houseboat in the middle of London, made such a success of budget trans-Atlantic flights that the prestigious *Wall Street Journal* ran an interview with him on its front page. A young computer wizard named Alan Sugar marketed millions of his low-priced Amstrad computers across Europe and the U.S.

The politics of the postindustrial kingdom was similarly impossible to ignore. Margaret Thatcher, the West's first woman prime minister, became the most widely known British leader abroad since Churchill, and she lent her name to a new ideology. "Thatcherism" was admired, copied, and occasionally despised throughout the industrialized world. Even the reform-minded new leader of the Soviet Union, Mikhail Gorbachev, was known to believe that there were valuable lessons in the Iron Lady's single-minded attack on the inefficiencies of a tradition-bound society.[10]

A war halfway across the world in the Falkland Islands in 1982 had restored a sense of nationalist pride. Despite the disintegration of British industry, a consumer boom was under way. "They used to call this country a nation of shopkeepers," one astonished British expatriate said after an afternoon struggling through crowded stores; "now, it's a nation of shoppers." Inflation had dropped from double-digit levels to below five per cent, a remarkable achievement for an otherwise battered economy.

The message delivered by Macmillan reached a newly receptive audience. Industrial decline did not have to be an epitaph for Britain. In a world preoccupied with postindustrial change, Britons could still be winners.

"Somewhere ahead lies greatness for our country again," Margaret Thatcher had said during the British national election campaign of 1979. "Look at Britain today and you may think that an impossible dream. But there is another Britain...a Britain of thoughtful people, tantalizingly slow to act, yet marvellously determined when they do."

Thatcher's scrappy optimism was one of the factors that contributed to her election as prime minister. It is no coincidence that the changes in British life and values recorded in the following chapters encompass the period of her government. Although this is not a book about "Mrs. Thatcher's Britain," some of the reasons for the surprising vitality of the British in the 1980s are directly traceable to the political revolution led by the daughter of a Lincolnshire shopkeeper.

Her supporters say Thatcher has already achieved the economic and social transformation of the country. Her critics regard her as disaster. No one has doubts about her impact. "Thatcherized" Britain would be largely unrecognizable to visitors whose last glimpse of the country was in the 1970s. Repeatedly, in interviews conducted for this book, I found a grudging acknowledgement even among her critics that many of the most hopeful developments covered in the following chapters would never have occurred without Margaret Thatcher. A large number of those developments, as it happened, were unplanned. Thatcher has failed in her attempt to forge a thrusting, entrepreneurial culture out of the wreckage of Britain's industrial base. But she has lent validity to the search for new alternatives, and the responses to her efforts revealed a new energy and sense of national accomplishment among a people who had been almost persuaded of their own inevitable decline.

There have been other periods during this century when Britain has hovered between crisis and transformation, only to sink back into the status quo. The significant fact about the 1980s was that the status quo was discredited, if not destroyed. Some of Thatcher's most vociferous opponents regarded this change in attitude as the best result of all: shorn of the last of its illusions, Britain now had a chance to build a new society.

The transition to such a new society has been far from easy. In a "job centre" operated by the National Manpower Services Commission in Newcastle-upon-Tyne, I met Jack Pallas, a dapper 59-year-old who had just lost his job in a shipyard. "I was working as a foreman for 29 years and the boss called me in to tell me I was surplus to requirements," he said. "I asked him for his reasons and he said, 'We don't give reasons.' I said, 'If you're going to cut my legs off, you've got to give me reasons.'" Pallas was about to attend a training course arranged by his union and former firm. But at his age, he didn't expect to find a job again. "Can you imagine being 'surplus to requirements'?" he said. "I don't even know what that means."

The deindustrialization of Britain left in its wake thousands of Jack Pallases in varying degrees of shock. During the Thatcher era, many Britons became angrier, poorer, more violent, and less tolerant of each other than they had ever imagined they could be. The safety-net welfare system conceived with such golden promises after the war had turned shabby and bureaucratic.

The term "British disease" entered the modern vocabulary in the 1970s as a synonym for chronic industrial conflict. During the 1980s, bitter strikes like the 18-month walkout by coal miners seemed to turn labour unrest into a malignant illness. Race riots, urban terrorism, and inner-city violence made Britons uneasily aware of their vulnerabilities. Their own leaders were not immune to the troubles usually associated with more unstable states: an attempt by Northern Irish terrorists to assassinate the British prime minister and her cabinet by blowing up the seaside hotel where they were attending a political conference came close to succeeding. The British even appeared to have lost control of their foreign policy. Their American allies had turned the soldiers of the former imperial army into guards of nuclear cruise missiles and had used bases on British soil to wage war on Libya. Decisions taken by their European partners in the Common Market further threatened the acute British sense of sovereignty.

But even the most troubling aspects of British national life in the 1980s contained signs of Macmillan's "renaissance." A rich inventory of responses to traumatic industrial change was evident. The British Isles, I discovered during my long stay as a guest, were filled with the most fascinating survival stories of a tumbledown civilization. "Something happened in the 1980s," I was told again and again by unemployed people, millionaire industrialists, political activists, Shakespearean actors, and peers of the realm.

The British experience seemed to prove the adage that, if you wait long enough, history will catch up with you. Despite being the world's first industrial power, Britain had always been suspicious of the industrial ethic. Even at the dawn of the machine age, English thinkers like John Stuart Mill looked forward to a time when the clamour for profit could be replaced by a more serene, inventive, and imaginative approach to life. Anti-industrial attitudes sharpened as the British industrial machine began to seize up. "We don't really need more technological gadgets," Nicholas Albery, a young London psychotherapist, told me. Albery, who founded the Institute for Social Inventions to find constructive ways of exploiting industrial obsolescence, argued that Britain needed to opt out of the race for a technological utopia. "We need to slow down, really. If you're on a cliff, it's crazy not to go backwards."

Albery was not alone. Across Britain's landscape of abandoned factories and shut-down steel mills, numerous lateral thinkers were looking for ways of making the concept of living with diminished expectations relevant to the British crisis. Heirs to the alternative politics of the 1960s, they had read Leopold Kohr's 1957 book, *The Breakdown of Nations*, and its successor, Edward Schumacher's *Small Is Beautiful*, which appeared in 1974. Theories and ideas born out of 1960s prosperity became living experiments in Britain. Questions such as the future of work, the relationship between technology and unemployment, and the role of government in maintaining public services — all of which had occupied some of the best minds in the West for years — became survival issues in Britain.

A few days after Macmillan's "renaissance" speech in 1985, one national newspaper claimed to see a "phoenix economy" already rising out of the ashes of deindustrialization, a self-reliant postindustrial society based on cooperatives, part-time business networks, and community projects that tapped the huge pool of unskilled and permanently unemployed Britons.[11] This was not quite the original Thatcher vision. But in the search for alternative routes out of their industrial dilemma, there was a strange convergence between Thatcherites and their most radical opponents. Sharply conflicting views of politics and society sprang from a similar rejection of traditional postwar economic thinking, and took a shared inspiration from Britain's past.

"A new set of values, resting far more on cooperative self-reliance and far less on either collectivism or individualism, is taking shape," claimed

INTRODUCTION

David Howell, a member of the Thatcher cabinet, in 1986: "Maybe these were always the predominant values in man's nature, lost somewhere in the ferment of the industrial revolution and its huge centralizing and massifying tendencies. Or maybe the vast power which the information revolution now disperses into individual hands gives fresh opportunities for this side of people's character and inclinations to flourish where it had been prevented and diverted before."[12]

Such ideas, coming from both the right and left of the British scene, challenged the traditional views of British decline as an inevitable and unproductive process. Fifty years before Macmillan's speech in the House of Lords, British historian Arthur Bryant could already see the handwriting on the wall for Britain's industrial supremacy — and he found little to complain about: "Now the wheel has come full circle again," he wrote. "The pursuit of wealth and power seems no longer to interest us. It may well be that the next 50 years may witness a return to our traditional British role of preaching and practising quality, and of once more teaching the nations how to live."[13] Bryant's prediction is a long way from fulfilment. But in the 1980s, observers from other industrialized societies began to look at Britain with a healthy respect.

"We Europeans have watched Britain waking up from her long sleep," said Giovanni Agnelli, president of Fiat.[14] International interest in Britain's experience was not just academic. In a revised version of his classic book, *Anatomy of Britain*, British commentator Anthony Sampson raised a question that could not be far from the minds of most Western policy-makers. "Britain, the first industrial nation, was the first [in the 1970s and 1980s] to show many ominous signs of the running down of an advanced capitalist society, and other countries were watching anxiously for their own symptoms of 'the English disease,'" he wrote. "Was Britain the forerunner of every late industrial state?"[15]

Symptoms of age, uncertainty, and weariness were already visible throughout Western Europe, North America, and even Japan in the 1980s. The West's largest economy, the United States, was showing early signs of the British disease. During this decade, according to one economist, the U.S. "experienced growth rates of output per head and industrial productivity as low as those in Britain."[16]

The experiences of the British in the 1980s could therefore tell something about the potential survival of the industrial West. Britain, to borrow a phrase coined by a Canadian friend living in London, was a sort of "Distant Early Warning line" for the rest of Western industrial civilization.[17] The British themselves would say they have been there before.

This book is not intended to be an addition to the already well-stocked library about the decline of Britain. Nor is it an attempt to underestimate the real tragedies that have occurred in the lives of many British people. Britons will continue to debate for years to come whether the traumas of this decade were necessary or avoidable. However, by concentrating on the British response to industrial catastrophe, and by telling the story of the past 10 years as much as possible through the perceptions, judgements, and experiences of British people themselves, I have tried to show that part of the explanation for Britons' curious contentment could be found in the ways they have chosen to respond — or not to respond — to the crises they faced in the 1980s.

The happiness poll is a lesson to observers of Britain — particularly those in North America — whose views are often shaped by the myths Britain weaves around herself. For those willing to look past the statistics and the headlines, there were growing indications that many aspects of British life in the 1980s no longer conformed to the mythology of decline. Britain's obituaries were in urgent need of revision, but new myths are as hard to discard as old ones. These pages are the record of a surprising shift of mood in a country thought to have had no more surprises left.

PART I
Mrs. Thatcher's Revolution

Being British isn't as much fun as
it used to be.

*— Dr. John Eatwell, economist,
1982.*

Chapter 1
THATCHERIZED BRITAIN

In the beginning was the mood,
and the mood became Thatcher.

— *Sir Alfred Sherman, former
advisor to Prime Minister Margaret
Thatcher.*

Soon after I arrived in Britain, I rented a furnished two-storey apartment
in Hampstead, a North London neighbourhood that shared a hilltop with
an astonishing tract of woodland and meadow called Hampstead Heath.
My lease was a passport to a very special world. The Heath was one of the
largest urban parks in Europe, and Hampstead's fresh air and villagelike
intimacy set it apart from the rest of London.

The community was a magnet for the best and the brightest in Britain.
Many of the country's most successful producers, actors, and writers lived
in the clutter of tiny streets and shaded lanes winding down from the
Heath. With its turn-of-the-century butchers, open-air vegetable stalls,
quaint pubs, fishmongers, and eccentric bookshops, Hampstead seemed
just as England was supposed to be: an oasis of civilized living in the
homogenized, consumerist culture of the twentieth century. But
Hampstead was also an introduction to some of the new currents in British
society during the 1980s.

When I moved in, my neighbours had just fought a successful battle to
keep the McDonald's hamburger chain from opening a restaurant in the
High Street. The rest of London enjoyed the spectacle. Trendy protest was
what Hampstead was supposed to be all about. The bourgeois, cause-con-
scious Hampsteaders aroused condescending remarks among my friends
in the upper-class districts of Sloane Square or in northern working-class
communities. Hampsteaders were not really British, were they? Sort of,
you know, *American.* "If you move to Hampstead," one Oxford-educated

1

old friend, a journalist who lived in Holland Park, less than 30 minutes away by Underground, warned me while I was still house-hunting, "I shall never come up and visit — it's just too far." I thought he was joking, but he never came.

Hampstead was more complex than it seemed. I lived across the street from a "council house," a building maintained by the local authorities for tenants on welfare. The Heath was no longer regarded as a safe place to walk at night. And despite its village atmosphere, the community was part of a bustling, suburban commuter belt that was entirely different from the typical conception of Britain. The prosperous boroughs of northern London shared a distinctively aggressive approach to life that the English middle classes had long tried to hide.

Since the nineteenth century, Britons had done all they could to atone for the material success of their country. Displays of wealth and competitive drive were regarded as disruptive to the social contract, if not in bad taste. Thus began the understated, stiff-upper-lip style and the concentration on past glories that created the myth of England so loved by foreigners. This myth placed a premium on preservation and continuity. Overt economic struggle was out. The distaste modern Britons felt for the industrial revolution created by their great-grandparents was palpable. "Most of us English still cherish an instinctive feeling that men come first and that machines should come a long way afterwards," writer J.B. Priestley argued proudly in 1970. "It is true we were the first machine people, partly because we enjoy inventing machines and still do — but the idea of serving machines did some injury to the British psyche."[1]

The antigrowth attitude stretched into the government. "Name a society whose economic advance delights the statisticians and you name one in which the good qualities of its earlier life are decaying and in which no new civilization has emerged," said a senior official of the British Treasury. In 1980, Martin Wiener, an American historian, published a provocative analysis that placed most of the blame for British decline on the psychological resistance of the middle class to further industrial success. "The period of economic crisis in Britain was preceded by a century of psychological and intellectual deindustrialization," he wrote.[2]

This attitude underlined the political shape and assumptions of postwar Britain. The principles of the welfare state were accepted as a means of containing the twin dangers of unbridled capitalism and communism. The compromise became known as "Butskellism," after its two most eager proponents from the two major parties, Rab Butler for the Conservatives and Hugh Gaitskell for Labour. Many Britons considered the "Butskellite consensus" to be the formula that had saved their country from the upheavals of other postwar societies.

It was no accident that the restless, suburban middle classes in Hampstead and similar communities around Britain were compared fearfully to Americans. Having outgrown, in a manner of speaking, the Butskellite consensus, they were entrepreneurial, combative, and consumerist — all qualities that represented a challenge to the anti-industrialists. Their politics were a similarly threatening bundle of contradictions.

The constituency in which Hampstead fell sent a Tory MP to Parliament, but Hampsteaders also voted in one of London's most left-wing Labour borough councils, thereby imposing upon themselves some of the highest real estate taxes in the city. The apparent political inconsistency was not just a matter of different electoral boundaries. The suburban middle classes were volatile, and they refused to follow predictable voting patterns. Beneath the surface of Britain's tired, otherworldly attitudes, a newly affluent and upwardly mobile society was having more of an impact than anyone realized.

Just north of Hampstead, for example, was the constituency of Finchley, a "bedroom commuter suburb" for London. After the war, it had attracted large numbers of Jews from the slums of East End London. These second-generation Britons, along with other self-made and self-employed people from working-class or immigrant backgrounds, were unashamedly entrepreneurial. Inevitably, they antagonized their middle-class neighbours.

In 1957, a racial controversy pierced the smug atmosphere of Finchley's wide, tree-lined streets. The Finchley golf club turned down several Jews who applied for membership. The affair discomfited the local Tory party, many of whose members belonged to the club. Belatedly, the Finchley Conservatives realized they needed to overhaul their image in the community. The result of their agonized reappraisal had significant consequences for British politics. A year after the golf club episode they chose a 33-year-old barrister named Margaret Hilda Thatcher to be their new parliamentary candidate.

Thatcher had no obvious links with Finchley. She lived in Farnborough, a prosperous middle-class suburb south of London, with her husband, Denis, an oil company executive, and her two small children. The energetic Oxford graduate was an intelligent if occasionally dogmatic speaker. She had already spent nearly a decade trying to get into Parliament. As a 23-year-old fresh out of university, she had run an unsuccessful campaign as a Conservative candidate for a constituency in North Kent, during the election of 1950. Since then, several constituency parties in other areas had turned her down. They considered her a poor political bet. Even though Thatcher was able to escape the economic and psychological pressures of most women in her position — Denis not only supported her political ambitions, he often funded them — placing a "working mother" on the hustings risked offending traditional Tory sensibilities of the Fifties. Thatcher's opponents in her campaign to become Finchley's Conservative candidate in 1958 were traditional old-line Tories: male and eminently safe and respectable. But Thatcher touched a chord with the hard-working suburbanites. Her poise and confidence, combined with her sense of party loyalty, symbolized what they hoped was the modern, forward-looking Britain of the postwar era. Whether the Tories of Finchley would ever have turned to her if they had not been worried and uncertain, is impossible to know. But the story of Britain in the 1980s might have been very different if the local golf club had been less racist in its membership policy.[3]

Thatcher was elected a Member of Parliament in 1959, the year Harold Macmillan swept the Conservatives back into power with a 100-seat majority. When Thatcher became Britain's prime minister 20 years later, the fact that she represented Finchley was often overlooked in the rush of interest at home and abroad in the new government. Commentators were intrigued by the first woman to hold Britain's highest elected office (and the first of her sex to reach power in a major Western nation), and they made much of the impression that the country had turned sharply to the right. But Thatcher's close identification with the suburban middle class was just as fundamental to an understanding of her victory on May 4, 1979. While "Thatcherism" was to become one of the most controversial political movements in the West, the election of a prime minister from Finchley was less a triumph of right-wing ideology than a confirmation of the growing political importance of those Britons who had been left voiceless and powerless for years by the rigid class politics of British society. The politics of Hampstead and Finchley had arrived as a national force. There had been other "middle-class" prime ministers, but none represented so well the concerns of the suburbanized middle and lower classes.[4] Britain had effectively been "Thatcherized" well before Thatcher arrived at Number 10 Downing Street, but few politicians had understood, or bothered to explore, the implications of the new currents in national life that had created Britain's fifty-sixth prime minister.

Margaret Thatcher was born in a room above her father's grocery store in Grantham, a quiet manufacturing town in the Lincolnshire countryside. By today's standards, her early childhood circumstances were humble. There was an outside toilet, and the house that served as both family home and business reflected the scrimping and saving of the lower middle class. But her father, Alfred Roberts, was successful by the standards of the time, especially in the eyes of his neighbours. He came from a family of rural shoemakers, but managed to work his way up from grocer's apprentice to the ownership of his own shop. Her mother, Beatrice, was the daughter of a railway cloakroom attendant. It was a sign of the family's relative afflu- ence that Beatrice could stay at home and raise the children. Roberts' stature in Grantham — he was a president of the local Rotarians, a town alderman, and a lay preacher in the Methodist church — testified to the opportunities open to a couple with ambition in the prewar years, and Thatcher was always intensely proud of what her parents had accomplished. "I'm a plain straightforward provincial," she boasted to author Anthony Sampson. "I've got no hang-ups about my background, like you intellectual commentators in the southeast (of England). When you're actually *doing* things you don't have time for hang-ups."[5]

Both parents were devout churchgoers, and they raised Margaret and her sister Muriel according to strict Methodist traditions. Sundays were reserved for church, and much of the family's social life revolved around church activities. One of the future prime minister's first public performances was as an angel in a church pageant, and young Margaret Roberts did not attend her first formal dance until university. In some ways, her background reflected an approach to life that could be traced to the England of the nineteenth century. The solid earth of provincial Britain had produced generations of schoolteachers, governesses, nannies, and nurses for the empire. Even today, a visitor can walk into any provincial school or volunteer charity office around Britain and find dozens of women who bear the unmistakable mark of virtuous English provincialism. They are stubborn, dogmatic but straightforward, intensely patriotic, and fervently respectable. It was no accident that the shopkeeper's daughter from Grantham was compared, usually unflatteringly, to a governess as her career in politics took off. But Thatcher's character, like her roots, was not so easily typecast.

Alfred Roberts' determination to rise above his origins eventually inspired his daughter to challenge the barriers of upper-class-dominated Conservative Party politics. Like her father and her future constituents in Finchley, Thatcher was not content to live by the rules of a system that did its best to prevent people from rising "above their station." As an ambitious young schoolgirl, she thought of joining the Indian Civil Service, then almost the exclusive preserve of the male upper-middle class. When her headmistress told her it was not available to women, Thatcher replied that that sounded like a good enough reason to get into it. The same headmistress unsuccessfully tried to dissuade her from going to Oxford, on the grounds that she came from the wrong social class.

Thatcher, however, was a child of the new welfare state. Although she would make her name as an opponent of statism, the egalitarian visions that transformed British society after the Second World War helped her to move beyond the confines of small-town England. After graduation, armed with a degree in chemistry, she got her first job in one of the new industries that flourished in Britain after the war. She became a laboratory assistant in a plastics factory, earning £350 a year. The salary was £50 less than a man earned for the same job, but Thatcher's early experience with "new technology" was crucial to her later outlook. Long before the great nineteenth-century factories began to go bankrupt, Thatcher was already a participant in the processes that were revolutionizing the British economy.

Thatcher, like many of the young people of her generation, had moved far beyond the narrow working and social horizons of her parents and their friends. The impatient youths who filled the universities in the years following the war were the first to achieve a peculiar "classlessness" in British society. They often looked across the Atlantic for their models. While they sneered at the American lust for profit, they were impressed by the prosperity and social mobility of postwar American society. Britain was still chafing under a regimen of wartime rationing (which continued into the 1950s) and the encrusted traditions of imperial England were embarrassing obstacles to change. The 1950s generation was to produce leaders of all parties determined to drag Britain out of stuffy backwardness and into the modern world, at almost any cost.

Most acted as if they had little time to waste. Thatcher, bent on a political career, realized that chemistry would not provide her the contacts she needed. Her friends suggested she enter law. She filled in the application for her bar exam when she was in hospital for the birth of her twins, Mark and Carol. Thatcher turned the decision, like everything else in her life, into a test of personal willpower: "I remember lying in the hospital . . . and I remember thinking, if I don't . . . actually fill in the entrance form for the final of the law, I may never go back to it. But if I fill in the entrance form now, pride will not let me fail. And so I did."

In Parliament, as a hard-working member of the "Class of '59," Thatcher was confronted with more barriers. A woman in politics was still rarely taken seriously, but she worked her way up through a succession of minor government posts. Grudging acknowledgement of her talents finally came when Prime Minister Edward Heath appointed her Minister of Education, making her the second woman to fill that post since the war. The job brought her to national attention for the first time, and provided an inkling of the controversy to come. Accepting a recommendation by her aides to drop a government-funded free milk program for schoolchildren, Thatcher found herself the target of an inevitable public furor. University students drew up signs reading "Thatcher — Milk Snatcher," and the *Sun* newspaper, eventually to become one of her most fanatical supporters, called her, in 1970, "the most unpopular woman in Britain."[6]

Despite her parsimonious image, Thatcher played a part in the massive expansion of government after the war. During her stint as minister, spending on education passed defence spending for the first time. The Sixties and Seventies were decades of social change in Britain. The abolition of capital punishment, the passage of laws legalizing abortion and homosexuality, and even changes in the archaic House of Lords formed part of a revolution in attitudes. Thatcher's generation, and the one that followed hers, had nothing but contempt for the Establishment's bemused acceptance of decline. The "classless" generation had been formed by the wealth and prosperity of Britain's service and managerial economy. Incredibly successful themselves, they saw no reason that the decaying industrial system could not be transformed. The principal obstacles to modernizing Britain were all too obvious to them.

While opportunities for professional job mobility had increased since the war, British society was still tribal and archaic. An "old-boy network" occupied most of the traditional power centres in the country, and it was off-limits to most Britons unless they could get into Oxford or Cambridge. A scholarship to one of the elite universities was the best passport to real status for middle- or working-class youngsters, but Britain's primary-school system, one of the most rigid educational systems in Europe, made the barriers even harder to crack. At the age of 11 or 12, British children took exams to determine whether they could try for university or whether they would be shunted off into dead-end classes until they were allowed to escape school at 16.

The politics of the 1970s reflected both the Establishment's fear of change and its complacency. Conservative leader Edward Heath and Labour leader Harold Wilson, alternating in power, tried as best they could to push Britain toward a new frontier while attempting to maintain the shaky Butskellite consensus. Heath's "dash for growth" and Wilson's invitation to Britons to bask in the "white heat of the technological revolution" fell victim to the opposition of unions or corporation directors anxious to preserve entrenched interests. Dave Clark, a student-protest leader of the 1960s, summed up his generation's painful sense of betrayal by the Labour Party, the beacon for generations of working-class Britons, like this: "There was the feeling that you couldn't do anything with the Labour Party. It was in the hands of evil, or at least corrupt and incompetent, people."[7]

Thatcher might never have used the same rhetoric, but she would have sympathized. She had more in common with the radicals of the 1960s left than with the timid postwar leadership of her own party. She was not just a Conservative but a radical populist. In 1968, at the height of the student-protest era, Thatcher gave a speech to a Tory meeting in Blackpool remarkable both for its early indication of her future style of government, and for its intellectual affinity with the reforming zeal of the late 1960s. "People have come to doubt the future of the democratic system and its institutions," she said. "They distrust the politicians and have little faith in the future. ...What is the explanation? Broadly speaking, I think we have not yet assimilated many of the changes that have come about in the past 30 or 40 years."[8]

Thatcher listed some of the important changes she believed had not yet been assimilated into mainstream political thinking in Britain: the growing scepticism toward politicians' promises, the "all-pervading development of the welfare state," and the new power of the media. All were changes she was to exploit with consummate skill less than a decade later. But even then, Thatcher had a clear idea of the direction reforms had to take. "It is our job," she said, "continually to retest old assumptions and to seek new ideas. But we must not try to find one unalterable answer that will solve all our problems, for none can exist." Thatcher's own scepticism about traditional solutions, and her warnings about the intrusion of "Big Brother" government, reflected the views of the voters of Finchley as much as they reflected the anger of students protesting in the universities. But the spotlight of the time was on reformers of the left, not the right.

Inevitably, as the frustrated "conviction" politics of the left moved reformers toward more open and bitter confrontations with the government, it created its radical antithesis. Growing sections of the new middle class, in hundreds of Finchleys around the country, perceived Britain as becoming dangerously unstable and polarized. Industrial disputes increasingly resembled the class war their parents and grandparents were supposed to have overcome. They had left their roots behind — why couldn't others?

Over one brief period, in 1979, for example, the entire country seemed to be out on strike. During the so-called "Winter of Discontent," grim news photographs of rubbish left uncollected by striking refuse collectors appeared in the international press along with stories of gravediggers who refused to conduct burials and civil servants who refused to collect taxes. A mixture of restrictive union practices, "I'm all right, Jack" attitudes, and general incompetence made "the British disease" a part of the century's political vocabulary. Nothing illustrated the malaise better than the comment of one striking worker, who, noting the fact that food supplies for his fellow Britons had been interrupted, said, "If I can't afford to buy food, why should anyone else have it?"[9]

There was a feeling that the choices for Britain had suddenly constricted. "A huge, icy fist, with large cold fingers, was squeezing and chilling the people of Britain," English novelist Margaret Drabble wrote in *The Ice Age*, a bitter examination of the British mood in the 1970s.[10]

The most chilling fact of all was inflation. British inflation during the 1970s was higher than anywhere in Europe except Greece. The idea that money represented value for work was seriously at risk. Between 1969 and 1975, the real value of salaries after taxes fell by 25 per cent for those earning £20,000 a year or more.[11] The effect of inflation was as much psychological as financial. "The whole notion of saving one's money and putting things toward a home, education, or whatever else began to disappear," reminisced British actor Simon Callow. "It was interesting, in a completely banal way, to see it in the theatre. People stopped booking seats in advance. I knew because I was in the box office, and up to the end of the Sixties and early Seventies you would have a good 50 per cent of your sales well in advance. It was part of an ordered life. Then people began to say, 'Fuck that, I feel like the theatre tonight, so I'll go.'"

The Labour government increased the middle class's sense of alienation with a punishing attack on individual initiative. Basic tax rates on the highest incomes were pushed to 83 per cent in an attempt to squeeze the rich until, as then-Chancellor Denis Healey put it in a memorable phrase, the "pips squeak." Conservative governments were little better. The landed Tories still regarded overt money-making with horror, and they made a fuss about the "unacceptable face of capitalism."

The suburban middle class did not know where to turn for help. "There was a general unformed fear that we were all ... going to the dogs, that society was breaking down," a former Labour minister, Lord Chalfont, recalled. In some circles, there was even talk of a military coup to prevent a "leftist" takeover. Few believed the rumours, but Britain's social fabric was becoming increasingly strained. Little by little, the middle class summoned up the courage to "rescue" Britain from itself.

In 1976, an organization called the National Association of Freedom (NAFF) was formed, consolidating many middle-class protest organizations, and it quickly became an ideal vehicle for members of the Conservative Party who were unhappy with the traditional "consensus" politics of the left and right. Margaret Thatcher was among the first to take advantage of this grassroots network. She spoke at NAFF's inaugural dinner in 1977. According to Lord Chalfont, she "struck a chord which was waiting to be struck. ... All those fears of bureaucracy, of too much government, of the erosion of freedom of the individual, ... of anarchy ... she just came at a time when all these fears began to coalesce."[12]

Fear would later come to be seen as a motivating principle of Thatcherism, but it was far from being the central one. A critique of the welfare state was long overdue. Thatcher captured its essence in her 1968 speech: "The great mistake of the last few years has been for the government to provide or to legislate for almost everything," she said. "But there came a time when the amount of intervention got so great that it could no longer be exercised in practice by government but only by more and more officials or bureaucrats. Now it is difficult if not impossible for people to get at the official making the decision and so, paradoxically, although the degree of intervention is greater, the government has become more and more *remote* from the people."

Thatcher went on to echo the calls of the new left for participatory democracy, arguing that "the way to get personal involvement and participation is not for people to take part in more and more government decisions but to make the government reduce the area of decision over which it presides."[13]

Returning "power to the people" had been a favourite slogan of the new left. Now it was captured by the new right. Often the transformation from left to right occurred in the same person. Roger Scruton, who was to become one of the foremost exponents of Thatcherite thinking in the 1980s, had been mildly left-wing in 1968. A 24-year-old Oxford graduate, the son of lower-middle-class parents, he found himself in the midst of the Paris student revolt when he went to study in France. "It outraged me so much that it was impossible to continue being a leftie," he remembered. "[The year] 1968 was a great eye-opener. I hated everything that was happening." Returning to England, Scruton began to feel that the ponderous welfare bureaucracy developed with such grand ideals had become a "cancer" on British society. "The welfare state was a good thing when it was meant to provide for people who could not provide for themselves, but it was not meant to guarantee everyone a job and income," he said. "It not only destroys individual responsibility, but opens the way to tyranny."

Scruton was not alone in his concerns. Many like him began arguing publicly for a reassessment of the postwar consensus. They were not taken seriously at first. Their study groups and published material, however, began to attract a wider audience when some of the leading Tory politicians of the day joined them.

Keith Joseph, minister of health and social security in the Heath government, was shocked by Prime Minister Heath's decision to increase public spending when unemployment began to rise. He decided that he had reached a personal and philosophical dead end with Butskellite Toryism. British politics needed to get out from under the "shadow of the 1930s," he believed. "We were haunted by the fear of long-term mass unemployment, the grim, hopeless dole queues and towns which died," Joseph told one interviewer. "So we talked ourselves into believing that these giant tight-lipped men in caps and mufflers were round the corner, and tailored our policy to match these imaginary conditions."[14]

Liberated from the need to maintain consensus politics, the new thinkers launched what was to prove the first institutional challenge to Keynesian thinking anywhere in the West. The most radical part of their argument was their questioning of the principle of economic equality. From Joseph again came some of the most forthright declarations of the new faith. "One of the central prejudices of modern British politics (is) the belief that it is the proper function of the state to influence the distribution of wealth for its own sake," he said in 1978. Joseph argued that the logical result of such a policy was a "society in which no one may advance an inch before another."[15]

Margaret Thatcher, by inclination and temperament, was attracted to the new ideas. She met Joseph, Scruton, and many of the other converts to antiegalitarian thinking at evenings organized at various private homes around London. She became particularly attached to Joseph, a wealthy businessman who was the son of poor Jewish immigrants and who reminded her of many of her own Finchley constituents. Joseph's senior position established him as the beacon of the new right, as well as the great hope of many other Conservatives weary of consensus politics. He was regarded as the next Tory prime minister by Thatcher herself. The best Thatcher privately hoped to achieve was a post in cabinet as Chancellor of the Exchequer. But even that seemed an improbable dream. She once confessed to a journalist her frustrations at the limited opportunities for women in politics. A woman would never become prime minister in her lifetime, she said. She sensed that arguing for such a possibility would have seemed like an impractical detour to the growing circle of Conservative revolutionaries.

The new right's opportunity came when Conservative Prime Minister Edward Heath lost the general election he had called suddenly in 1974. Heath's smugness in office and his arrogance toward his backbench MPs came back to haunt him in defeat. He was forced to concede demands for a review of his leadership. The most ambitious candidates for his job, however, were unwilling to make an open assault. The Tories had always prided themselves on their unity. Joseph announced that he would run for the leadership, but within a few months his star had faded, thanks to a misguided speech in which he suggested that the poor were breeding too fast. There were no others who seemed willing to challenge Heath, until a group of Tories suggested to Margaret Thatcher that she should stand.

Thatcher was never intended to be anything but a stalking-horse, submitting her name on the first ballot in order to give others the room to oppose the prime minister in later ballots. As even she admitted later, she would never have consented if Joseph had not been ruled out of the race. Few people, including Heath, took her seriously. When she walked into his office to announce that she would run, he didn't bother to look up from the papers on his desk.

But Thatcher's apparent lack of party support was misleading. The architects of the new right, as well as some of her close friends in the backbenches, orchestrated a brilliant campaign. They solicited votes from Heath's allies by telling them it was a way of stopping some of the most threatening right-wing candidates, and they got support from the right by painting Thatcher as the last hope of reform. In 1975, Thatcher stunned the party and the country by her election as leader. The reformism of the left had produced a new reformer on the right.

The Conservatives' years in opposition, watching the country become convulsed in strikes and inflation, convinced the philosophers of the new right that their time had come. Similar ideas to theirs were gaining ground in other parts of the West. The thoughts of Friedrich von Hayek, an Austrian-born philosopher who warned that freedom was endangered by the corporate state, were widely quoted. So were the theories of an American economist named Milton Friedman, who argued that massive government spending distorted the working of a free economy. "Monetarists" like Friedman and their eager disciples in Britain saw inflation as a more serious threat to modern democracy than unemployment. They believed that British governments' propensity to borrow funds on a diminishing industrial base to pay for labour peace and social stability was ultimately ruinous.

As it turned out, the first monetarist government in Britain was a Labour one. In 1976, the Labour government of James Callaghan was faced with an exchange crisis and imminent bankruptcy. It was forced to negotiate a rescue loan from the International Monetary Fund on the strict condition that public spending was to be sharply reined in. Callaghan, defending his policies before angry party members, sounded as if he were repeating the arguments of the new right. "For too long, perhaps ever since the war, we've postponed facing up to fundamental choices and fundamental changes in our society," he said. "For too long this country ... has been ready to settle for borrowing money abroad to maintain our standards of life, instead of grappling with the fundamental problems of British industry."[16]

For all its limits as an economic theory, monetarism provided a workable analysis of contemporary British problems. Britain, like most democracies in the West, was in danger of becoming an overcentralized state, at the mercy of entrenched interest groups and a mammoth bureaucracy. The evident structural inequalities of the British economy made monetarism doubly attractive as a way of returning wealth (and power) to the people.

All the separate strands of Margaret Thatcher's life and philosophy — her small-town patriotism, her scepticism about big government, and her outsider's determination to break down barriers — came together in the election campaign of 1979. She had an uncanny ability to make her opponents feel that they were simply on the wrong side of history. Joan Ruddock, an unsuccessful Labour Party candidate in the Thames Valley commuter belt near London, sensed during that election she was witnessing one of the mysterious shifts which occur from time to time in the national life of a people. "Thatcher captured people's imagination, by telling them they could control their own lives," she remembered. "The Labour governments of Wilson and Callaghan had ... regulated people's lives in a dull and dismal way. They hadn't given people any sense of pride in having one of the best welfare states in the world, and certainly the best health service in the world. People had not embraced that in a way [which] led them to feel that being British, with those things, was good."

Ruddock, who was to achieve national and international fame in the 1980s as a leader of an antinuclear movement that tapped the same stratum of middle-class restlessness, was often startled by the whining tone she heard on the doorsteps of her prosperous middle-class neighbours. "I remember hearing the kind of comments I had never heard before," she told me several years later. "It was all about being selfish, about not allowing people to get anything off the welfare state; it was all about having choices, how *she'll* give us the money in our pockets and *we* will be able to decide what to do."

Like Ronald Reagan in the United States, who was to sweep to power on a similar platform the following year, Thatcher did symbolize a certain selfishness and single-mindedness. She was a representative of the "silent majority," fearful of the country's drift toward industrial crisis and selfish about its own privileges. But she was also firmly in the tradition of the moralists and social reformers who were anxious to transform British postwar society. In Margaret Thatcher's hands, Thatcherism was less an ideology than a moral instrument, a way of defeating "aggro" — the ubiquitous 1970s British slang word for hassles and aggravation — at home and abroad. "Thatcherism," wrote one political observer, "was essentially an instinct, a series of moral values and an approach to leadership."[17]

For that reason, it was hard at first to see her election as the revolution it was to become. In 1979, it seemed little more than a temporary detour from the comforts of Butskellism. Thatcher was by no means the choice of a majority of Britons. The Conservatives won 44 per cent of the vote in 1979, one of the lowest percentages earned by a Tory government since the war. The real clue to her significance was the support she found among an astonishing variety of Britons, ranging from trade union members to London commuters. Her election indicated that the postwar coalition of the working class and liberal middle class that had made the Labour Party a potent national force was falling apart.

Thatcher was often too easily confused with Thatcherism. While the prime minister brought a new economic policy into government, she was much more cautious than her advisors in promoting sophisticated new theories. Her politics were often based on an intuitive emotional grasp of her electorate rather than zealotry. Her political idol was Winston Churchill, the great war leader of her youth, and the symbol for her of the era of national unity and purpose that was her most stirring girlhood memory. To the irritation of many older Tories, she often referred to him in speeches and in private conversation as "Winston."

Many of those who realized what Thatcher represented didn't like what they saw. They muttered that the Thatcher government was dominated by shopkeepers and immigrants. She was as disturbing to the upper-class image of who belonged in Number 10 Downing Street as loud voices in a St. James club. "This was the first time that the working classes [had] been in power since the war," said Scruton. "It was always either the landed establishment or Oxford public school radicals. For the first time, you had somebody who was Oxford-educated but [bore] all the marks of the English lower-middle classes, and it was a great shock to people."

Her public personality, including the affected "posh" accent of the Tory hinterland, a hectoring speaking style, and even her way of striding through a room, rubbed people the wrong way. Cabinet ministers and the press called her by the slang names used by public schoolboys, such as "Atilla the Hen" and "The Leaderene." She annoyed and fascinated civil servants. "I'd made some bad mistake which caused her a lot of trouble," a staff member once recalled. "I expected a real dressing-down. Instead, she gave me this *look* which meant: 'Nanny is not cross. SHE is just very, very sad.' It was ghastly." Northern working-class radicals had a way of pronouncing her name as if it were an imprecation, and to most other people in the country, Thatcher was simply known as "she." No postwar political leader since Churchill has had such an impact on the minds and digestions of Britons. "The reaction to Margaret Thatcher by friends of mine who are strongly left-wing is one of absolute hysteria," said Simon Callow. "There's a kind of madness that overtakes them when they start to talk about her."

At close quarters, Thatcher is very different from her austere public image. Many people who have met her come away remarking at the warmth of her personality. The public saw some of the hidden Thatcher for the first — and only — time when her son Mark disappeared during a motor rally in the Sahara Desert in 1982. Talking about her fears in the days before he finally turned up safe, she wept openly. The Thatcher persona is perhaps a direct response to the pressures of being a female leader in a country where men still refuse to take women's aspirations seriously. My own most vivid memory of her came during a brief interview she granted to a group of Canadian journalists in her Number 10 Downing Street office. She walked into the room where we were seated and fixed each member of her audience with a chilly blue-eyed glare, as if she would simply forbid any unfriendly question. One reporter, temporarily nonplussed, began a question with the words, "Mr. Prime Minister." We laughed to fill the awkward silence. Thatcher frowned, and then, noticing the reporter's discomfort, she smiled at him. "It's an office, not a person," she said.

The new prime minister made her priorities clear almost as soon as she took office. "The mission of this government is much more than the promotion of economic progress," she said in 1979. "It is to renew the spirit and solidarity of the nation. ... At the heart of a new mood in the nation must be a recovery of our self-confidence and our self-respect."

At first, the opposite occurred. Between 1979 and 1981, the first two years of the Thatcher administration, Britain experienced an economic upheaval. Most people expected the new prime minister to follow her predecessor Edward Heath's example and move back toward middle-of-the-road conservatism, but Thatcher refused to pump more money into the economy. The "Iron Lady" tag given her by the Russians when she was still leader of the official opposition took on a new meaning. Loyal cabinet ministers and officials saw the experience in military terms. John Hoskyns, an aide recruited from the private sector to reorganize Thatcher's office, typified the bunker attitudes of the men and women who imagined they were fighting a new Battle of Britain. "She doesn't say, 'Well, I'd rather survive, so I'll fudge and compromise,'" Hoskyns recalled. "She'd say, 'On that basis, I'd rather not survive.' That was clearly understood by everybody who worked with her, and of course that did make the thinking so much easier. I mean, people knew, you know, that the lines of retreat were cut off."[18]

By 1981 Thatcher's popularity had sunk to 25 per cent, the lowest ever recorded by a British prime minister in this century. Even her own cabinet ministers worried that she was destroying the country with the "economics of the madhouse." They met in secret to plot ways of overthrowing her. But while outsiders watched in disbelief, the attempts at a coup won remarkably little support. Britain, the first country to experiment with a complete monetarist program, seemed willing to weather the blows. The economist J.K. Galbraith once pointed out that Britons were the ideal "guinea pigs" for monetarism. "Britain's political and social institutions are solid, and neither Englishmen, Scots, nor even the Welsh take readily to the streets," he said.[19]

Perhaps the "counter-revolution" never happened because a majority of Britons felt that the revolution was being waged in their name. Thatcher's firmness had encouraged those Britons who felt stifled by the Butskellite consensus. According to Sir Alfred Sherman, director of the Centre for Policy Studies, one of the Thatcherite think tanks, millions of voters had been waiting for the chance. "There was a hunger for fresh thinking, new ideas and — human nature being what it is — new certainties," he wrote in 1985. "In the beginning was the mood, and the mood became Thatcher."[20]

For many, the gamble paid off in increased disposable income. Inflation dropped to under 4 per cent, coinciding with a consumer spending boom.

Those who were employed benefited from a 10 per cent increase in the standard of living. The middle classes in Finchley (and would-be middle classes elsewhere) were able to take advantage of generous tax subsidies for home ownership. In 1983, mortgage interest relief amounted to £2.15 billion. The upwardly mobile working class who lived in public housing were given the right to buy their own homes at discounts of up to 50 per cent, helping to create another million homeowners between 1979 and 1983.

Thatcher herself described her ultimate goal as "popular capitalism." She defined it at a Conservative party conference in 1986, in rhetoric hardly changed from her speech to the conference in 1968, as being "nothing less than a crusade to enfranchise the many in the economic life of the nation. We Conservatives are returning power to the people."

"Popular capitalism" indeed looked as if it could fulfil the Thatcher goal of making Britain a share-owning as well as property-owning democracy. Thousands of Britons took advantage of the sale of nationalized industries to buy stock for the first time. Most of them had little difficulty agreeing with Thatcher's claim that they had regained control of their own lives. The people of Thatcherized Britain were bolder, richer, and less willing to accept being held for ransom by the tribal institutions of British society, whether they were on the political left or right. On the shop floor, the popularity of legislation prohibiting secondary pickets and automatic dues checkoffs to political parties, and requiring open strike ballots, took union barons and shop stewards by surprise. It was one more sign of the weakening of class allegiances. Some 59 per cent of the working class had become Thatcher voters.

Even the former rebels in cabinet now acknowledge it was they, rather than the prime minister, who misjudged the mood of the country. "I failed to recognize that the mood of the country had changed," said Jim Prior, whose open opposition to Thatcherite economics had sent him from the senior Employment portfolio into exile as Northern Ireland minister. "Mrs. Thatcher was much more in tune with people than I was. I was much more worried about the impact those policies would have on people's political thinking and on the social structure of the country than apparently the people were themselves."[21]

While Thatcherized Britain was enjoying the novelty of success, its principal representative continued to be insecure. Even after years in power, the prime minister of Britain still seemed an outsider. She could sometimes be heard in the Commons cafeteria criticizing the government as if she had nothing to do with it. Thatcher often resembled a foreigner roaming through British society, opening gates that were not supposed to be opened, ignoring No Trespassing signs and asking questions that only outsiders would be awkward enough to ask.

Many Britons, including some of her supporters, suspected that the victory of the woman from Finchley was a fluke. In 1983, however, Thatcher was swept back to power in one of the biggest electoral landslides in post-war history. Although her popular vote had fallen slightly, she passed an important historical landmark — becoming the first Tory prime minister since Lord Salisbury to win a second consecutive term. In January 1988, following her third election victory six months earlier, Thatcher became the longest-serving British Prime Minister this century and consolidated her place as one of the world's most well-known political leaders.

As a middle-class revolution, Thatcherism has been extraordinarily successful. The ambitious grocer's daughter from Grantham has created a new politics of affluence on the ruins of the West's oldest industrial society. The people in Finchleys around the country gained an access to power they would never have had otherwise. Thatcher's closest nonpolitical friends and associates remained the entrepreneurs and self-made people who had once, like her, been shut out of the British class structure. Even the number of millionaires has increased during her tenure.[22]

Those with talent, ambition, and skill in the lower middle class were similarly able to exploit the underlying changes in British society. Britain now began to reflect the economic and social realities of Thatcher voters. The number of those employed in manufacturing in the 1980s was 25 per cent; 50 years ago it had been 50 per cent. Services were soon expected to employ 70 per cent of the workforce, the same proportion of people who were in agriculture in 1830, at the dawn of the industrial revolution.[23] "So completely has Margaret Thatcher's government transformed Britain," said Lord Whitelaw, one of her admiring cabinet ministers, "that our main problem is that so many people take for granted what she has done."[24]

That may have been true, but the new landscape of Britain did not necessarily resemble the sketches drawn up with such fervour by the new right of a few years before. A British journalist once described the kind of society Thatcher hoped to create as a "cross between nineteenth-century Birmingham and contemporary Hong Kong," but the "new realism" Thatcher advocated had as much of an impact on the spending of money as the making of it.[25]

The peculiar and innovative British genius for living was strengthened during the 1980s. Entrepreneurs received new prominence in the society, but they were not always those who built new factories or better mousetraps. As the decade progressed, lifestyle and leisure industries became some of the most successful offspring of Thatcherism. A company aptly named First Leisure, which owns a range of West End theatres, discos, snooker clubs, and seaside piers, saw its pretax profits go from £6.75 million in 1983 to £12.7 million in 1986.[26] Also, in 1986, one out of every four British households owned a video recorder, and nearly one out of every ten a home computer. Were these signs of health, or of a country in decline, determined to enjoy its last hours as a modern industrial nation? Sometimes, it was hard to tell the difference.

Under Thatcher — and occasionally in retaliation to her — the British accommodated themselves well before other Western nations to a world where growth and progress could no longer be measured in GNP. In 1980, one young writer predicted that the "newly emerging lifestyle of the middle class ... might offer the only way of curing the British disease and of coming to terms with the world as it is likely to be in the twenty-first century."[27]

Did her popularity mean the Thatcherization of Britain was complete? Thatcher herself knew that her major struggle was the battle of ideas. "The comfortable illusions that accompanied our gradual decline have been shattered," she claimed. "The nation has woken up to the reality of the need to earn its place in the world." But in her drive to create a new Britain, there were bound to be victims. The sobering presence of an old, decaying society, seemingly beyond the reach of Thatcherism, took some of the glow off the prosperity of Hampstead and Finchley. Derelict factories and armies of unemployed youth were the darker side of Thatcherized Britain.

A visitor to Britain in the 1980s could see a people still deeply worried about their future, preoccupied with their country's diminished role in the world, and uneasy about the growing economic divisions in their society. Although a new consensus had replaced the tattered old one, glimpses of "the other Britain" raised serious questions about the nature of the transformation achieved by Thatcher. Even the fiercest supporters of Mrs. Thatcher's revolution had to acknowledge the existence of two separate nations: one steaming ahead toward a bright future, the other apparently grounded on the reefs behind.

English-speaking countries in particular watched Britain's troubles with the mixed emotions the illness of a once-arrogant aunt inspires in relatives. They wanted her to get well, but they *were* rather tired of her pretensions. Like most journalists who arrived in the United Kingdom at the start of the decade, I was initially more interested in covering the funeral service than rumours of a resurrection.

Chapter 2
IRON IN THE SOUL

How do you respond to your client's long-term
unemployment? What can you do when you are
faced with your client's massive loss in
confidence, paralyzing fear for the future, despair,
and possible suicide?

*Advertisement for a practical
skills handbook for the caring
professions*, New Society,
April 25, 1986.

In February 1982, seven months after I moved to Britain, I travelled northeast from London to the port of Newcastle-upon-Tyne, on an assignment
that depressed me even before I began it. I was to look for the "human
reality" behind the unemployment figures that were then rising to dizzying
heights. It was one of the formula stories for a foreign reporter in Britain
during the 1980s.

The trip was to provide me with the first clues that there were encouraging signs of life in the part of Thatcherized Britain that lay almost buried
beneath the rubble of the 1980s economic catastrophe, but I hardly noticed
them at the time.

Statistics told the story in brutal terms. In 1900, Britain ruled a fifth of
the world's land surface and a quarter of its people. Between the 1890s and
the outbreak of the First World War, the United Kingdom produced half of
Europe's coal, the major portion of the world's steel, and 60 per cent of the
world's ships. Britons enjoyed a standard of living 40 per cent higher than
that of the Germans, their nearest commercial rival.

Nearly a century later, Britain's share of world trade had plummeted
from 33 per cent to 7 per cent and she had become a net importer of manufactured goods for the first time since the industrial revolution. Living
standards had fallen below those of Italy, and looked likely to drop below
those of East Germany before the century was over.[1]

Time appeared to be running out on Britain's industrial future. "We need
a sense of urgency [about] the regeneration of industry in this country,"

19

said Prince Charles, in a widely quoted comment that illustrated the despair of the period. "What worries me is that otherwise we are going to end up as a fourth-rate country."

A sense of urgency was precisely what had been missing for years. The worldwide economic boom of the postwar years, and the start of profitable exploitation of rich oil and gas reserves in the North Sea during the 1970s, had allowed the British to ignore their most serious structural problems. Second-hand prosperity and the flush of being an oil power permitted them to brush off inconvenient realities — such as, for instance, the fact that between 1945 and 1970, the rate of investment in British industry was two-thirds of that in the rest of the developed world.

Successive British governments had talked about meeting the economic "challenge," and many, in fact, had honestly tried to do more than talk. But they were hampered by an industrial culture that had turned its face resolutely away from real change. Correlli Barnett, in a book analyzing the causes of British decline, noted the widespread contempt for industry in a country that had once been an industrial trailblazer. Instead of applying new scientific and managerial processes to improve the manufacturing base, he said, Britain suffered under "the stultifying authority of customary practice and traditional wisdom."[2] In foundries and factories, machines that were new in 1910 strained to meet production quotas. They had been built to last forever; why, the typical response went, bother to replace them? When the world economy went into recession in the mid-1970s, Britain inevitably suffered more than any other country in the West.

As British goods became more expensive to make and harder to sell abroad, managers reacted by laying off increasing numbers of workers. Unemployment rose until, by the winter of 1979, it was increasing at the rate of 100,000 a month. But the process of decline did not stop with the loss of jobs.

First individual companies, then whole industries, folded. Entire regions of Britain were left ravaged by the implosion of one traditional industry after another. The collapse of the iron and steel industry alone in the late 1970s and early 1980s, according to one group of historians who produced a documentary for the BBC, "approached an industrial holocaust."[3] Even areas of the economy based on newer industries suffered. The West Midlands engineering city of Wolverhampton, for example, lost 29 per cent of its construction jobs and 38 per cent of its metal engineering jobs between 1978 and 1983.

The search for blame led to the new Conservative government. Prime Minister Thatcher, armed with what she considered an election mandate to end economic stagnation, refused to help floundering industries or to deal with union barons who were demanding job protection for their members. A decision to allow the pound to float higher made British goods even more expensive overseas, deepening the crisis. But a single government could not be held responsible for the endemic problems of a worn-out industrial system, problems whose blurred outlines could already be sighted before the Second World War.

Although they could not avoid pouring funds into some of the most troubled state companies, or making concessions to powerful unions, the Thatcherites were more consistent than governments had been in the past. So many Britons accepted the prime minister's often-repeated phrase, "there is no alternative" that its initials, TINA, became another of the private nicknames for her.

Even more important, the Tories had given a long-wished-for signal to British business leaders. Company chairmen had been drained by the years of industrial conflict. The government's iron resolution lent them a touch of steel as well. They began cutting payrolls that had long been inflated by union feather-bedding practices. The scale of the catastrophe, nevertheless, took even the government by surprise. "We were," one of Thatcher's cabinet ministers admitted in a rare moment of candour, "neither intellectually nor emotionally prepared for [unemployment] increases of this magnitude."[4]

At a time of world recession, no British government could have headed off a rise in the numbers of unemployed, but it was hard to avoid the conclusion that at least some of Britain's depression had been planned. In 1981, prominent Swiss economist and noted monetarist Jurg Niehans was commissioned by the government to find out what had happened. He charged that economic policy had been tighter than it needed to be. His report was never made public. Another analyst calculated that at least one million of the three million unemployed by the mid-1980s had lost their jobs because of government strategy. A journalist remembers talking to cabinet-level sources who argued that unemployment would put powerful unions "in their place." "We all know there is no prospect of getting down unemployment," wrote John Hoskyns in a private memo in 1983. "We need to look at new forms of activity."[5]

In the end, it no longer seemed to matter why the disintegration of the economy had happened. When I began travelling around Britain, I sometimes imagined I was in a third-world country. I had spent many years in Latin America, as both a journalist and an American Peace Corps volunteer, and Britain's combination of apathy, bureaucracy, and physical decay was disconcertingly familiar. Third-world problems were evident even in London. Beyond the leafy comforts of Hampstead and Finchley, and far from the monuments, parks, and tourist sites, the great metropolis offered Dickensian landscapes of grey apartment buildings, boarded-up warehouses, and vast derelict tracts. When the producers of the British film *1984* were looking for locations that could express George Orwell's bleak vision of a future urban desert, they found them in recognizable London neighbourhoods.

"Everyone can see that the country . . . is falling to pieces, the cities growing dirtier, the railways rustier, the pavements crumbling beneath our feet," wrote Peter Jenkins, a political columnist for the *Guardian* .[6]

In both senses of the word, Britain just didn't seem to be working any more. The breakdown of essential services was surprising even to someone like myself who had grown up in the battered environment of New York City. The London "Underground" municipal railway was one of the first built in the world. Some stations still carried the elegant Victorian wooden banisters that had once made the system a model of cheap, luxurious transport, but elevators and escalators were continually out of service. An escalator in the station near my office in central London went unrepaired for more than two years, one among countless examples of the national failure to invest and modernize.[7]

British Telecom, the country's telephone and telecommunications network, continued to be one of the more frustrating public utilities in the West even after it was sold off by the state and became a private company. The company illustrated the classic gap between innovation and service in Britain. At a Western economic summit staged in London during the 1980s, British Telecom was able to arrange modern satellite communications and telephone facilities for thousands of journalists and officials in record time. It trumpeted the fact proudly in full-page newspaper ads to prospective business clients. But the quality of its service to ordinary customers was quite another thing. A conversation across town was often an adventure: either it was unintelligible because of static or numerous attempts through crossed lines were necessary to connect with the right number. The problem, as company officials and employees alike freely admitted, was that too little money had been set aside too late for investment in improved switching and relay equipment. A system built for the early twentieth-century could not cope with the demands of the 1980s. According to one survey, as many as 12 per cent of all long-distance calls failed to provide satisfactory quality.[8]

"I find myself exasperated by all sorts of things," said producer-director Jonathan Miller. "I find myself exasperated by the dirt, by the inefficiency of things, by the crammed inelegance and the grubbiness of cities, and the dirt and the litter and the destruction of the countryside." Miller, like many successful Britons, had retreated into his own private space. His home in the upper-middle-class St. John's Wood neighbourhood of London was comfortable and airy. Shuttling between his parlor and theatres and opera houses on three continents, he could keep the decay and inefficiency at arm's length.

Throughout the country, in pockets of affluence, certain Britons lived as if they were part of another nation. My assignments bridged the two worlds. Even in northern Britain, I could pass through an apparent time warp in half an hour, from the computer age of a modern automated plant into an open-air museum of industrial civilization, where abandoned factories dotted the green landscape like medieval castles. Invariably, as I travelled through the landscape of Thatcherized Britain, I felt as if I were entering a country as distant from the contemporary world as nineteenth-century Manchester or Birmingham.

The assignment in Newcastle lived up to my bleak expectations. I stepped outside the Newcastle railway station on Neville Street into a damp, foggy day. The news vendor who sold me the local paper was as listless as the weather, and the Victorian buildings that my faithful "Blue Guide" to Britain described as "dignified" were closer to shabby. Newcastle had been one of the launching pads for the industrial revolution. From the "Geordie" workshops had come the world's first steam locomotive and the first incandescent lamp. By the time I arrived, the city's past accomplishments were obscured by its present despair.

I soon found the "human reality" I was looking for. I was introduced to John Foster, a man apparently washed up at the age of 30. He had lost his job as a pipefitter the year before, and shortly before I met him his wife had lost the part-time position at a shoe store that had been keeping the family solvent. The couple was struggling to meet a mortgage, the cost of school clothes for their eight-year-old son, and the food bills, on an unemployment insurance cheque of £62 a week. The way Foster saw it, things could hardly get worse. "Every place I look for a job tells me they don't need my specialty any more," he complained. "And there's a two-year waiting list for training courses in the skills I want to have to get a new job."

It was disturbingly easy to come across similar tales. The biggest employers in the region — British Steel, the shipyards, and the coal mines — were then casting off thousands of workers as if they were old clothes. Men who had followed their fathers and grandfathers into the coal pits — "It was as natural as breathing," one told me — wondered what would happen to their sons. Newcastle had fallen on hard times before in its history. Memories of the Depression had left scars in the older generation, and as late as 1964 frightening increases in unemployment had forced the government of the day to appoint a special minister for the North. Nevertheless, many people acted and spoke as if this were the Final Crisis. They were exhausted. "As fast as you fill the bath," one worn-out government official told me, "the water seeps out of the holes."

Yet there were intriguing exceptions to the general mood. Looking back over my notes several years later, I realized that my visit to Newcastle had provided me with different images as well. I interviewed, for instance,

Jim Goodman, a 49-year-old Glaswegian who had started a private engineering firm in Newcastle after losing his job with a large company. He built his first machine after doodling the design on the back of a cigarette package. "We sold six of those machines," he boasted, with an energy that seemed to call back the genius of Newcastle's past. "I went to my designer and he had it ready in a few days. Of course, he came from the unemployment queue, like me. That's one of the things that happen to you when you haven't got a job. You become inventive with what you have left."

Goodman started his company with engineers, designers, and skilled and unskilled labourers, all plucked from the unemployment rolls at the local government job centre. "You get a chap who's had a good work record and he suddenly finds himself out in the streets for months — he's ready to climb the walls. When you offer him a job, the response is just what you'd expect ... he'll work his backside off, and to be honest, we exploit that," Goodman explained. Goodman had a vision of Newcastle as a place for the gleaming high-technology industries of the future. "There has to be a new style of work. Our survival really depends on having leaner, fitter companies with a workforce that is no longer tied to the old ways. Of course, I don't see a lot of chance of that happening at the moment."

I didn't either. I had fully absorbed the defeatist atmosphere that seemed prevalent in Newcastle and the country at large, and I felt reservations about Goodman's glib confidence. His tiny, nonunion company seemed to exploit the decline, rather than offer a way out of it. While "twenty-first-century" technology represented an opportunity for a lucky few, most of Newcastle's unemployed already seemed beyond help. Goodman's story was fascinating, but it was an isolated case among dozens of human failures. The report I finally sent home never mentioned Jim Goodman at all.

In my unwillingness to credit Goodman's optimism, I was following the lead of Britons themselves. "I don't think that the next 20 or 30 years or what's left of this century [are] going to be very good for England," Jonathan Miller said. "I think there's no sign of a regeneration of the ingenuity and energy." Most centres of intellectual and political opinion similarly refused to accept the claims of the government that a revival of British enterprise was underway.

If there had been a "revival," it had certainly bypassed the millions of Britons who remained out of a job, and it had exacted a terrible price from the hundreds of thousands who were not likely ever to work again. "You see a lot of men around here just walking around the streets fairly aimlessly," a young community worker named Barry Clark said one afternoon in the northern city of Bradford. It was nearly two years after my visit to Newcastle. By then, the British crisis had become a mirror in which it seemed possible to see the approaching senility of Western industrial society.

Clark looked tired and cynical as he showed me around the Bierley Estate, a public housing project built for textile workers on the edge of Bradford. In the 1920s, this estate represented the height of progressive care for workers. The houses were clean and comfortable, and they were located in fresh air and green pastures away from the belching smoke-stacks. Now that the textile mills had closed for good, the estate was a trap. It was too far away from downtown areas where food and services were cheaper, and where people could look for new jobs, had there been any. "They don't have the bus fare," Clark explained.

More than 30,000 people lived on the estate, but I saw few cars. The conditions, in a city that had been the nineteenth-century woollen capital of the world, were appalling. Unemployment stood at over 20 per cent. Before I arrived, a dysentery epidemic had swept through the area, gener-ating more than 2,000 cases among ill-fed schoolchildren. Teachers reported youngsters falling asleep in class after lunch, a sign of poor diets and squabbling at home.

Poor nutrition was one of the most shocking results of the economic crisis. In a 1984 survey conducted by the Food Policy Unit of Manchester Polytechnic among 1,000 low-income people in northern England, some 37 per cent admitted they had at some time been forced to go without a meal due to lack of money. The sample included young people, the unem-ployed, and the elderly. The average weekly income of those surveyed was less than £50, out of which they could afford about £10 a week on food. They were asked to list what they had had to eat in the previous day. A 37-year-old unemployed man with a wife and two children reported hav-ing five cups of tea, two slices of white bread with margarine, a plate of chips, peas, and an egg. An unemployed labourer said he had had seven-teen slices of bread with margarine, butter and jam, tea, soup, and bis-cuits. An unemployed nurse had had four cups of coffee, one can of chicken-and-mushroom soup, and three slices of brown bread with butter. A 79-year-old woman living alone on a pension listed her previous day's food as tea and toast in the morning, fried fish, fried potatoes, canned peas, and a cup of tea for lunch, and bread and jam for supper. In the evening she allowed herself one cup of cocoa.[9]

The children of Bradford were poorly dressed and craved attention. Arguments at home were another reflection of the tensions caused by unemployment. "Couples get into a trap with each other, especially the younger ones," said Clark. "They have nothing to fall back on, and when they have to budget week by week to make sure the electricity doesn't get cut off, it makes it harder. There's a feeling of helplessness; people fall into a pit from which there is no way out. When you haven't worked for several years, any crisis which you or I would be able to cope with is a major disaster."

Bierley Estate and countless communities like it were neither Brazilian *favelas* nor the "garbage cities" of Cairo. The new poor of Britain had once been solid working-class citizens, with paycheques coming in every week; now they suffered the impact of downward mobility. The welfare system ensured that no one died of hunger, and it usually provided people with a roof over their heads. It was therefore often difficult to tell the extent of unemployed people's alienation. They often wore the same clothes, watched the same television programs, and drank at the same pubs as those who had a job.

In Bierley, the houses looked almost fussily neat inside. The inhabitants, sitting by their TV sets, were more wistful than angry. They often spoke as if they had been unaccountably robbed of some lost utopia. "When I left school in 1953, you could get a job anywhere," said Dennis Lofthouse when he and his common-law wife Nina met me in the sparse sitting room of their two-bedroom house. "Even up to the last five or six years, if you didn't like your job you could walk off. Now a man is ruled by fear at work. If he answers back, the gaffer can tell him where to go."

Lofthouse was a tall, slow-spoken truck driver who looked as spare as the room. He was 48, and had been out of work nearly three years until recently. He had just landed a job driving nine-tonne loads of coal around the country. It was messy work that kept him away from home for long periods of time, but he knew he no longer had any choice. Nina had also lost her job. The eldest of her three children was 11, and she found the pressures of insulating them from the indignity of poverty hardest to bear. "I walk miles around the markets to find clothes for the kids that I can afford, and that are not going to last anyway," she said.

The family of five was doing better than most. Dennis came home with £89 after working a 52-hour week. Nina earned £44 a week from social security, plus another £92 a month in family allowances. They had bought a colour TV and a video machine. "You've got to have luxuries," she explained. "Most of us end up on credit now. You keep thinking you're going to get out of this, but the more you go into it, the deeper you get."

Nina's complaint was repeated by the social service professionals who worked daily with the new British poverty. An entire industry had grown up around the problems of the long-term unemployed. Social workers needed special courses in how to deal with problems that were often more psychological than financial. In the words of the advertisement for a practical skills handbook for professionals quoted at the beginning of this chapter, the problems ranged from "paralyzing fear of the future" to "possible suicide."

"What makes me really angry," said Peter Milligan, a credit advisor in Bradford, "is that 86 per cent of my clients have financial commitments that were all made before they were unemployed. One of my clients, for instance is a butcher. He's 35 years old now, and he once had three shops in the centre of town. When people started to lose their jobs, he lost business. He had to give up one shop, then the others. His bills started to accumulate. He sold his house and all the furniture in it, and declared bankruptcy. Now he drives a taxi part-time and lives with his mother-in-law. But the one thing he keeps worrying about is whether he will have to go to prison for his debts. He was brought up as a person who pays his bills and lives a frugal life."

The only consolation available to the butcher was that he was not alone. "In ten years," noted a report prepared by the Bradford Metropolitan Council in 1984, "the [Bradford] district has moved from full employment, a superficially healthy-looking economy, and relative prosperity for virtually everyone to massive factory closures, 37,000 unemployed, 50,000 people on supplementary benefit — and for thousands, the apparent end of their hopes for a decent career, income, and lifestyle."[10]

The report, signed by the leaders of all political parties in the city council, read like an obituary. In numb phrases, the authors noted how once-thriving centres of industry now stood empty and derelict. They described the fierce competition from overseas that had killed the textile trade. Many Bradford firms had simply moved their operations outside of Britain, to developing countries where labour costs were lower. The district's manufacturing base had eroded.

Some of the social statistics they cited could have come out of the third world. In two inner-city areas, 17 out of every 12,000 babies died before their first birthday, compared with an average of 10 in other areas in Britain. Of the 37,000 unemployed, 12,500 had been out of work for more than a year in 1984, and 7,000 had been jobless for more than two years. "An average Bradfordian can expect to live two years less than the national average," the report said. Few sentences could have illustrated more poignantly how the conditions of the early industrial era had returned to plague Britain at the era's demise.

Maggie Pearse ran Ginger Ale, an advice centre for single parents in Bradford. I met her in her office down a shabby side street in the downtown area. Despite the resemblance of many of the problems in her caseload to past British crises, she was aware of a change. "My parents come from the mining area in Newcastle and grew up in the poverty of the Twenties, and it seemed to be happening all over again," she said. "I would hear about houses catching fire, for instance, and I would wonder, was that family using candles because their electricity was disconnected? But I think what we're seeing here is something new.

It's fourth-world poverty in Western society."

During the 1980s, employment became the principal arbiter of character and social status. You were, as the phrase went, either "in work" or you weren't. In even the most depressed parts of northern Britain, there were people who had held on to their jobs. Skilled workers and craftsmen were able to move from one factory to another. In their ability to command a living wage, they now had little in common with their former workmates. This disparity accounted for a marked decline in British working-class culture. The contrast between the militant, proud workers of the 1950s and 1960s, and the resigned unemployed of the 1980s was another sign of how much had changed in Britain.

"There used to be a literate working class in this city," said a Glasgow woman in her early forties. "But that type of man no longer exists in this city. My father, for example, was an ordinary steelworker. He and his friends drank heavily and worked very hard, but they read a lot. My father read three or four newspapers a day, every day. He was very political. He had an opinion on everything, and they would argue it over in the pubs. At one o'clock on a Friday afternoon, after the men picked up their paycheques, you could hardly get into the pubs. Now the shipyards are gone and the steel mills are away, and you've got a working-class population which basically doesn't work. I can't even find a good working-class pub any more."

The possibility that thousands of men and women like John Foster and the young Bradford butcher were the casualties of a planned depression did not seem to bother most Britons. Every family either knew someone who was out of work or felt the pressure of the constricted job market on their children. They had developed a wartime fatalism. Joblessness was accepted as a cruel fact of life, like death on the battlefield. "The only surprising thing about unemployment," said a Liverpool sociologist, "is that it's no longer surprising." There were still battles between unions and management, but the energy of the struggle was sapped by the knowledge that a growing army of the unemployed was waiting to take scarce jobs. More than 85 per cent of the population still worked. The "unwaged" became a normal subgroup of the population, along with students and the elderly. They rated special discounts for movies and museums, and created what one American journalist termed "the unemployment culture."[11]

The solidarity of the unemployed was a poignant substitute for the cohesiveness of the old working class. Nevertheless, the "unemployment culture" provided evidence of life among the industrial ruins. Many Britons treated their state of joblessness as a permanent subsidized university. "If I hadn't been unemployed," said one youth, "I never would have had time to learn to play the guitar." The two young men of Wham!, one of Britain's most successful pop groups in the 1980s, said the "dole" payments they earned as unemployed teenagers gave them the time to rehearse and write the music that made them millionaires.[12]

Their wealth was earned from thousands of jobless youngsters like themselves who bought their records and paid to attend their concerts. State benefits and subsidies amounting to more than £8 billion annually made the unemployed one of the fastest-growing and richest consumer markets in Britain. One advertising-agency executive said that the marketing success of the Sony "Walkman" tape cassette player in Britain was due almost entirely to trend-setting youth who spent their unemployment payments on "conspicuous fashion and personal technology."

Unemployment statistics rarely told the whole story. The thriving "black economy" — consisting of unemployed or underemployed people who provided, for cash, services like cleaning windows and plumbing — was worth an estimated £25 billion a year, nearly eight per cent of the official national income.[13] In the beery gloom of the Westerhope Workingmen's Club in Newcastle, I met a master plumber named George who hadn't held a steady job for seven years. He refused to give me his full name because he didn't want the tax department to know he was illegally picking up odd jobs while receiving unemployment money from the state. It was his private guerrilla war against a system that had locked him out. "In this corner," he waved a callused hand in the direction of his mates, "the most skilled tradesmen of Britain are sitting. And we're invisible."

The black economy and the unemployment culture were hardly examples of the "enterprise economy" the Thatcherites hoped their policies would create. But in their willingness to accept permanently high levels of unemployment, the British have changed some of the postwar assumptions of Western politics. More than 50 years after the worldwide Depression that had traumatized their parents and grandparents, they had learned to exploit economic catastrophe.

The Bradford Council survey noted signs of attitude change below the grey surface of poverty and alienation. Of those Bradfordians who were working, some 44 per cent were women. "The traditional view of a family consisting of a male breadwinner, a dependent wife at home, and two children is no longer the pattern for most people," the report said, noting that without women's earnings, three times as many families would be living in poverty.

The report suggested that a new set of policies was needed to deal with the new situation. If, as seemed likely, the mass employment provided by traditional industries never returned, communities would have to begin working out ways to handle a permanent core of unemployed or underemployed people, and "turn more and more attention to dealing with [the situation's] consequences in society."

My final appointment in Bradford was at City Hall, a wonderful Victorian building that conveyed the power and majesty of Britain's city-states in their heyday. The clock tower looked like Big Ben at Westminster, and it even rang like Big Ben. Gordon Moore, the gruff chief executive of the town, took up his post in 1965, at the height of the boom years. He found the city administrators living in a dream world. "They kept saying to me this was the world metropolis of the wool trade," he said. "But they were living in the past. Even the equipment the mills had was appalling."

Moore claimed that Bradford's depression contributed a healthy realism to the town. The region's economic crisis had destroyed so much of the traditional infrastructure that the normal British resistance to change was impossible to maintain. As a result, he said, the city was on the brink of a development boom. A campaign to attract new industry, including high-tech companies, was showing success. One of the new computer industries had just received the Queen's Award for Exports. Two new hotels were being built. Bradford was now confident enough to restore some of its old landmarks. The Alhambra, an Edwardian music hall that had hosted entertainers like Laurel and Hardy, was getting an £8-million facelift. "It's no good deceiving ourselves," Moore was careful to say. "We have massive problems, but when I go to Liverpool, for instance, I feel much better. Now that's a city which is beyond hope. In Bradford, I don't find the same despair and despondency."

The optimism of people like Jim Goodman, Dennis Lofthouse, and Gordon Moore was admirable, but it seemed unreal, even fantastic, to think that individual initiative could flourish in the litter of broken dreams I had encountered in many parts of Britain. The odds, in particular, against someone with a working-class background seemed to make it impossible. It was not until I met Linda Echlin that I changed my mind.

I found her in the cramped back office of a tiny shop in downtown Glasgow. The shop was indistinguishable from the row of stationery sellers, hardware stores, and grey houses lining the busy thoroughfare of Old Dunbarton Street. A gas station faced it on the other side. It was hard to believe that the storefront was the "head office" of a £40,000-a-year knitters' cooperative that employed three part-time salesclerks and a bookkeeper. But it was even harder to imagine that the plump woman in owlish black-rimmed glasses who faced me across a desk laden with balls of wool had created the business out of pure spunk.

Just over a decade ago, Echlin had been a cleaning lady. Now she had the confident aplomb of a businesswoman. Something had happened to her in the 1980s. Instead of accepting the narrowing horizons that the British crisis offered her class, she fought back. "I was obsessive — well, demented really," she said. "I knew it was a matter of finding help even if it killed me. I got tunnel vision. Everything else fell by the wayside, even family and keeping the house clean."

Linda Echlin was as iron-willed and stubborn in her way as the woman in Number 10 Downing Street. She proved to be one of the most remarkable people I met during five years of reporting from Britain. She had somehow mastered the art of survival in a male-oriented and failure-prone society. Hers was a story almost too good to be true.

Echlin grew up in a tough, working-class Glasgow neighbourhood in the 1950s. Her father, like most Glasgow workers of that era, regarded a job as virtually a birthright. Echlin absorbed his attitude. She was so confident of her ability to find work that she didn't bother to finish school. Echlin dropped out of classes and went to London at the age of 15. It was the era of the "Swinging Sixties," and a job was not the sort of thing a lively young person needed to worry about. "I could leave a job on Friday, and be in another one on Monday. That was the game," Echlin recalled.

At 20, she returned home, married, and began a family. In the early 1970s, her husband lost his job as a millworker. Echlin, with four children and a husband to support, was not too proud to do what working-class women had always done when their men fell into the troughs of the economic cycle. She went back to work temporarily, scrubbing the offices of doctors and dentists in upper-class Glasgow to tide her family over the bad times. She would leave the house at six in the morning, rush back at nine to prepare breakfast, and then head off to find other menial work.

At the time, it did not seem like the end of the world. Although neither Echlin nor her husband possessed any real skills, unemployment was regarded as a temporary setback. True, the Scottish shipbuilding industry was now providing less than one per cent of the world's ships, compared to twelve per cent in 1954, but hadn't oil been discovered off the Scottish coast?

The "temporary" family crisis lasted longer than it should have. It was nearly five years before her husband found work again, and moved the family to the little town of Saltcoats, 30 miles south of Glasgow on the Ayrshire coast. By then, the easy confidence of her early working career had faded. Over the next six years, Echlin discovered how many other women had been through the same experience. While her husband's anxieties about the permanence of his new job grew, she began helping local authorities in her town as a volunteer community organizer. In 1980, unemployment in Saltcoats was climbing to frighteningly high levels. Echlin formed a committee of women whose husbands had lost their jobs.

Looking around their depressed community for ways to earn money, the women decided to take advantage of the British talent for tinkering. Nearly every home in Saltcoats had a makeshift workshop where men carved lamps or tables, and there was always a sewing machine in the front room or a pair of knitting needles tucked away by the family picture album. Echlin persuaded the local council to provide an empty store that could be used to sell local crafts and second-hand clothes. But she still needed advice on how to run the business.

She became a familiar sight in the colourless waiting rooms of Glasgow officialdom. Planting herself stolidly before one desk after another, she would adjust her thick glasses, inhale one of her ever-present cigarettes, and direct an anxious smile at her captive. Times were hard for everyone, Echlin admitted. But in Saltcoats, nobody could survive on the welfare payments arriving every week. Could someone help them?

Hard-luck stories were nothing new to the overworked Glaswegian bureaucrats. Defeated and sullen people were crowding into their offices every day with accounts of lost jobs, hungry children, and broken marriages. In the winter of 1980, the cases were multiplying. However, the tenacious Echlin rarely left an office empty-handed.

The social workers, impressed by her apparently unlimited energy, went out of their way to help. They often had nothing better to offer than advice. Occasionally, a box of stationery, or perhaps a sheet of postage stamps, would find its way to Saltcoats to help the women with their accounts. But more importantly, each time Echlin took the evening train home to Saltcoats, she possessed a little more knowledge to add to the shop's growing inventory of ideas. "I still don't know how those bureaucrats put up with me," she recalled. "Sometimes, in front of them, I would just break down and weep. All those words they were using — cash flow, projections, board of directors — were like a foreign language."

The group of women had to learn how to run a business the hard way. "We would even take the clothes and items they couldn't sell in church bazaars," Echlin remembered. "Once, we ended up with a shop full of black bags. We had to throw them all away." But the little shop slowly began to make enough to provide a few pounds a week of extra income for nearly 100 home knitters and woodcarvers. With Echlin as the energizing force, the women soon went from selling old clothes to making new ones.

The shop in the Saltcoats High Street also gave Echlin an insight into the extent of the transformation of British society. Saltcoats was apparently filled with people cast adrift by the economic crisis. "A lot of old people used to come into our shop," she remembered. "I would get all their worries about lights being cut off and the pension cheques coming late; in our community, there are a lot of social workers and social work agencies, but for some reason the elderly weren't going to them to complain.

"Then I realized it was because they weren't frightened of a shop; a lot of them just wanted to come in and talk. The advent of the supermarket wiped out a lot of wee shops in our community, and people in supermarkets don't talk to you. They fill shelves and wait on you at the checkout counter, but they don't talk. In the old people's day, you would buy two rolls and a pint of milk, and you would stand and talk for half an hour."

From her social agency friends in Glasgow, Echlin heard about a program that was providing funds and advice to a number of businesses like theirs. Called the Local Enterprise Advisory Project (LEAP), it received funding from the Scottish Office in Westminster and the Strathclyde (Glasgow region) authorities. The acronym LEAP was appropriate. The young community organizers in Glasgow wanted to provide depressed communities with the skills necessary for making their way through the government bureaucracies, skills that most middle-class businesspeople and larger municipalities already had. But their most important aim was to change the entrenched defeatism of people who had been hurt most by the slowdown in the economy.

"Everyone always assumed that you needed large, new industries in order to have an economic recovery, but we felt that wouldn't necessarily affect unemployment at local levels," explained Colin Roxburgh, a 34-year-old Glasgow community organizer who worked with Linda Echlin. "People haven't the skills to take advantage of it. In many cases, the people who really need help don't have the basic knowledge that entrepreneurship requires. They have only been trained as employees. They may have been damn good welders, but they were employed by people who already had those skills, which are tools of power. What we were interested in doing was passing those tools of power back into the community — by teaching them simple things, like being able to do their own books. That's the community business process."

The little shop in Saltcoats qualified as a "community business," and the LEAP officials had an eager pupil in Linda Echlin. The Saltcoats cooperative was one of the first to apply for new "management grants" designed to help neophyte business operators in impoverished neighbourhoods learn how to manage their accounts and find markets for what they produced. With LEAP's help, in 1984, the Saltcoat knitters received £28,000 a year for three years to put the business on its feet.

The money allowed them to hire a "business consultant," but the advice they were getting from their new consultant, a young woman from Glasgow with a business degree, wasn't easy to swallow. If the knitters and craftspeople wanted to succeed, they would have to drop those who weren't producing. It was the kind of harsh decision hundreds of British managers were forced to take throughout the lean years of the early 1980s. Such decisions often provoked resistance in the larger British economy, but the knitters had few second thoughts. The knowledge that they were working for themselves and not some distant manager produced the sort of coming-to-terms-with-reality that the LEAP concept was meant to achieve.

With their grant money, they decided to move to Glasgow. They kept their old clothes and crafts operation in Saltcoats, but they now wanted to capitalize on the one skill, knitting, they were best at. They pared the operation down to 40 knitters and began making knitwear they thought they could sell to buyers from big stores. Under the weighty name of the "Home Production Sales Organization," they set out to meet the real world.

When I met Linda Echlin, she was preparing new designs for the fashions she hoped would soon be selling in London department stores. The piles of red and blue yarn, balls of wool, swatches of fabric, and heaps of paper surrounding Echlin's antique typewriter were testimony to the drive that had brought this little company into existence. The woman who less than five years before had had no idea what "cash flow" meant now said confidently, "We should achieve viability over the next two years."

I asked Echlin if she thought many people could follow in her footsteps. She pulled a serious face. "If you can find a wee, hard core of people that can somehow be sparked into making a better life, it's bloody better than nothing happening," she said. "The more nothing happens, the less likely anything is to happen." She began to giggle. "In bad English, worse can only get worser."

I realized, looking back over many of the people and situations I had encountered over the previous five years, that Echlin's experience was part of a pattern of courageous survival existing below the apathy and resignation I had been seeing in my visits around Britain. The clues were hard to pick up because they seemed so singular at the time. Toward the end of 1985, a reporter from the *Observer* newspaper in London travelled north, as I had done three years earlier, to sketch the "human face" of Britain's industrial crisis. He went to Wakefield — like Newcastle, a crucible of the industrial revolution — and interviewed Graham Wood, a skilled 28-year-old auto mechanic who had lost his job years before.

With a friend, Wood had scraped together savings and government grants to start a small, successful glass-fibre-moulding business. The reporter asked him why he seemed so sure of his ability to rebuild his life. "When you are skilled and hard-working, yet have experienced unemployment," Wood replied, "an iron enters the soul."[14]

PART II
The Postindustrial Kingdom

Learn, good soul, to think our
former state a happy dream.

— Richard II, *Act V, Scene 1.*

Chapter 3

LOOK BACK WITHOUT ANGER

Damn you, England. You're rotting now,
and quite soon you'll disappear.

— *John Osborne, "A Letter to my
Fellow Countrymen," 1961.*

Jeremy Irons began his acting career with the wrong face. In the 1960s, his drama school teacher informed him, sadly, that his delicate features would never get him a leading role in Britain. It was the golden era of the "angry young men," when actors like Albert Finney and Tom Courtenay, with their strong working-class faces and rough accents, were making the British school of so-called kitchen-sink drama famous around the world. "My instructor said I would have been great 30 years before," Irons remembered, smiling. "He told me there was no place for someone who 'spoke right' and looked faintly elegant." Two decades later, however, Irons discovered he owned one of the most successful faces in Margaret Thatcher's "new" Britain.

In the autumn of 1981, a television series called *Brideshead Revisited* appeared. The 11-part series was adapted from a postwar novel by Evelyn Waugh that focused on the long and ultimately tragic friendship between a young English painter named Charles Ryder and a spoiled aristocrat named Sebastian Flyte. Irons, then an unknown 33-year-old, played the role of Charles Ryder. Within the year, he was an international star. The "faintly elegant" faces of Irons and his co-star Anthony Andrews captured the fancy of a worldwide audience. The popularity of *Brideshead* made it one of Britain's most profitable cultural exports in the 1980s and contributed to a global fascination for British popular culture not seen since the 1960s.

Waugh's novel chronicled the decline of an era and the decay in particular of Britain's Catholic aristocracy. In the television production, the theme of decline was partially obscured by a fascination with baroque manners and opulent settings. *Brideshead* tapped a special British emotion. The image conveyed by the central characters was one of self-confidence and poise in the midst of a disintegrating environment. It was another paradox of the decade that Britons found some of the strength they needed to tackle their contemporary problems by updating the images of their past.

The modern *Brideshead* era actually began with a rejuvenated treatment of one of the most powerful of all elements in British mythology: the monarchy. On July 29, 1981, Prince Charles, heir to the British throne, married his young fiancée Lady Diana Spencer with the pomp and majesty of a nineteenth-century monarch. Britain lovingly took down from the attic its imperial props and symbols, dusted them off, and staged a one-day spectacle of living history to the delight of 100 million television viewers around the world. The royal wedding turned out to be an event with far-reaching cultural significance for Britain in the 1980s.

At first, the splendour of the royal wedding seemed a sad counterpoint to Britain's declining fortunes as a commercial and cultural power. Occasional British voices pointed out that, enchanting as the spectacle was, it couldn't bring back the industrial competence that paid the bills. But those voices were soon lost in the din outside Buckingham Palace. Television turned the "village wedding" into a global event, and Britons basked in its reflected glow. "Anyone who wonders what happened to British patriotism will see it alive and well on the pavements of Britain today," one BBC commentator enthused.

The night before the wedding, I slept on the couch of my tiny office overlooking Fleet Street in order to watch the wedding procession to St. Paul's Cathedral. Many other occupants of my building made similar decisions to stay the night, after having been warned by police that offices along the wedding route would be locked at dawn. The next morning a collection of tired journalists, secretaries, and accountants pressed against the window railings high over the narrow street to get a view of the day's events. "I can't believe I'm doing this," said the manager of the office next to mine. The gilded carriages carrying the Queen, the bridal couple, and assorted royalty passed beneath us in a glittering instant, and the crowds closed in again. Reluctantly, we went back inside to watch the rest of the day's events on TV. A loudspeaker erected nearby was even then relaying the organ music from St. Paul's to the hushed masses below.

Even Britons watching at home felt the same inexplicable sense of giddiness. Nicholas Albery, a one-time Sixties radical, was prepared to be angry — or at least bored. "I remember I was lying in bed watching the ridiculous wedding on the telly, and my neighbour came in, a woman I didn't particularly like and who didn't particularly like me. We began watching it together, and we fell to sort of hugging and kissing. It was just sort of a sexual atmosphere."

The wedding anticipated the success of the *Brideshead* style. By the end of that day, when the royal couple walked out onto the balcony of Buckingham Palace, kissed, and waved shyly to the crowds below, all the world was at Britain's feet.

But what kind of Britain was it? The royal couple's youthfulness contrasted poignantly with the times. Paolo Filo della Torre, an Italian journalist based for years in London, detected signs of a midlife crisis in the mythology of contemporary Britain. The appeal of Britain in the 1980s, he believed, told us almost as much about ourselves as it did about the British. "The mood of the Western world has swung toward middle age — middle-aged disillusionment, middle-aged conformity, and middle-aged repressiveness, leavened perhaps by a dash of middle-aged pragmatism," he wrote in 1985. "This is the mood that has voted in and supports the 1980s Britannia, a strong and authoritative lady resolved to re-create the glory of the days of the British Empire, and who, by being in step with the times, has captured the imagination of the entire Western world."[1] *Brideshead* and the royal wedding were examples of the sorts of things the British knew they had always done well. But they were also proof against the inevitability of decline: the national talent for historical pageantry and pomp had survived the breakdown of the industrial machine.

Inevitably, the "productions" of the 1980s carried a strong sense of emerging nationalism. Like the Americans who elected Ronald Reagan in 1980, the British wanted to feel good about themselves again. Thatcher, who promised to restore Britain's place in the world, was the political counterpart of the scriptwriters, film producers, and royal wedding planners. The decade witnessed an auspicious marriage of culture and national pride.

A year after *Brideshead* appeared, Britain's new look abroad received an official endorsement from the acknowledged experts in the manufacture of dreams. On Academy Awards night in March 1982, British film-maker Colin Welland won an Oscar for the screenplay of *Chariots of Fire*, a small-budget film that became a "sleeper" success around the world at the same time as *Brideshead* in 1981. Based on the true story of two British runners who swept the 100- and 400-metre track events in the 1924 Paris Olympic Games, the film concentrated on the friendships and rivalries between a young aristocrat and his working-class or immigrant contemporaries. Its emotional finale, which proved that hard work and determination could overcome class differences and win prizes for Britain, could very nearly be described as Thatcherite. The real-life success of the film underlined the point.

When Welland's name was announced at the Academy Award ceremonies, the portly former actor bounded onto the stage of the Hollywood Bowl. Beaming, he held up the golden statuette like a war trophy. As the cheers and applause died down, he stepped to the microphone and inadvertently blurted out a phrase his compatriots would learn to live with for the rest of the decade. "The British are coming!" he shouted.

His film won three other Oscars that night. British newspapers, taking their cue from Colin Welland, reacted as if the Academy were giving the prizes to Britain herself. In a way, that was exactly what Hollywood was doing. The Academy could not give an Oscar to the royal couple for their balcony scene, but it could recognize the artistic excellence in part inspired by the national pride they embodied. Wrapped in sequinned Union Jacks, the old Empire had duly arrived as an international celebrity for the 1980s.

The renewed absorption in the nation's aristocratic heritage was in contrast to the free-swinging egalitarianism of the 1960s. The British seemed to have changed gears. "Suddenly we didn't want to go to see plays and films about the problems of today," Jeremy Irons said. "We wanted to hark back." Britain's economic distress was the key explanation for the change. "Over the last 20 years more people had more opportunities to be socially mobile than ever before," wrote Peter York, a young magazine writer who became an internationally known interpreter of 1980s Britain. "It gave them a taste for things — the things the rich really had. Then the economy got worse again, and it looked as if the changes of the Sixties and Seventies might have been bad, as if the future might not work. When that happens, people want roots and rules — or at least the symbols of them."[2]

There was no better symbol of roots and rules than the British aristocracy — and something odd happened to its members in the 1980s. After years of keeping a low profile, the British upper classes suddenly seemed to be everywhere. They were seen unashamedly enjoying themselves at foxhunts and debutante balls; they were photographed leading charity drives, opening their estates to tourists, raising money for political causes, and making serious speeches about the nation's future.

The claims of the aristocracy to a special moral or political influence in national affairs had ended for all practical purposes in 1918, when an act entitling every British male (and some females) to a vote became law. Aristocrats have lived ever since with the threat of being taxed into extinction or legislated into oblivion. As late as the 1970s, they were still an easy target for reformers and egalitarian-minded governments.

Until the 1980s, those aristocrats who were successful were usually careful to confine their influence to private gatherings and their enjoyment of luxury to the privacy of their homes. The same free-enterprise values that propelled the new government into power liberated those who had money from any sense of guilt. Prince Charles and Diana, Princess of Wales, emerged as the acceptable faces of inherited privilege, and they pulled along many others in their wake. Titled personages appeared in magazine ads or TV commercials as high-class salespeople. Lord Mansfield was photographed in front of his estate with a new Volkswagen car. Lord Lichfield promoted Burberry's raincoats. Complimentary stories about enterprising "aristos" regularly appeared in every Sunday glossy magazine. A marquess could attract sympathy with a tale of how he had managed to make ends meet at the ancestral castle by turning it into a convention centre. Where once he might have been the focus of angry attempts to use his grounds for public housing, he now won praise for preserving Britain's heritage.

One historic British landmark, Castle Howard, played a starring role in the aristocratic revival. The late Lord Howard of Henderskelfe, chairman of the BBC, rented the family pile to television production crews looking for a place to film *Brideshead Revisited.* The success of the series attracted thousands of tourists to the magnificent property in Yorkshire and ensured that the old building would remain intact for generations to come. Like other stately homes that attracted new interest in the 1980s, it represented values that Britons thought were important to their survival.

Charles Brocket, the elegant, Eton-educated third Baron of Brocket Hall, who allowed himself and his American wife to be photographed in *Brideshead*-style evening clothes on the lake in front of his massive family home, explained to a Sunday magazine reporter that he and his counterparts, in going public with their wealth and their lifestyles, were merely following a path already trodden by the royal family. "The Queen is Britain's most effective promoter [and] peers have the same sort of attraction," said Brocket. He was right. The royal wedding was a triumph of promotion for Britain. The Queen frankly used her tours abroad as marketing trips for British goods and industry. She lent respectability to the feeling that there was no harm in making — and enjoying — a profit. "In point of fact, surely," wrote Auberon Waugh, the son of *Brideshead's* author, in the *Spectator* in 1986, "it has been rather a jolly time. Many of us have grown richer. I certainly have. Others may have something to complain about, but I don't."[3]

Waugh's "*Brideshead*-ism" was one of the delicious ironies of the decade. Britain was culturally and geographically such a tight little island that pretending to be ignorant of Britain's growing industrial sickness was less an example of complacency or selfishness than the purposeful adoption of a style — and the aristocrats fit right in.

Lord Colwyn is one of the few who could see what was going on from both sides, so to speak, of the ballroom. The baron, a dentist who leads a part-time dance band, is at home in the upper reaches of British society. At least 60 nights a year, he and his trumpet can be seen in the homes and watering places of the rich and the noble, from Windsor Castle to exclusive Mayfair hotels. At charity balls, twenty-first birthdays, and scores of other occasions where honourable lords and ladies gathered in the 1980s, he detected a new feeling in the air. "When I look down from the stage, I can see how confident some of these people are, even the young ladies of 18; and there's almost an arrogant look to some of the men," he said. The confidence of the aristocrats made it hard to tell them apart from the new Thatcherite entrepreneurs.

"You can see the leisure society getting larger," he said. "There's a lot of money about. Sometimes it can be embarrassing." He and his band played at a ball held to celebrate the change-over to new financial technology in the City of London. It was a charity auction for a holiday trip to the West Indies. "They were bidding more than some of my band members earn in a year, and I found that hard to reconcile," Colwyn said, "but I don't lose sleep over it."

Even for those without the money to attend charity balls, style was important. Britain's new pop stars bridged the gap between the affluent society and the unemployment culture. Boy George, who was born George O'Dowd, piled up millions in export earnings for his country through the sheer novelty of dressing and performing in long skirts and makeup. He brought the style-conscious underground culture of London discos and clubs into the open, but like many of his contemporaries he carefully stayed away from the images of sexual and political rebellion presented by previous generations of pop stars. Mothers were reassured when he explained he wasn't even interested in sex.

Britain, according to *The Economist,* was once again the "undisputed leader of youth culture" around the world in 1985. In that year alone, 12 of the 27 top single records in the U.S. were British.[4] The industry earned a record £1.5 billion in foreign earnings.[5] Youngsters who regarded the Beatles and the Rolling Stones as museum pieces mobbed British pop groups from Sydney to Toronto.

Most of the pop stars of the 1980s shared with other successful cultural phenomena of the decade a disavowal of national politics and a desire to flout the obituaries written about Britain. Collectively, they made a most energetic comment about contemporary life. Unlike their 1960s and 1970s predecessors, who identified with the alternative politics and "down-market" lifestyles of their affluent audiences, the glittering pop musicians of the 1980s publicly indulged in fantasies of wealth.

In the clubs and discos of Britain, and in the depressing public housing estates in the inner cities, it was hard to distinguish the employed from the unemployed. Everyone dressed "up," in the absence of any other visible proof of success. Anybody could improve himself by adopting the clothes, attitudes, or style that represented his personal response to the uncertain society around him.

The story of a young radio disc jockey illustrates the point. In less than two years, 30-year-old Gary Davies moved from a job in a radio studio in Manchester to national prominence as host of London's BBC1 pop station. His lifestyle changed accordingly. Davies owned a red Porsche 911 and a plush North London apartment with floor-to-ceiling mirrors, a whirlpool bath, and a bed with built-in radio and television controls. His nights were spent going from club to club, sipping champagne and trading gossip with other "celebrities." "My greatest problem," he told one admiring reporter who accompanied him on a night's tour of London clubland, "is deciding what to wear."[6] Such public displays of hedonism were part of the "style" of British popular culture in the 1980s.

On the other hand, Sloane Rangerdom, the British answer to North America's "yuppie culture," emphasized the nonacquisitive lifestyle and conformity of a certain section of the British aristocracy that had been mocked during the Swinging Sixties. *The Official Sloane Ranger Handbook*, written in 1982 by Peter York and Ann Barr, editors at the glossy *Harpers* magazine of London, focused on a small group of upper-middle-class youth whose social life revolved around Sloane Square, a southwest London neighbourhood that had once claimed international fame as the location of the King's Road, the capital of the beaded, psychedelic London of the Sixties. The King's Road was now commercialized and bland, while Sloane Square, considerably helped by the rise to prominence of the most well-known "Sloane," Diana, Princess of Wales, became a worldwide symbol of a certain English way of life. "Sloane Rangerhood is a state of mind that's eternal," wrote York and Barr. "You might believe it's all different now, that nobody's like that anymore. You'd be wrong. ...Good manners, nursery food, the same shirts for five years. ...This is the...eternal stream of English life."[7]

And so it seemed. The acceptance of limits, a subtle disdain for material goods, a love of the past, and a close-knit community — *Brideshead* values that helped the aristocracy ride out the storms over the years — were well suited to the new uncertainties of the 1980s.

The fact that Britain's lords and ladies felt free to exhibit their lifestyles openly, along with Sloanes and pop stars, was the most visible evidence of a national shift in attitudes. Class, as Peter York once put it in a felicitous phrase, "came out of the closet." During the Falklands War, for instance, class became synonymous with competence and authority. "Suddenly, everyone on TV was officer class, authoritative, *posh*," York wrote. "The easy, classless world of chat show presenters and disc jockeys was peeled away for generals and admirals, the right people for serious times."[8]

Sometimes even Britons could not understand why they were suddenly everyone's favourites. One evening in 1985, Simon Callow and other members of the cast of *A Room with a View*, a film based on E.M. Forster's Edwardian novel, assembled in New York for its first screening to an American audience. They waited nervously for the show to begin. The reaction after the lights went out startled them. "The audience roared with laughter from the moment it started," recalled Callow. "We thought the novel it was based on was a kind of clothing for a parable of human behaviour, not an evocation of a particularly British way of life. What *they* were shrieking about was how English, how exotic, how 'another world' it was."

A self-described "renaissance" of the British film industry was under way, largely built out of movies and television productions that took a fresh look at the myths of Britain's past. Callow held a cynical view of much of the work produced during the decade. "It's got great style," he said, "which is the thing that generally starts to predominate when people don't believe in anything."

Yet the overseas success of British videos, films, and other products of popular culture demonstrated that, even if Britain's conquests began in cutting rooms and recording studios rather than the playing fields of Eton, British vitality was real. The intensely competitive Thatcherian environment produced cultural entrepreneurs with a talent for success that was notably absent in other areas of British life. Many of the most successful films and TV productions were begun by refugees from the world of advertising. "I learned — at a point in life where it was not offensive to learn — that the key to having a successful product was in tailoring product to market," said David Puttnam, a former maker of TV commercials who went on to produce *Chariots of Fire* and many other successful British films of the decade.[9] It was a message Margaret Thatcher would have endorsed wholeheartedly.

Instead of rebelling like the "angry young men" of the Fifties against the arrogant, class-conscious society of the (original) *Brideshead* years, many young middle-class Britons sought reassurance in its atmosphere of self-confidence and stability. "I have a great love of style and a great distrust for new things," remarked Jeremy Irons in a comment he believed applied to many in his generation. "In Britain, there's a sort of weight, a lodestone which keeps things smooth no matter how rocky they get. That's why we'll never have a revolution here."

Born the son of a prosperous company director on the Isle of Wight, educated in a Dorset public school, Irons became interested in the stage after reading theatrical histories. He described it as a "backward-looking decision" that paralleled the voyages of rediscovery to the past taken by many other Britons. Despite being dressed in jeans and a shapeless grey sweatshirt, Irons still managed to look the personification of the *Brideshead* style when we met in a lovely 1930s house outside Stratford-upon-Avon, in the summer of 1986. The actor had rented the house for his family while he appeared for a season with the Royal Shakespeare Company. Slender, courteous, with a hint of dreamy grace, he could have stepped out of the drawing room of a Noel Coward play. Our conversation was held in what seemed to me an appropriate setting: a 26-foot wooden Edwardian sailing punt moored to a rickety dock on the Avon. The punt is Irons's fondest possession. "It's the place I go to think," he said, leading me down a brambly path to the river. As I gingerly stepped in behind him onto the punt's velvet cushions, he was already pouring tea. Distant birdsong filtered through the gentle light of a perfect English summer afternoon. Here, I imagined, Charles Ryder and Sebastian Flyte would have been at home.

Irons offered one explanation of *Brideshead*'s attraction to the British psyche of the 1980s. There were many Charles Ryders still walking around Britain, he said. The actor was first offered the part of Sebastian, but he refused. "I was more interested in the Englishness of Charles, the dilettante quality of him, that quality of never really committing his full self to anything, which means of course that he ends up without anything. In a way I always felt that Charles Ryder was the man I was educated to be. Since leaving school, I have been dis-educating myself, and trying to open up, to cut away that reserve, to stop relying on that charm and to give more of myself. When I meet some of my old school contemporaries, I see what I could have been."

It was an intriguing comment, and one that partly explained Irons's open admiration for the prime minister. She had, he said, helped Britons to realize that traditional English charm was no longer sufficient to pay Britain's bills. The actor believed Thatcher had laid the groundwork for a more realistic approach to Britain's problems. "This is a period when we are leaving the Victorian work ethic," Irons said. "At the moment it seems too many people are working too much, and too many people are not working at all. As an actor, I can see this clearly because I don't have that [Victorian] work ethic. I work extraordinary hours; sometimes it's an 18-hour day, sometimes I don't work at all.

"I see work as not being a habit, yet we all need a job for our self-respect, as something to base our lives around. A job gives us structure. It's not a good feeling that one has been given money for doing nothing." He paused, and smiled. "But I have to tell you it's very easy to fill seven days a week with not working. When people say to me they don't know what they would do [without steady work], I know damn well what they'd do. They'd walk, they'd fish, they'd ride horses, they'd work in the garden. And this is beginning to happen."

Irons was not indifferent to the millions of his fellow Britons unable to afford horses. But he was sure that the political changes of the decade would in the long run improve the lives of his compatriots.

Britain's film "renaissance" was in tatters by the late Eighties. Some of the major production companies closed, and a few leading filmmakers such as David Puttnam took important jobs in Hollywood or went on to non-British themes. The government was blamed for refusing to back up the fledgling companies and directors with grants and training support. In the theatre, there were bitter arguments with politicians about diminishing arts subsidies; and in the entertainment industry at large, there were warnings about the growing American presence. Colin Welland's confident prediction at the Hollywood Bowl now evoked embarrassed laughter.

But the achievements concentrated in such a short period of time were remarkable. Of the themes that dominated British movies and plays in the 1980s, the *Brideshead* version of nostalgic realism played a central part. It fostered a tough-minded optimism and a liberating nationalism as relevant abroad as it was at home. Its vitality accompanied Britain's change from an industrial culture to a full-blown leisure society.

Dr. Jonathan Miller paced back and forth between the kitchen and the study in the basement of his Victorian home near Regents Park in London. It was the day after the July 1986 wedding of the young Duke and Duchess of York.

The wedding had been produced by the same hard-working publicity and promotional machine that had done yeoman service in 1981. Thousands of journalists had come to Britain for the occasion from all over the world, and an audience of millions watched the Westminster Abbey ceremony on television. For weeks, television and newspapers had been providing so many details about the couple and the ceremony that the Great Event — when it occurred — seemed like an anticlimax.

Miller wondered whether his country would ever grow up. "We still broadcast all sorts of outdated pieces of nostalgic self-promotion," he complained. "We don't apply ourselves to the problem of becoming a modern country."

It was not surprising to find Miller a dissenter from the *Brideshead* ethic. The sad-eyed neurologist had earned a special niche in British cultural history after teaching an entire generation of Britons how to laugh at their obsessive preoccupations with ritual and glory. In the early 1960s, with Dudley Moore, Peter Cook, and Alan Bennett, he created the satirical revue *Beyond the Fringe*. The four, just down from Oxford and Cambridge, uncurled the British stiff upper lip with anarchic, hilarious sketches of modern life. *Beyond the Fringe* was among the most successful British cultural exports in the postwar period. It went directly from London's West End to Broadway, where it played for 673 performances. I saw the show in a packed theatre in New York when I was an impressionable teenager. The dry-witted quartet were the first Britons I had ever observed outside a movie screen, and a British accent could send me into strange bouts of uncontrollable laughter for months afterwards.

Some British writers on the period contend that the social criticism and satire of the "angry" 1950s and 1960s never really challenged the Establishment.[10] The four humorists of *Beyond the Fringe* certainly found themselves patronized by the very targets of their wit. Princess Margaret invited the young Miller for dinner, and when the Queen visited the show, Miller complained, "If we had wounded the Establishment as much as we intended, the Queen's advisors would not have let her come." But to many of my generation, Britain was the symbol of a liberation from humbug. Much of the best humour produced in North America in the 1960s seemed to draw its inspiration from British models.

"We were on the edge of making revolutionary changes in sensibility in the 10 years following the end of the Second World War," said Miller. "There were already signs of a 'San Andreas Fault' around 1956, a relaxation which allowed certain things previously unmentionable and invisible to be made visible. I always say England was stuck in the Thirties until the Sixties."

The year 1956 was a watershed in British political as well as cultural life. In 1956, British troops tried — and failed — to punish the Egyptian government of Gamal Nasser for its temerity in nationalizing the Suez Canal. The "Suez crisis" was the beginning of a steady retreat of British troops and influence from former colonial outposts around the world. *Look Back in Anger,* a play by John Osborne staged at the Royal Court Theatre in London in 1956, was considered the first work of art to reflect both the pain and promise of Britain's altered status. Writers on British postwar theatre decided much later that the play was not really "angry" at all, and they found it hard to explain the controversy that greeted its appearance.

Nevertheless, Osborne's attempt to treat working-class life as the subject of drama represented a break with the drawing-room, "upstairs-downstairs" art that had relegated the majority of Britons to walk-on parts as butlers and maids. According to Miller, the break was long overdue. "Our decline, if you like to call it that, began much earlier than we liked to think," he said. "We see it as a postwar phenomenon, but in many ways the war disguised changes which had already started a long time ago. A lot of England's ingenuity and energy was invested abroad. When we withdrew our connections and markets from the empire, we were left with no firm foundations for capital investment in this country. It may well be that the energy and power and pride and potency that we had was misspent running an empire which perhaps we ought never to have had in the first place."

The England of Osborne's day was a stifling world of class resentments. The "proper accents" of the public school system dominated the country's culture as well as its institutions. The angry young playwrights and intellectuals perfectly captured the hopes and frustrations of the postwar generation. For them, the decline of British influence and prestige abroad allowed Britain to be honest about itself and its society for the first time. "Damn you, England," Osborne wrote in an exultant "open letter" to his compatriots in 1961. "You're rotting now, and quite soon you'll disappear. My hate will outrun you yet."[11]

By the 1960s, the struggle against the England of the inbred aristocracy that had aroused Osborne's hatred appeared to be won. The joyful satire of *Beyond the Fringe* set the tone for a decade that called into question every shibboleth of national life, from sex to the monarchy. But within two decades, the sense of liberation had palled. The "rot" that had once seemed liberating had begun to eat away at British industry and livelihoods. There was no longer much to laugh at. Osborne was still angry — but the focus of his bitterness had changed. In a series of interviews given in 1986 to promote a West End revival of his 1957 play, *The Entertainer*, he sounded almost nostalgic. "When I wrote *The Entertainer*, life for most people seemed excruciatingly dull, but [there was] a vitality and courage then," he said. "Thirty years ago, there was a fugitive hope *not* that we were going to change the world, but that *people* would become more aware. Instead . . . everybody is so vile and unpleasant. Half the nation is dumb and stupid."[12]

Miller echoed some of Osborne's disenchantment. "It's a cold-hearted, opportunistic England," he said. Lines of disappointment now showed on Miller's face, and his carroty hair had greyed. The rich, articulate voice contained traces of wistfulness. In the 1980s, Britain still awakened many emotions in the former comic, but laughter was not one of them. The doctor no longer felt at home with what he saw around him. "The welfare state is under suspicion," he complained. "It's on probation. Instead, [we have] the Thatcher world, the world of the upwardly mobile, of fast-moving entrepreneurial figures who see the welfare state as simply a cadgers' and scroungers' charter. I think it's absolutely fatuous."

But even Miller did not share Osborne's blanket disavowal of the culture that descended from the Fifties. "*Beyond the Fringe* opened up the possibility of a much more radical and anarchic type of criticism," Miller admitted. "Things have opened up and relaxed a great deal more in almost every area. Look at the things you can talk about on television. You can say 'fuck' if you want to, and you can show working-class life of a very real sort. I mean in many ways it's idealized and slightly sentimentalized, but it used to be inconceivable that the lives of working-class people could receive any kind of real public representation."[13]

Not all of the popular culture of the 1980s was sentimental, excessively preoccupied with style, or drenched in nostalgia for the past. Postwar British discontent had not necessarily been buried in the different cultural atmosphere of the 1980s. Sometimes it took a more open and honest form.

A successful low-budget film called *My Beautiful Laundrette*, produced by a young British Asian, managed the surprising feat of tackling in less than two hours the themes of racism, inner-city poverty, and homosexuality. *The Boys from the Blackstuff*, a series written for television by Alan Bleasdale about unemployed northerners living in a recognizably grim urban environment, gave the decade one of its political slogans. "Gissa job," the anguished appeal of Yosser, the central character, was scrawled in graffiti on the London Underground, printed on shirts worn by unemployed teenagers in Glasgow, and painted on the walls of boarded-up Birmingham factories. Miller predicted that the "revolution in sensibility" his contemporaries began was far from expended. "It [the 1980s culture] is enormously refreshing," he said. "It's much more honest than it's ever been before, and it's much grittier and grainier and grubbier."

But the two strands of popular culture — *Brideshead* and *Blackstuff* — were not as different as they appeared. Bleasdale, for instance, was very far from being an "angry young man." His play turned on the struggle of men desperate to regain their place in the social structure. They were not interested in pointless gestures against the Establishment. Like most of Bleasdale's audience, they were anxious to recapture a sense of community and continuity with the past in an environment whose links with history had broken. They wanted nothing more than to live dull, decent lives. "If this was a decent society, there'd be no need for me," Bleasdale said.

One day in 1982, the Queen and Prince Philip came to the backlot of a Manchester television studio. They were on a mission very different from their usual tasks of opening new businesses or lending their royal blessing to the kingdom's charities. Stepping regally past the outdoor toilets and peeling water pipes of a mock English working-class neighbourhood, they looked remarkably at home. The street they walked on was called "Coronation Street." After Buckingham Palace, it was the most famous address in Britain.

Coronation Street, the longest-running television soap opera in the world, attracted 13 million British viewers twice a week. Abroad, it was packaged with subtitles ranging from Chinese to Hindi. The royal couple, in Manchester to inaugurate *Coronation Street*'s refurbished set, were paying a genuine professional tribute from one venerable British landmark to another. Like the monarchy, the series was one of the few cultural institutions uniting Britons in the 1980s. It often showed a formidable streak of black British humour. "You have to suffer to achieve real happiness," commented a character over a pint of beer at The Rover's Return, the *Street*'s local pub, in one typical episode. "Yes," responded her companion, "and some of us never get past the suffering."

The soap opera started life long before the 1980s, but its continuing appeal was another significant fact of contemporary British culture. When it first appeared on the airwaves in 1960, *Coronation Street* represented a bold experiment in working-class "realism." Inspired by the kitchen-sink drama of the postwar era, it delivered through the medium of mass entertainment an unprecedentedly accurate portrayal of the real lives of millions of Britons.

The show's formula barely changed over the decades. But its continued success in the 1980s demonstrated that even the once-discredited working-class drama could be transformed by *Brideshead*-ism. Although it was no longer completely accurate as a contemporary portrait, *Coronation Street* seduced Britons with a picture of a lost world as compelling as that of *Brideshead.* It was one of the few places on the British landscape that appeared unaffected by the industrial crisis of the 1980s.[14]

Other British television "folk operas" in the 1980s, such as *The East-Enders* and *Brookside*, were harsher in language and in their reflection of political realities than *Coronation Street*; however, they all successfully exploited the same rich seam of nostalgia for the community values of working-class Britain. With their closely drawn characters and "true Brit" spirit, the programs delivered a weekly reassurance to the British that the qualities they considered important still had a place in the modern world.

Long before the industrial crisis set in, Richard Hoggart, a working-class-born British academic, predicted that escapist entertainment would come to dominate postindustrial Britain. In a classic 1957 study about the development of mass culture, he suggested that the entertainment media were already creating a new class of apathetic worker–consumers whose leisure activities were as hollow as their assembly-line jobs. The "corrupt brightness" of sensationalist tabloid newspapers and magazines would eventually destroy the roots of working-class culture, he wrote. "Many who seek the money and favour of working-people approach them constantly along the lines to which they are most receptive and exposed, with material whose effect is likely to be debilitating."[15]

Both *Coronation Street* and *Brideshead*, at first glance, fulfilled Hoggart's prediction. Mass unemployment, however, created a different kind of audience, with different needs. "Brightness" — whether corrupt or not — was infinitely preferable to despair. Something had been lost in Britain's passage from a successful industrial society to a struggling, deindustrialized one, and the entertainment of the 1980s filled the gap. While much of popular culture might be condemned for the way it anaesthetized Britain, it also gave the patient valuable time to recover.

"With all those opinion polls telling us how Britain is changing out of sight, the wonderful world of the *Street* is the only reality we've got to cling to," sighed a TV critic in the London *Daily Express* in 1983. "The *Street* survives while Britain becomes a bad soap opera."

"It's so good that it's dangerous," countered Alan Sapper, the militant, left-wing head of the TV technicians' union. "It gives an image of the working class which is totally unlike reality."

But by the late 1980s, reality was precisely what most people had had enough of.

Chapter 4

LOVE ME DO

While we were fighting, we were
getting somewhere. People had
to listen.

*— Jimmy, a 20-year-old unemployed
black.*

"They'll shoot somebody tonight for sure," Gary Cuthbert said. "It's tit for tat now."

Riding in the back seat of his taxi down Belfast's Shankill Road in the fall of 1981, I gazed nervously out the window. Groups of youths and older men lurked with what seemed to me purposeful menace in the shadows of the neat row-houses of the city's Protestant neighbourhoods. I didn't think Cuthbert, a chatty young man in his early twenties, was trying to be dramatic. His prediction was offered in the casual tones of someone who was suggesting it might rain; but after just a few days in Northern Ireland I was ready to believe the worst.

In fact, Cuthbert was off by only a couple of hours. The following morning, a member of the Protestant Ulster Defence Regiment was shot down in cold blood as he emerged from his house in Londonderry. It was the tenth killing in as many days. A wave of revenge killings among Protestants and Catholics, triggered by the Irish Republican Army assassination of a Unionist MP, was threatening to plunge Ulster into another round of civil disorder.

After 10 years of "The Troubles," it was hard to imagine anything less surprising than mayhem in Britain's northern province. But the game of "tit for tat" being played with such murderous intensity in Ulster that fall was part of a new pattern of violence across the United Kingdom in the 1980s. The mainland was beginning to have more in common with Northern Ireland than anyone cared to admit. Ulster's periodic convulsions have always been considered a part of the sad political geography of the north, but I had already observed Cuthbert's matter-of-fact approach in Britons who lived in the south. Violence had become an acceptable response to conditions in many depressed parts of Britain, a way to disgorge the bile of being confined to a disintegrating, hopeless environment.

The infection of social decay was spreading. During the decade, unemployment in Northern Ireland reached a staggering 20 per cent, raising the possibility that industrial crisis had almost as much to do with the atmosphere of easy violence as politics. Statistics comparable to those of Northern Ireland could be found in the inner cities of mainland Britain. I had barely unpacked my typewriter, in my first English summer of 1981, when many depressed urban neighbourhoods exploded in an orgy of rioting and looting as angry young people rampaged through burnt-out sections of London, Manchester, Liverpool, and Birmingham.

Each night, for 10 remarkable nights, there was news of another outbreak of rage and riot somewhere in the British Isles. No one had seen anything like it for a hundred years. Black-uniformed police, drawn up behind thick Plexiglas riot shields withstood barrages of bottles, stones, and homemade explosives. In Nottingham, Newcastle, and Preston, the sound of breaking glass and the glow of burning shops overwhelmed the summer evenings. The great, grimy industrial centre of the country seemed to be collapsing under the insurrectionary anger of the young. Liverpool, which had last hit the international headlines as the home of the Beatles, earned a special footnote in British contemporary history. During three nights of rioting, it became the first place on the mainland where police used tear gas. Comparisons with Northern Ireland were drawn by frightened Britons themselves. The Liverpool riots left 700 police officers injured. I met one of them on the streets of Toxteth, the worst-hit neighbourhood, holding his bloodied head after a rock had hit him. "To think this is England," he said. "This is more like Belfast."

Theories explaining the outbreaks filled the newspapers, but the explanations usually shed more light on the politics of observers than on the actual causes of the riots. The Labour Party blamed unemployment: "Whatever the causes and remedies, nobody can doubt that the riots' background is one of mass unemployment, and particularly unemployment among young people on a scale which most of us believed had been banished from our country forever," said Labour Party leader Michael Foot. Prime Minister Margaret Thatcher, who had served as education minister in an earlier Conservative administration, was uncharacteristically shaken by the turmoil. However, she saw it as an outbreak of criminal behaviour. "She felt sorry for all the shopkeepers who'd had their windows broken," confided one civil servant.[1]

Many of the rioters happened to be nonwhite. Not surprisingly, blacks and Asians traced the trouble to the underlying racism of British society. Newspaper headlines such as "Race War Flares" confirmed the impression that the riots were racially motivated. The fears of minorities were endorsed by voices from Britain's articulate right wing, who blamed the disorder on the influx of immigrants from new Commonwealth countries in the 1950s and the resulting changes in what they liked to call "British life." Britons waking up to morning BBC broadcasts at the time heard calls to stop the "wave of immigration" from the third world. Such appeals to emotion lost nothing from the fact that immigration had already been sharply cut back since the late 1960s. A Tory MP named John Stokes neatly combined two pet right-wing peeves. He said that the Liverpool riot was caused by "the vociferous immigration lobby who seek excuses all the time for the excesses of blacks." It remained only for Charles Parker, an organizer for the neo-Nazi New National Front, to deliver the final verdict. "I'm sure," he said, "there will be an all-out racial war in this country." The reasons advanced for what newspapers called the "worst social crisis" Britain had experienced since the war only heightened the general insecurity. Most Britons couldn't believe it had happened in their own backyard. "Why us?" complained Finula Heffernan, a white Liverpudlian who had watched her family store smashed during the riots. "We have no enemies here."

Surprise and confusion reached into every corner of British society. The Duke of Westminster remembered seeing Toxteth burning from the rooftop of his elegant home in the north of England. The rioting in the quiet town of Chester a few days later seemed proof that outside agitators were involved. "Chester has the highest spending per capita outside London," he said. "Can you think of a less likely place to have a riot?" Westminster claimed to have discovered that "CB radios were used by people with London accents" to whip up trouble. But he admitted that the intensity of the violence shocked him. "It came as a terrible jolt to those not involved at the hard end of race relations," he said. "It was a terrible surprise and a very ugly one as well."

The trauma continued after the riots were over. As the royal wedding procession wound its way through London two weeks later, one group of black children standing on the pavement suddenly began to cry in fright. They thought the Union Jacks passing by in martial splendour were the insignia of the white-supremacist National Front, who used a similar motif in their banners.[2]

Up in Dundee, Scotland, Bashir Okhai, a 28-year-old Asian immigrant who was helping to build a family business that would eventually be worth millions of pounds, was so jolted that he wondered whether it was worth staying in Britain. "I thought to myself, do I really have a future in this country?" he recalled years later. "People go through life saying they don't think something like this will ever happen to them, and then it's a surprise when it does." Okhai decided to stay, but he doubted Britain's ability to adjust to the fact that it had become a multiracial society. "If Britain wants peaceful integration, it has to work for it. You can't say I'm going to make a cup just by watching a piece of glass."

Nevertheless, it was hard for an outsider to understand the British hang-up about race. Britain was still a white-dominated society. Of the United Kingdom's 56 million people, fewer than 2.5 million were considered nonwhite. True, entire neighbourhoods — in some cases, towns — had nonwhite majorities. In Bradford, a Koran shared space with a Bible in the rooms of the main hotel. Without the new Asian and Caribbean British, Britain would probably be a much less efficient, and less interesting, society. Nonwhites take the tickets at British Rail stations, run the all-night grocery stores, and have considerably broadened British eating habits. Nearly every High Street in the country boasts at least one well-frequented Indian curry house. And not every nonwhite was a recent immigrant. There has been a large, cohesive black community in Liverpool for over a hundred years.

Part of the problem was native English xenophobia. The Irish, Scots, and Welsh were despised with equal ferocity less than two centuries earlier. The worst "race riots" in the eighteenth century occurred when English labourers attacked Irish immigrants just off the boat in Liverpool. During any period of economic depression, the English easily saw the Irish as a threat to their jobs and way of life. During the industrial crisis of the 1980s, the pattern was repeated. Nonwhites from Caribbean and Asian countries who came to Britain after the war often took the low-paid and unskilled jobs Britons refused. They were often the first to be laid off, but a large number of white Britons found minorities an easy scapegoat for the underlying changes in their society.

Their fears were exacerbated by several political leaders. A speech by a former Conservative minister, Enoch Powell, on April 20, 1968, became a notorious rallying cry for successive generations of British "patriots." With the memory of American inner-city riots still fresh, Powell predicted that "rivers of blood" would flow in Britain as a result of the clash between white and black. He quoted a constituent who believed that "in this country, in 15 or 20 years, the black man will have the whip hand over the white man," and then went on to draw a lurid picture of the effects of British multiculturalism. "For reasons which they [white Britons] could not comprehend, and in pursuance of a decision by default, on which they were never consulted, they found themselves made strangers in their own country," he said. "They found their wives unable to obtain hospital beds in childbirth, their children unable to obtain school places, their homes and

56

neighbourhoods changed beyond recognition, their plans and prospects for the future defeated." Conservative leaders were outraged and embarrassed by the speech. They were even more concerned by a Gallup poll that appeared the following month, in which 74 per cent of the respondents agreed in general with Powell's remarks.[3]

Powell had been regarded as a strong candidate for the party's leadership, and the speech effectively ruined his chances of ever holding a major national office, but it also turned him into a kind of underground hero. The maverick MP made a subsequent career out of a forthright, articulate defence of British "traditions," whether they were threatened by European common marketeers or American hegemonists. It was no coincidence that Powell resurfaced as an independent MP for Northern Ireland, one of the many places where he considered the integrity of the kingdom to be at risk. After the outbreaks of 1981, reporters eager for a quote went to Powell again. He was obliging. "We haven't seen anything yet," he maintained. It seemed pointless to suggest that his own diatribes had played a role in worsening the social climate of the 1970s and 1980s.

Powellism, in fact, played a role in the rise of Thatcherism. Margaret Thatcher was one of his unabashed admirers. She made a widely publicized remark, as leader of the opposition in 1978, following the release of official figures that indicated that Britain's nonwhite population would reach four million by the end of the century. "Now that is an awful lot," she said piously in a television interview, "and I think it means that people are really rather afraid that this country might be rather swamped by people with a different culture. You know, the British character has done so much for democracy, for law, and done so much throughout the world, that if there is any fear that it might be swamped, [people] are going to react and be rather hostile to those coming in."

The "swamping" remark horrified her advisors, who remembered what similar sentiments had done to Powell's career. Aides hastened to tell the press that her comments had been off-the-cuff. However, according to insiders' accounts, Thatcher had shown copies of her remarks to her staff beforehand. She told them brusquely that if that was what people thought, why shouldn't she say it? She was proved right. Thatcher's remarks drew more than 10,000 letters, most of them approving, and many of them from Labour voters. It was an early, if rather unpleasant, illustration of Thatcherism's ability to form a new coalition between suburbanites and the white working class.[4]

Such long-simmering attitudes inevitably poisoned the atmosphere of the 1980s, when the competition for scarce jobs turned violent. A government-commissioned inquiry into the disturbances in London's Brixton neighbourhood warned that Britain would have to face up to its most obvious failure in human relations. "The evidence which I received leaves no doubt in my mind that racial disadvantage is a fact of current British life," wrote Lord Scarman, a senior member of the judiciary who was appointed head of the commission. "Urgent action is needed if it is not to become an endemic ... disease threatening the very survival of our society."

The 168-page "Scarman Report" stands as one of the few efforts made during the decade to take a cool-headed look at what was really going wrong. It concluded that racial discrimination, police harassment, and unemployment were major factors in the riots. But even Lord Scarman backed away from the problem represented by the young people themselves. Only a few Britons thought of the rioters as more than examples of one social ailment or another. "We need to offer [them] a sense of hope and a sense that they have a real personal stake in our society," argued Leader of the Commons Francis Pym. The comment won him few friends among his colleagues, but it was prescient.

The lack of a "personal stake" in Britain was shared by rioters of all colours and ethnic backgrounds, by those who were employed as well as by those who were jobless. Several nights after the Liverpool riots, a group of young people agreed to talk to me about their experiences on the condition their full names weren't used. We sat in a run-down youth centre in Toxteth. A worn pool table was the main piece of furniture in the room. As they described in flat, unemotional tones their skirmishes with police, younger children listened with rapt attention.

"Personally, I felt like killing them," said Kevin, a personable, sandy-haired 20-year-old. "Everybody says the riots were all about racism. Well, there was some of that, but it's mainly the police, believe me." Kevin rolled up his sleeve to show an ugly scar he said was inflicted by a bottle that cut him during an arrest. Dressed in a clean sweatshirt and jeans, he didn't look like a hooligan. But there was an unspoken menace in the way he sat, his feet firmly planted on the floor, as he talked about himself.

Kevin shared a public housing flat in Toxteth with his girlfriend and their two-year-old child. In and out of jail and reform school for most of his life, he had been a willing soldier on Toxteth front lines, even though it had cost him his job as an apprentice glazier. "I was arrested on Sunday night, the biggest night of the riot, but they let me go after charging me. The next day, I was walking to work with my tools, and the same copper who arrested me Sunday picked me up on Monday for carrying dangerous weapons. When I finally came to work, the boss said, 'Where have you been?' I told him. He said, 'There's plenty more where you came from,' and he sacked me. You can't win. We're failures and we all know it."

Jimmy, also 20, sitting calmly beside Kevin, followed with his own story. He had a wife and three young children, and had been unable to get a job since he finished school at 16. His young family was trying to survive on less than £70 a week in unemployment benefits from the state. An articulate, witty youth who smiled often, he blamed all his troubles on the fact that he was black and unemployed. "There's nowhere you can go when you're black," he said earnestly. "The city university has a big athletic gym but you can't get in. When I was in school, nobody pushed me and I never got anywhere. The only way I could get money now is to take it — and I'm really not that kind of person." The riots, he said, gave him an opportunity to release his frustrations. He had never felt so free as when he was tossing bricks and chasing police up the streets. "I'm sorry it stopped," he said of the street battle. "While we were fighting, we were getting somewhere. People had to listen."

The young rioters of Liverpool personified the failure of 1980s Britain to keep its society together under the old rules. Their plaintive appeal for attention, for someone to "listen" to them, made me think of the title of one of the earliest Beatles songs. "Love Me Do" was written, ironically, by Liverpudlian youths who had been only a few years older than the ones I had been speaking to. The combination of pathos, alienation, and violence showed the extent of the change over two decades.

A British "underclass" began to appear at the end of the 1970s. In Scotland, Linda Echlin became aware of it soon after she moved to the village of Saltcoats. With several other women, she decided to do something about the large number of idle youths in the town. The local authorities gave the Saltcoats women permission to start a disco. They rented a hall hardly bigger than a store and borrowed a record player. On opening night, 300 teenagers squeezed into a room that was supposed to hold no more than 80. Echlin was surprised by the numbers who showed up, but she was even more astonished by the personalities of the young people themselves.

Supposedly the town roughnecks, the teenagers were frequent guests of the local jail and "borstals," the notorious youth reformatories. (The local police chief noticed an agreeable slump in the crime figures on nights when the disco was open.) But Echlin couldn't figure out why the youths aroused so much dread. On close acquaintance, the young proto-criminals rarely exhibited the energy that would have justified calling them delinquent. Once, she suggested they get together a soccer team. The following Sunday morning, a group of them appeared at her front door. "What are you lot doing here?" shouted Echlin, rubbing sleep from her eyes. "You're supposed to be off playing." They looked at each other in confusion. One of them at last explained patiently, as if it were too obvious for words, that they couldn't start a game without her, could they?

Fresh from her own experience of scrabbling for work, Echlin was irritated by the fact that many of the youngsters no longer even considered getting a job. They spent their "dole" money idling in the pubs. To Echlin, they seemed more helpless than menacing. "A lot of them couldn't read. I was horrified. I really didn't think that here and now, they were turning out kids of 16 who couldn't read or write. On Friday nights, if I had the time, I would try and read some of them comics."

Most of the time, however, she just felt sorry for them. "They wanted more and more attention from me, but they were totally devoid of imagination," Echlin said. "They didn't have a clue what to do with themselves. I remember one of the boys, Derek, got married. He was only 17, and she was 16, pregnant. I took them home for a talk. 'What are you going to do?' I said. 'Neither of you have money.' They weren't worried. They got a council flat, and lived on the dole, like their parents. The wee girl that Derek married, Eleanor, would buy two [frozen] chicken suppers for their dinner. That's two pounds each, which even I can't afford. I said, 'Eleanor, for two pounds you can buy a chicken at the butcher's and boil it; you get a pint of soup and two full days' food.'

"She just looked at me.' I said, 'Go and buy a bloody chicken.' But she had no idea. She asked me, 'Do you get it with the head on?' It's things as basic as that they don't know. They were from families that lived on chips and bottles of lemonade, and never sat down to a meal."

Although she couldn't tolerate their helplessness, Echlin began to enjoy her "wards." She discovered that they did have the capacity to rouse themselves, although it surfaced in bizarre ways. Once, planning for a village fête, she recruited a group of them to help hang bunting over the main street. She left them with ladders and material, only to return half an hour later to discover them gleefully hanging from the ladders, the bunting mostly ignored, giving pedestrians below the shock of their lives. "They were," Echlin said with an embarrassed laugh, "pissing all over the people."

Her encounter with the teenagers of Saltcoats sharpened Echlin's fears for her own children. "Looking at those kids in the disco, I had this feeling we were never going to see full employment again. Working-class people are educated to come out of school and get a job. It's difficult for us to change. But I could see the system falling down, and kids still being educated for the same thing: getting a job and working for someone else."

Echlin's pessimism was confirmed by a report published in 1986 by the Labour-run Wolverhampton local authority. The report was unashamedly partisan, blaming the region's problems on government policies, but it contained some startling glimpses of the new world inhabited by the young.

The authors of the report said that unemployment in their region had hit 20 per cent. For young people, however, there had been a "virtual collapse of the labour market." About one-third of 16-to-24-year-olds who wanted work could not find it. Many of these young people were already experiencing future shock. Their lack of money and security had forced them into psychological early retirement. For working-class youngsters, in particular, the normal routes to self-esteem were blocked. "It is the working class for whom getting a job and [a] wage has been the main liberation at 16," the report said. "[Middle-class] students have their own way of being creative between childhood and adulthood [and] this may now be in its own form of crisis. But it is nothing like the abrupt 'chop' that working-class young people face if they are cut off from the world of work at the age of 16."[5]

Unemployment had even changed the teenagers' courtship rituals. Only a third of the young unemployed in the survey saw a girlfriend or boyfriend every week, compared to 60 per cent of employed youth. Unable to afford going out, they sat at home watching TV or videos. The "Englishman's castle," the report suggested, had become an "electronic prison house" for the young.

"On the best available economic data and analysis, it does not seem that jobs will come back to the area in the foreseeable future," the report predicted. "We may be witnessing the beginnings of social transformations and upheavals which will stretch into the next century."

A series of polls published by *The Times* under the headline "Thatcher's Children" noted that the 6.5 million young people who had reached voting age between 1981 and 1986 were a distinctive generation. They showed marked tendencies toward apathy. In 1981, 40 per cent of young people under 25 blamed the government for the industrial crisis. Five years later (when unemployment was much higher), only 21 per cent did. A large percentage of the youths in the survey believed that they would be out of a job at some time over the next 10 years, but they all accepted the crisis without question. A few blamed local bureaucrats, job centre personnel, or occasionally themselves (for not working hard enough at school), but none appeared to agree when they were asked whether politicians were responsible for their situation. "Everybody ... seemed taken aback by the question," wrote the reporter who summarized the findings. "It was as if it had never occurred to them to ask it."

The reporter, perhaps revealing more of his own biases than he intended, found the contrast with the committed generation of the Sixties disturbing. He was shocked that more than a quarter of the youths in the survey said they wouldn't bother to vote in the next election. "This political apathy is surely something more than a listless unconcern for the issues of the day: rather a positive opting out of the whole political process." More than 60 per cent agreed with the statement that "people like me are powerless to change things in Britain."[6]

Echlin's hapless wards, the apathetic young of *The Times* poll and the Wolverhampton surveys, and the rioters in the streets of Britain's cities had at least one element in common. They were marginalized by industrial change. Proportionately few went out into the streets to throw bricks at police, but the predicament of British youth added to the general insecurity of the decade.

"There was a period in this country when you could leave your car unlocked, your front door open, when you could trust anybody across the whole social scale," insisted Prince Philip in an interview with a woman's magazine marking his sixty-fifth birthday in 1986. "Now you can't even trust your neighbour."[7] By most objective criteria, Prince Philip was wrong. Despite constant headlines about "rising crime rates" and inner-city violence, the actual level of violent crime in the Eighties compared favourably with that of other periods in British history. Nevertheless, there was a pervasive feeling of vulnerability.

A report by two London researchers discovered that fear of crime was so widespread in some neighbourhoods that half the people interviewed admitted they never left their home except for work or shopping. A professor at the University of Reading blamed rising crime rates on young criminals who were "able to evade personal responsibility for their actions." He added: "What we [have been] witnessing is the growth, maturity, and strange death of respectable England."[8]

Robert Chesshyre, a correspondent for the *Observer*, returned home to England in 1985 after three and a half years spent reporting from Washington. He noticed that even in the short time he'd been away his fellow Britons had grown desensitized to violence and social decay. "We often look haunted and hunched as if expecting very little out of life," he wrote. "We don't fight back enough, and it shows in our demeanour."[9] Life even in London occasionally showed signs of the atmosphere in some U.S. cities. He recalled an episode on an Underground train in his first month home, in which "skinhead" youths terrorized a well-dressed subway rider while other passengers calmly read their newspapers.

"Antisocial disorders appear to be the short change of the arson, looting, and murder of inner-city riots," concluded Chesshyre, writing just after another outbreak of fighting and arson around Britain. "They, like the riots, tell of frustration and alienation — symptoms of a society losing coherence and tolerance under economic strain. Even motorists suffer from a futile, dangerous aggression."[10]

One morning in 1983, Britons woke up to find a photograph in their newspapers of two police constables striding down the street with guns at their hips. The constables were part of a specially trained Manchester force, but the tradition of the "unarmed" bobby had taken a severe beating. Even after seeing the riot police with their truncheons and shields during the disorders of 1981, Britons were not prepared for a spate of stories about police use of guns and violence. In one particularly nasty example, two London detectives stopped a car in Kensington and pumped bullets into the head of the hapless driver, a 26-year-old film editor. The incident turned out to be a case of mistaken identity. The driver looked similar to an armed criminal the police had been hunting for weeks. He managed to survive, but the image of the friendly police constable didn't.

Ironically, the increase in insecurity occurred under the nose of a government that had staked a special claim to the issue of "law and order." In her first election campaign, Thatcher promised to reduce crime with more efficient and better-funded policing at Scotland Yard. Her cabinet continued to make tough pledges, sometimes frightening the people they intended to reassure with apocalyptic warnings on the forces of evil besieging British society.

One such pledge was made at the annual Conservative Party conference in Blackpool in 1983. At the following year's conference, held in Brighton, Thatcher and her entire cabinet nearly fell victim to the same forces themselves when a bomb planted by Northern Irish terrorists exploded in the Grand Hotel on October 12, 1984.

During the 1970s, there had been isolated bombings and terrorist incidents in Britain, mostly claimed by Irish paramilitary organizations. But, starting in 1979, when a Tory MP named Airey Neave (a close friend of Margaret Thatcher's) died after a bomb exploded in his car as he left the House of Commons parking lot, a new, undiscriminating form of violence began to terrorize ordinary British people.

In October 1981, Lt. Gen. Steuart Pringle, head of the Royal Marines, lost part of his right leg when a car bomb exploded outside his London home. The attack, a response to British treatment of the hunger strikers in Northern Ireland, injured several passersby. "We suspect it's the start of a new campaign," said one Scotland Yard detective. He was right. In the same month, a booby-trapped van exploded outside Chelsea Barracks, spraying large iron nails through a passing bus filled with Irish Guards. Eight soldiers needed major surgery and one was blinded. But even more menacing, two children had been seriously hurt. Appeals were broadcast to Londoners to be "vigilant."

Throughout 1982 and 1983, London felt like a city under siege. Several explosions rocked London shops. Passersby as well as police were injured or killed. Even harder on the nerves were constant bomb hoaxes. At the height of the terrorist scare, the normal city noises were punctuated several times a day by the ear-shattering wail of bomb disposal vans. Traffic jams took hours to unsnarl. Often, it was impossible to know whether police were racing to the scene of an actual or threatened explosion, or merely responding to a crank call.

A corrosive feeling of danger accompanied the normal activities of living in London. Whether shopping on Oxford Street, or visiting museums and other public attractions, people became accustomed to having their bags searched. Signs on the Underground warned commuters to watch out for "unattended packages." Inquiring strangers were not to be trusted. The British had faced the Blitz during the Second World War with courage and good humour, but random violence in the midst of affluence, conducted by an enemy who used the same streets and buses, caught them unprepared.

When a new outbreak of riots occurred in 1985, it only confirmed Britons' bleak view of the landscape around them. The disorders were even worse than the riots four years earlier. On October 5, 1985, four police officers questioned a woman in a North London public housing estate with the deceptively rural name of Broadwater Farm. The woman's sons had a connection with illegal drugs, and the police, as they told investigators later, were trying to find out where her two boys were. The woman, upset over the police visit, collapsed with a fatal heart attack. Local residents, most of them black, were infuriated. The next day and night saw some of the worst rioting Britain had ever seen, and the murder of one police constable — the first death of a police officer this century in a civil disorder on the mainland.

There were equally fierce riots in Brixton, in Toxteth, and in the Handsworth neighbourhood of Birmingham. Once again, the press concentrated on the fact that many of the rioters were black, unemployed, and living in the decaying inner city. But there was more confusion about the causes. A year before the second Brixton riot, for example, reports in Brixton had concentrated on the new "spirit of enterprise" in the community. More than 300 new businesses had started up with the help of local authority and central government funding, contributing to what one London magazine called a "facelift."

Neither unemployment nor racism could completely explain what had happened. Some commentators began to see the violence in Britain's inner-city neighbourhoods as a political response, and they compared it to the actions of alienated groups in more overtly political settings. "South Africa has come to Birmingham," declared Shirley Williams, president of the Social Democratic Party, shortly after Handsworth. A British writer named Jeremy Seabrook added, "In more inner-city areas than I can number in the last few years, I have heard the words 'It's getting like Belfast round here.'"[11]

Some government ministers began to hear the message. Home Secretary Douglas Hurd said that aimless youths with no stake in the society they lived in were the "helots" of the 1980s. Those who worked provided much of the unskilled labour. Those who didn't were permanently unproductive wards of the state. "In the modern world, a society which depends on helots is condemned to disorder and dissolution," he told a London seminar on violence.[12]

In May 1985, thousands of Liverpool soccer fans travelled to Heysel Stadium in Brussels to watch a European Cup Final match between the British and Italian teams. Before the day was over, 39 people — most of them Italian — were dead. The British fans, most of them young and nearly all of them drunk, had charged the area of the stands where the Italians were sitting and forced the bleacher area to collapse.

The rest of Europe was stunned and outraged. English teams were banned by World Soccer officials from playing on the Continent for a year. Britons were not the only ones guilty of soccer violence. Dutch fans had burned down a stadium in 1982, and the passions of the soccer field once started a war in Central America. But the English somehow symbolized the worst excesses.

After the Heysel tragedy, the British government duly expressed shock. It threatened football clubs with legislation limiting the activities of fans. But Whitehall reacted testily to suggestions that the violence was anything more than a bad case of hooliganism.

In fact, the young British "soccer hooligans" came from a surprisingly broad cross-section of British society. Ian Stuttard, a television producer who completed a documentary on a football "gang," discovered that it included two solicitors' clerks, an insurance underwriter, a bank manager, and even soldiers on leave. "They are certainly not the mindless, drunken louts of the headline stereotypes," said Stuttard. "They do what they do not because of drink, or poverty, or poor education. They do it because basically they enjoy a good fight." Members of one organized football fan club called "Intercity Firm" showed the characteristics of a tribe. "Fighting is a clear way to gain respect in their community," he said.[13] Those most directly involved had a simpler explanation. "Our violence," explained one convicted football fan, "is all about defending and invading territory."

The long history of British imperial violence, in which generations of young British men set out to conquer the Zulus or Pathans, puts some of the brawling turbulence of the decade into a clearer perspective.[14] Racism, urban terrorism, football hooliganism, and inner-city crime together made Britain a more insecure nation in the 1980s, but they were the predictable symptoms of frustration and alienation in a society whose native energies, formerly expended in the service of the Empire, no longer had any constructive outlets. British political culture, according to a Canadian writer, Michael Ignatieff, has always been regarded as "one of the most venerable and successful instruments ever devised for the containment, suppression, and adjudication of social conflict." In the 1980s, that culture was breaking down, and there was little on the immediate horizon to take its place.[15]

Chapter 5
JOHN BULL AND THE ARGIES

We are a very formidable lot
when we have moral right
on our side.

*— Bernard Ingham, Press Secretary
to Prime Minister Thatcher,
May 1982.*

On the first Saturday afternoon of April 1982, Britons listened with wry amusement to a BBC announcement. A solemn voice said that the weekly radio program, "Sorry, I Haven't A Clue," was being interrupted for a live emergency debate on the Falkland Islands from the House of Commons. Amusement, however, was short-lived. It was the first time the Commons had called a Saturday session since the Suez crisis. And as the nation eavesdropped on a painful moment in British history, the comparisons with Suez quickly became ominous.

The debate opened with cries of "Resign!" and "Betrayal!" Prime Minister Thatcher rose from her seat on the front benches to describe in a tremulous voice the strange events of the previous two weeks. On March 19, she said, a party of 60 Argentine scrap merchants had landed on South Georgia, an island in the Falklands archipelago. Britain duly protested what appeared to be just another move in the 150-year-old diplomatic struggle between the two countries over competing claims to sovereignty in the Falklands.

But on March 25, another Argentine vessel had dropped off supplies. "Later that day," the prime minister said, "we received information which led us to believe that a large number of ships, including an aircraft carrier, destroyers, landing craft, troop carriers, and submarines were heading for Port Stanley [the Falklands colonial capital]." Thatcher said she had asked U.S. President Ronald Reagan to intervene. "We promised in the meantime to take no action to escalate the dispute," Thatcher continued, as a roar of outrage swelled from all sides of the Commons, "for fear of precipitating the very events that our efforts were directed to avoid."[1]

For the rest of the three-hour debate, the "Mother of Parliaments" was overcome by a boiling flood of rhetoric. Members spoke as if the eyes of history were on them. Douglas Jay, a former Labour minister, drew uncomfortable comparisons between the Argentine landing on the islands and the outbreak of the Second World War. "The Foreign Office is too much saturated with the spirit of appeasement," he said. "The whole history of this century has shown that if you give way to this sort of action, things will not get better, they will get worse."

Sir Bernard Braine, a Tory backbencher, caught the Commons' mood of stunned anger. "The very thought that 1,800 people of British blood and bone could be left to the hands of these criminals is enough to make an Englishman's blood boil," he said, adding quickly, "and a Scotsman's and Welshman's blood boil too."

The most surprising speaker of all was Michael Foot, the white-haired leader of the Labour Party, a renowned pacifist and antinuclear campaigner. He threw his party wholeheartedly behind any government action to wrest the Falklands back from the Argentines. "We should not see foul, brutal aggression successful in our world," he said majestically. "Because if that happens, it will be a danger not only for our islands, but for all this dangerous world."

In that first parliamentary debate, historians are likely to find the real origins of the Falklands War. The fury and aggrieved sense of nationhood in the Commons carried the country into a battle in the South Atlantic that dominated the world's front pages for the next three months. More than 255 British soldiers died in the conflict, and another 777 were wounded. Argentina sustained an estimated 1,800 killed or wounded.

By sheer good luck and fighting skill, Britain emerged as the victor. Although, years later, the Falklands War has become a source of embarrassment to some Britons, it was a crucial phase of British regeneration in the 1980s. If the Falklands adventure had been inconclusive, or if Britain had lost, the history of the decade would have been entirely different. Like the royal wedding and the Hollywood Oscar, the episode triggered a cathartic emotional release. Years of bottled-up frustration over Britain's diminished role in international affairs found an outlet in an explosion of national pride that astonished the British as much as the rest of the world.

No government could have resisted the patriotic fever of 1982. Conflicting postimperial visions of Britain — as a strong and influential team player in the Western alliance, or as a wise, experienced teacher of moral values — united behind an issue that most Britons in a quieter moment would have ignored as a bad colonial joke. Members of Parliament had taken six days to debate Britain's entry into the Common Market in 1973, one English observer reflected scathingly, but they led Britain to war over the Falklands in three hours.[2]

The crisis touched the most vulnerable part of Britons' mental makeup: the memory of Empire. Since the Second World War, Britons had been watching their influence in the world fade and crack, like the old photographs of relatives in the colonial service some middle-class families still kept in their scrapbooks. "The proprietary sensation with which I had once watched the unfolding of international affairs gave way to a sideline diffidence," Jan Morris confessed in the 1973 introduction to her trilogy about the Victorian British Empire. "Where once the great stakes at risk were all my own, by virtue of my passport, now I was only a casual investor."[3]

Nevertheless, the imperial heritage was not easily discounted. At the peak of British power, the Falklands were an insignificant part of one of the grandest multinational enterprises the world had ever seen. The Queen of England, nominal ruler of some 400 million people, extended her royal influence over a fifth of the world's surface. As late as 1964, after the last British troops had been withdrawn east of Suez, and long after Empire Day had been dropped from schoolchildren's calendars, Prime Minister Harold Wilson reassured the British people, "We are a world power and a world influence, or we are nothing."

The Falklanders were the direct beneficiaries of those grand visions. The majority of the "1,800 people of British blood and bone" who were living tranquilly on the islands, a few hours' flight from the coast of Argentina, in the spring of 1982, were sheep farmers. Most were descendants of nineteenth-century British settlers, but their ties to Britain were more cultural than juridical. Recent legislation at Westminster had granted only those whose fathers or grandfathers were born in the United Kingdom the right to claim British citizenship. The legislation was aimed primarily at stopping the immigration of nonwhites from new Commonwealth countries, but it was equally applicable to the Falklanders — as they discovered to their dismay when they applied for an exception to be made in their case only a few months before the invasion.

Life on the islands was indisputably British. Car drivers kept to the left, pictures of the Queen and the royal family decorated every home, and the colonial governor — a diplomat sent out from Whitehall — used a black London taxicab as his official car. Most Falklanders lived a feudal existence. Their wages and living quarters were supplied by absentee landlords in London. But they valued a lifestyle that kept them far off the beaten track of civilization. The only real threats to their existence were the Argentines, who had never stopped claiming the territory since British warships uprooted an Argentine settlement there in 1833, and the British Foreign Office.

For the businesslike foreign policy managers in Whitehall, the Falklands were an awkward reminder of Britain's imperial past. The islanders' persistent refusal to contemplate closer economic and political links with Argentina, together with the support of a tiny, vocal Falklands "lobby" in Parliament, complicated British relations with Latin America, while more strategic twentieth-century holdovers of Empire, like Hong Kong, Belize, and Gibraltar, occupied London's attention.

It was hard, at first, to take the "Falklands crisis" seriously. It seemed a minor power play, 8,000 miles from London, intended to push Britain into a decision she had long been contemplating anyway. In the 1980s, archaic arguments over national sovereignty appeared to suit the excitable Argentines better than the phlegmatic, pragmatic Britons. Several officials had even publicly cast doubt on the British claim. "The fact remains," said a junior foreign minister named Lord Trefgarne, shortly before the Argentine invasion, "that the Falklands are not and never have been part of the United Kingdom."

The first to reap profit from the crisis were the British press barons. Fleet Street enjoyed itself hugely at the government's expense. Newspapers ran lurid tales of reporters in Argentina phoning their home offices with guns at their back. They gave the affair a tone more reminiscent of *Scoop*, Evelyn Waugh's classic send-up of British journalists, than a prelude to serious conflict. "It's War," announced the headline in the *Sun*. "Shamed," wept the *Daily Mail*.

There were implausible rumours of preparations to send a British naval armada to retake the islands. "We no longer rule the waves, but we still have one of the world's most powerful navies," thundered *The Times*. It sounded impressive, but vague. Even if the Falklands were worth fighting for, it was hard to imagine a country less psychologically equipped than Britain for a military confrontation halfway across the world. Northern Ireland, urban riots, terrorism, and mounting economic catastrophe seemed burdens enough for any nation.

Britons who happened to be abroad at the time were as sceptical as most foreigners. A senior Royal Navy commander on a spring training exercise off Gibraltar was astonished at communications traffic that suggested his ships might be joining a task force to the South Atlantic. "In the back of our minds, we were saying, 'No, there isn't going to be a war, for goodness' sakes,'" he later recalled. Sir Ranulph Fiennes, a former military officer who was leading a historic four-year expedition to circumnavigate the earth, was languishing on an ice floe near the North Pole when a member of his team heard over the weak battery radio that Britain was "at war." "I said to him, 'That's a load of rubbish,'" Fiennes remembered. "'Who could Britain be at war with? France?' I couldn't think of any other country that was more likely. We thought it was a BBC spoof. Sometimes the BBC had these April Fool-type things. This one had been carried on well along because it wasn't anywhere near April first, but we forgot about it."

There were some Britons on the home front who refused to get carried away. The first reaction of Campaign for Nuclear Disarmament leader Joan Ruddock was cynicism. She believed the crisis was a political ploy. "All the things Thatcher had appealed to, to try and get elected, were things easily linked to jingoism. We were a nation supposed to have gained something through experience. We have had all the experience that any nation could have wanted . . . and we couldn't resist the impulse to go and crush a tin-pot regime." Listening to the Commons debate on her radio at home, Ruddock was sickened. "Apart from personal tragedies, it was the worst moment of my life," she said. "I felt nausea."

Spinning the globe in his cavernous office in Whitehall a few days before the Commons debate, Defence Minister John Nott hunted for the Falkland Islands. He couldn't believe it when he saw how far away they actually were. "I was shattered," he wrote later. Not for the last time that month analogies with Suez came to his mind. It had taken five tense days for British forces to reach Cyprus, their jumping-off spot for the Suez landing. How much more difficult would it be to sustain a military expedition 8,000 miles from home? "During the critical week between the first intelligence indicating the Argentine invasion . . . to the sailing of the fleet, the memories of Suez played a greater part in my own hesitations than almost any other single factor," Nott recalled.

Nott was a young army officer, just returned from service in Malaya and beginning his undergraduate studies at Cambridge, when the Anglo-French-Israeli attempt to "liberate" the Suez Canal was abruptly terminated by American financial and political pressure. Like most of his contemporaries, Nott was shaken by Suez. "The notion that we might seek to act militarily except in alliance with our friends seemed pure delusion," he wrote. "I believed that we could not and should not be a rather ill-equipped military policeman for the world."[4]

When Nott joined the Thatcher cabinet, he was passionately committed to reasserting British global prestige, but he was very far from sharing the imperialist presumptions of his predecessors. With the other economic evangelists who had come to power in 1979, he believed that British prestige and the ability to exert influence abroad, like the ability to control events at home, depended on a more rational allocation of resources. A few months before the Argentines landed on the Falklands, Nott secured cabinet support for two key policy decisions. Nearly one-fifth of Britain's frigates and destroyers would be scrapped; there would be a reduction of 20,000 military personnel. At the same time, final approval was given for a program replacing Britain's aging Polaris nuclear submarine fleet with new American Trident nuclear missiles in the 1990s.

Both decisions were at the heart of the debate raging about the country's defence structure during the decade. Britain's large, cumbersome Royal Navy reflected the continuing appeal of colonial traditions. But today the principal British overseas military commitment was the defence of Europe. The northern sea and air corridors were the only conceivable sources of any military threat to the United Kingdom in the late twentieth century. Since the 1950s, Britain had also been shouldering an expensive independent nuclear weapons establishment, partly from pique at being left out of American nuclear development in the postwar years, and partly from the conviction that Britain, like France, needed her own system of nuclear deterrence as a safeguard of sovereignty.

The price of such an extended military posture was an increasing strain on the nation's resources. Something had to give. To Nott and his contemporaries in government, there could be no doubt about the choice. Ironically (as later events would show), one of the ships affected by the cutbacks was the HMS *Endurance*, assigned to patrol the Falklands waters. Its withdrawal provided a fateful signal to the Argentine junta.

Most of the new "Thatcherite" thinkers in the foreign policy establishment approved the decisions. Purchase of the Tridents would guarantee Britain continued membership in the club of nuclear powers, and assure her a place in superpower strategies. An "imperial" Navy equipped to operate in three oceans was an agreeable luxury, but it could no longer be considered an essential element of Britain's pretensions to global influence. Nott, like his opponents in the peace movement, had no doubts about Britain's right to claim such influence. The habit of Empire was so ingrained among most Britons that they rarely recognized its signs. Few people doubted that Britain had a special moral role in the world.

The Falklands crisis at first threatened the hard-headed Thatcherite aspirations to British prestige as much as it did the moralists in the peace movement. "High out of the sun, almost invisible amidst the great issues of economics and social policy that cloud so much of the sky, a thunderbolt has descended from nowhere to shake the government," wrote journalist Max Hastings, who was to become a "celebrity" as the first British war correspondent to enter liberated Port Stanley. "The logic of events appears inexorably to demand that Britain must fight surely its last imperial battle in the South Atlantic for the protection of our citizens and the credibility of our country. It will be a national tragedy if we are obliged to do so. Yet the alternative — capitulation — would destroy not only Mrs. Margaret Thatcher, but the last tatters of Britain's position in the world."[5]

In one of his first conversations with the prime minister about the crisis, according to one knowledgeable source, Nott warned her, "You do realize that if you [send a task force], there's going to be no pulling back until the Argentines have given in."

On that fateful spring weekend in London, the nation was drifting steadily toward war. Outside the Argentine embassy, where two young hooligans had been arrested for venting their patriotism by hurling cans of Argentine beef through the windows, a few helmeted bobbies were keeping a tense watch. I wandered over to chat with some well-dressed young men who said they had seen the incident. They sympathized with the vandals. "I don't understand why those two blokes were the only ones who came out," said 17-year-old Kevin Skelton. "I thought this country had more bottle than it had." Perhaps Kevin had been reading too many Fleet Street headlines. But "bottle," or, as the Latin Americans might put it, machismo, was on just about every Briton's mind as the Falklands crisis began to escalate. "Those people out there want to remain British and we should bloody well help them," sputtered Paul Fishlock, a mild-mannered 36-year-old computer analyst. "I'm just bloody mad."

Similar expressions of wounded patriotism were aroused in the most unlikely quarters of the realm. A supermarket chain announced that it was stopping sales of Argentine corned beef in its 500 stores around the country. Ossie Ardiles, an Argentine football star playing for the London Tottenham Hotspurs, was hissed and booed when he walked onto the field. Prince Charles grappled with the problem of whether to go ahead with his plans to hire an Argentine groom for his polo ponies, and even the Queen was reported to be reconsidering an official trip to Ottawa, where, ironically, she would preside over the cutting of the last formal constitutional tie between Britain and its former Canadian dominions. At the newly opened Barbican Theatre, Canadian-born administrator Henry Wrong refused to refund a ticket paid for by the Argentine ambassador. "We give nothing back," he said. "We are at war."

A quieter, but no less strident, chauvinism was taking hold of the government. Bernard Ingham, the prime minister's press secretary, whose florid face, bushy eyebrows, and bluff Yorkshire manner made him a modern caricature of John Bull, was in a bombastic mood at his regular briefings for foreign reporters. He met questions about the contradictions in Britain's Falklands policy with undisguised hostility. "We have moral right on our side," he said, "and we are a very formidable lot when we have moral right on our side."

On the Monday following the Commons debate, Lord Carrington, the aristocratic foreign secretary, handed in his resignation. He was followed by two junior foreign office ministers. Under the tradition of parliamentary accountability (usually honoured more in the breach than the observance), they took responsibility for the "failures" of their department. They were also reading the mood of the country. Newspaper polls showed that more than 25 per cent thought Thatcher should quit as well. About 70 per cent said they agreed with the notion of sinking Argentine ships or attacking the mainland if necessary.

Tension built up through an extended "phony war" in which Britain tried to negotiate indirectly with Argentina, using the shuttle services of then U.S. Secretary of State Alexander Haig. Meanwhile, the biggest naval armada ever assembled in postwar history was chugging laboriously across the Atlantic. Even then, few people believed it would have to be used. Britain's decision to establish a 200-mile "exclusion zone" around the Falklands appeared to make a serious conflict less likely. On April 27, the British confirmed their control of the military situation with a bravado mission. News came that a British force had recaptured South Georgia. The victory had been achieved in classic British *Boys' Own* style. A Special Air Services (SAS) squadron stole ashore in a blizzard, followed by a small force of Royal Marines who stealthily surrounded the Argentine garrison. Gunboats kept up a deafening bombardment. The Argentines surrendered after a brief exchange of fire. There were just two casualties, a wounded Argentine sailor and an Argentine conscript killed accidentally the next day. After it was over, the British officers in full dress uniform sat down to a very correct dinner with the Argentine officers who were now their captives.

The victory lifted spirits at home, and it was particularly important to Margaret Thatcher, who had monitored the South Georgia operation during a tense night at British command headquarters at Northwood near London. The prime minister was under increasing pressure from the international community to step up negotiations for a compromise solution. The operation was chosen for psychological and political reasons, rather than for any tactical purpose. Britain, and the Thatcher government, needed to be seen to be doing something. "Just rejoice at the news," the relieved prime minister told a crowd of journalists waiting for her when she returned to Number 10 Downing Street after the victory was announced.

However, her remark turned out to be one of the few political mistakes she made during the war. Even some of those who had earlier criticized her for giving in to the Foreign Office "appeasers" were horrified at what seemed to be Thatcher's newly discovered relish for combat. Britain was supposed to win, of course, but one wasn't supposed to harp on it. Instead of striking the Churchillian note that was so essential to her self-image, she impressed people as acting like a "warrior queen." In any case, the war of nerves had ended. Less than a week later, the real war arrived.

On May 2, an Argentine carrier, the *General Belgrano*, apparently steaming away from the exclusion zone, was torpedoed and sunk by a British submarine, with the loss of hundreds of Argentine lives. The Thatcher "war cabinet" explained that it had given the order to protect the task force that had by then moved into position around the Falklands, but the first taste of blood took a toll on national unity. Labour's Michael Foot began to regret his own fiery rhetoric about Britain standing up for little countries around the world. Historian E.P. Thompson warned that British society would never be the same if violence was allowed to prevail over the cooler emotions of the bargaining table. "We shall pay for it a long time," he predicted, "in rapes and muggings in our cities, in international ill will, and in the stirring up of ugly nationalistic sediment which will cloud our political and cultural life."

Britain's armed forces were much more hesitant in private than anyone realized at the time. In 1986, I interviewed one of the leading military figures of the Falklands War. His superiors, still sensitive to the issue years afterwards, made it a condition of the interview that his name not be used. He told me point-blank that few of those in the inner circle realized they were beginning an unstoppable chain of events. "While there was a clear military and official understanding of the escalation process, and plenty of opportunity for the Argentines to say, 'No, I think we've had enough,' there was a political inevitability about the whole thing on both sides which I don't think very many people understood," he said.

"We, the cold, cool thinkers, the strategists if you like, were just as much interested in turning the crisis down and getting it under control, but [we] didn't take into account the fact that the media tend to make an issue of things. If you make an issue of things, people take sides — witness any good football game — and you have a punch-up. A politician can't resist national pressure for very long, and the media these days can actually cause an entire nation to take attitudes very quickly.

"The message I took from 1982 was that deterrence and escalation theories can be extremely dangerous, because they give us a warm feeling that we can afford to fool around on the edge of war, like sailing a task force and thinking that we can turn it around. It's jolly dangerous."

The "edge of war" was crossed with devastating speed. On May 5, Nott stood up in Parliament to report that the Argentines had avenged the *Belgrano*. The destroyer HMS *Sheffield*, he said, had sunk with a crew of 270 officers and men, after exploding in flames from a direct hit by an Argentine Exocet missile. Thirty British sailors were feared dead, the first major casualties of the war. Sitting alone in my office that night, watching the TV broadcast, I felt a chill. Until then, "covering" a war 8,000 miles away had seemed unreal. Now there were victims and grieving families.

A few days later, I travelled by train to Portsmouth. The mood of flag-waving hilarity that had prevailed when the armada was sent on its way had been replaced by a cold sadness. Rev. Trevor Lynn, a navy chaplain, spoke with me at his home, after having been to see the parents of a cook aboard the *Sheffield* who had been killed in the attack. "It was difficult," he said, shaking his head. "They were inconsolable." The chaplain's wife, Paddy, said the sleepless nights of parents around the city had just begun. "People are wondering what ships are next," she said. "When I heard the news on television, my stomach turned over. But now the general feeling is we can't let those sailors die in vain."

The war added a sinister quality to national life. Shortly after nine each night, television screens would flash a list of phone numbers for anxious relatives of servicemen in the South Atlantic. The country seemed to live on nerves. "Let's go in and win this one, but quickly, please," pleaded a London disc jockey.

Britons of all backgrounds found themselves drawn in, sometimes against their better judgement. "I thought it was incredible that we showed so much restraint early on," said social analyst Nicholas Albery. "I was becoming terribly aggressive; I was thinking we should have said to the Argentines, 'Look, for every ship of ours you sink, we're going to bomb one of your mainland airports or something.'"

Every pub and parlour was the proving ground of amateur naval strategists. Television news announcers moved ships and planes around huge table-maps in their studios with the steely aplomb of Admiral Nelson. The *Sun* offered to sponsor missiles to "wipe the smile off [Argentine leader General] Galtieri's face." Vicars debated the principles of a "just war" in the pages of *The Times*. John Robinson, assistant bishop of Southwark, complained that Britain's clergy had abdicated their roles as spiritual counsellors. "I think we shall look back with shame on this business," he said.

Long after the event, most Britons could remember being shocked by friends who were swept up in the militarism. "I thought this was a country I didn't want to be part of," said Craig Brown, a young journalist. "Friends of mine were saying, 'What a great war,' but there was something uncomfortably spurious about it." Jonathan Porritt, then the leader of Britain's Ecology Party, remembered "people ... I thought were quite reasonable suddenly longing to bash the Argies." He felt deeply uncomfortable. "There was this naked, aggressive, militaristic, deeply unpleasant British character emerging all over the place, and it was frightening to behold."

In fact, some Britons were less militaristic than it often appeared. They felt as trapped by events as the government. "I thought the Falklands was crazy, but you couldn't let the old Argies just walk on our soil," recalled Bill Tennent, the young managing director of a computer firm in Scotland. "It may have felt at first like just a World Cup football match, but I think the general reaction was that when you put the guns out, you've got to be behind our soldiers." Tennent was at a computer fair in Hanover,

Germany, the night the *Sheffield* was sunk. "The people we were with — I don't know whether it was a joke — they took us to an Argentine restaurant," he said. "It was quite embarrassing really. We felt like traitors. I think most people in this country felt the Falklands [War] was unnecessary, it was Maggie being belligerent, but at the same time, you were still behind them and you wanted them to win."

Margaret Thatcher felt every twist and turn of the war. Despite the public image of belligerence, her closest aides remember that she took the deaths deeply. After strategy sessions broke up in the evenings, she would retire to her private quarters upstairs at Number 10 Downing Street to write letters to the parents of the dead servicemen until the early hours.

An exchange between Thatcher and a broadcast journalist during one lull in the campaign revealed the tensions she was experiencing. The interviewer had innocently wondered whether the whole affair was superfluous. The islanders could not expect permanent protection from British troops. "I beg your pardon?" said Thatcher, her voice rising. "Did you *really* say that eventually Britain would leave those people to be under the heel of a junta if they did not wish it? These are words I never thought to hear."

The interviewer quickly backed down. What did the prime minister hope to achieve, then, once the war was over? The answer was fired back with the directness of an Exocet missile: "We shall have the quiet acclaim and approval of all who believe in democracy, and they'll think, 'Thank goodness, someone stood up for international law. Someone's done it at last.'"

Foreign diplomats had an equally hard time trying to engage Thatcher on her postwar plans. Giulio Andreotti, then foreign minister of Italy, recalled, "I tried to put to Mrs. Thatcher the idea, which I had already discussed with the French foreign secretary, Claude Cheysson, of the reopening of negotiations about the future of the Falklands, and she cut me dead. I had the impression that she felt it was almost an insult to her to mention this."[6]

By late May, there was no turning back. As the Commons gathered for its sixth full parliamentary debate, Thatcher warned that she was ready to seize the Falklands by force if there were no progress on negotiations. In fact, even as Parliament was sitting, British forces were moving into position off San Carlos Bay in East Falklands.

On May 21, at 8:20 p.m., John Nott appeared at the Ministry of Defence briefing room. Reporters suddenly sprang to attention at his words. "Seven weeks after the Argentine aggression, British forces are tonight firmly established back on the Falklands Islands," he said.

The explosion of national pride at that moment made Joan Ruddock wonder at first whether she had seriously misjudged the audience she was trying to reach with the antinuclear movement. She had been attacked everywhere, even by friends in the peace movement, for speaking out against the war. They worried that her campaign against the planned deployment of American cruise missiles at British bases would alienate some of their middle-class supporters. In the midst of the current fervour, there was no room for arguments about nuclear weapons. Driven to communicate in furtive whispers with others who opposed the war, Ruddock describes those days in the conspiratorial language used by dissidents behind the Iron Curtain. "You didn't know how even some of your best friends felt, and it was difficult to ask."

As the final push to Port Stanley began, with Royal Marines "yomping" across the islands, the peace movement was faced with a crucial decision. Earlier that year, Campaign for Nuclear Disarmament (CND) organizers had made plans for a June rally at Hyde Park in London. The demonstration was intended to coincide with the opening of the United Nations Special Session on Disarmament in New York, and to begin raising public consciousness for the scheduled arrival of cruise missiles in Britain, still a year away. Considering the war fever in the country, many wondered whether it would be political suicide to stage a public protest against government policy toward nuclear weapons. A peace rally conducted before the eyes of the world press, while British soldiers were dying in battle, was likely to be interpreted as an act of treason.

The organizers could have found many reasons to postpone the rally. "Strickly speaking, we were not a peace movement," said Ruddock. "Our constitution was entirely based on opposition to nuclear weapons and other weapons of mass destruction. Theoretically, you could be an ardent CND supporter and [a supporter of] the Falklands War. But we were taking one hell of a chance with a demonstration."

The CND leaders took the gamble. They announced that the rally would go ahead as scheduled. On June 6, 1982 — a thundery Saturday — 250,000 people filled Hyde Park. Millions held "peace" demonstrations in other cities around Europe and the U.S. on the same day, but the unexpectedly huge British turnout — it was the biggest antinuclear rally ever held in Britain — provided an unforgettable contrast to the atmosphere of war on the home front.

Joan Ruddock and the rally's other organizers were vindicated. Only five CND members in the entire country resigned because of the rally. Hyde Park convinced observers — and the peace movement itself — that their side of the great postimperial debate had not lost ground.

On June 14, a week after the Hyde Park rally, British paratroopers descended into Port Stanley. The weeping Argentine commander surrendered his untrained recruits without a further fight. The Union Jack flew again from the colonial governor's mansion. A brigadier general rushing anxiously over to an officer he saw in a dangerously exposed position above the town was told cheerfully, "It's O.K. It's all over."

The newspaper headlines back home registered the kingdom's relief. With a self-conscious glance back at the Second World War, the *Daily Express* ran an eight-inch-high *V* on its front page. But as the first contingents of sailors and soldiers returned to Britain over the next few weeks, there was a different edge to the flag-waving and cheering. The men who had gone out to fight for Queen and Empire were reluctant to be turned into heroes. "All I remember," said one grumpily, "is being muddy, cold, and wet." The mother of one sailor who was killed put her feelings soberly. "I am proud of my son," she said. "But not proud of the fact that he died for his country in a war which was not necessary."

A debate over the causes of the war, however, never got off the ground. "The soundness of the operation must be judged by its success," was the brisk conclusion of Max Hastings and Simon Jenkins, who wrote one of the flotilla of journalists' books about the Falklands.[7] A special government inquiry a year later absolved the prime minister of any direct responsibility for the mistakes and misjudgements that began the affair, although it agreed that the withdrawal of HMS *Endurance* in the midst of the Royal Navy cutbacks had probably spurred the Argentine generals' invasion plans.

The Falklanders were jubilant, at first, but their mood gradually changed. The Falklands cost Britain more than £2 billion (including £700 million spent on the war effort) between 1982 and 1986. Much of the money went toward building a garrison and a new airfield, and strengthening the islands' military defences. But the islanders had little reason to feel any more secure about their future.

"In the long run, the British are going to say 'Be buggered with those bastards,'" Stuart Wallace, a former Falklands councillor, told a *Guardian* reporter in 1985. Wallace could not imagine leaving the islands and being forced to live in a "terraced house in Britain, scared of vandals," but he acknowledged that the Falklanders could not determine British foreign policy forever.

If Falklanders had mixed feelings, at least foreigners were glad to give Britain the adulation she seemed to need. Henry Kissinger invoked the courageous spirit of the Blitz at a speech to the Royal Institute of International Affairs in London. The Falklands, he said, reminded the world "that certain basic principles such as honour, justice, and patriotism remain valid and must be sustained by more than words." The reminder may have proved more useful to the U.S. than to Britain. Several observers wondered whether Britain's successful pursuit of the war made small-scale interventions by the U.S. fashionable again. The Falklands might well have been a dress rehearsal for the invasion of Grenada and the attack on Libya. At any rate, it was hard to prove that Britain's moral authority was in any way enhanced.

"A Czech friend of mine said that [the Falklands] was the first time in his experience he'd seen a Western power reacting without any regard to diplomatic consequences," said Roger Scruton, "without any regard to law, or any of the usual hesitations that tie our hands behind our backs, acting from sheer, straightforward offendedness. That was to them the clearest message to the Soviet Union that we're not going to be messed around with." But even Scruton, who was teaching in Canada for most of the war, admitted that the biggest benefits were reaped at home. "The Falklands showed the end of our postcolonial guilt," he declared. "I didn't think it was an embarrassment. It was a great triumph."

From the comfort of retirement, former Defence Minister John Nott was unrepentant about his original hesitations, pointing out how close Britain had come to failure. "We were imperfectly equipped to undertake such a task," he admitted, "nor, with the diminished size of our national budget, can we ever hope to do so." It was still Suez, he maintained, that demonstrated the facts of life for Britain: "The Falklands changed nothing."

A senior Falklands commander who spent much of the battle on the treacherous Antarctic waters worrying about the Argentine air force felt the same. "I don't think that the Falklands issue is particularly relevant to what our broad attitudes to the world at large should be," he said. "It was a very particular case . . . another unexpected future."

For Joan Ruddock, the war proved the mettle of the peace movement. Although the anti-cruise campaign had been unable to prevent cruise missiles from being deployed in 1983, she argued that the protesters had introduced a new sense of realism into the country's affairs, and given a new generation a voice in choosing the path Britain needed to take in the postindustrial world. "The reason we succeeded in coming back after cruise deployment, and after the government, the media, and everyone else wrote us off, was [that] I think we articulated our concerns in a way appropriate to the Eighties," Ruddock said. "A lot of things have come together to indicate to the British people that the risks of war are real."

The greatest impact of the war was, inevitably, on the home front. "The Falklands . . . didn't prove we are a bloodthirsty lot, just aching to carve up Argies," wrote columnist Katherine Whitehorn in *The Observer*. "It did prove that people are invigorated by feeling they've won something." Whitehorn cited as evidence the words of an engineer interviewed by her newspaper. "[Thatcher] showed 'em, didn't she?" the engineer said. "She showed they couldn't just walk in."

It was left to Margaret Thatcher to make the real link between victory in the Falklands and Britain's industrial problems. A month after the Argentine surrender, the prime minister spoke to a Conservative rally at Cheltenham Race Course. "Now that it is over, things cannot be the same again," she said. "We have learned something about ourselves — a lesson which we desperately need to learn. When we started out, there were the waverers and the fainthearts, the people who thought Britain could no longer seize the initiative for herself, ... those who believed that our decline was irreversible. . . .

" . . . Well, they were wrong. The lesson of the Falklands is that Britain has not changed. [But] why does it need a war to bring out our qualities and reassert our pride? Why do we have to be invaded before we throw aside our selfish aims and begin to work together? We have to see that the spirit of the South Atlantic — the real spirit of Britain — is kindled not only by war but can now be fired by peace. We know we can do it. We haven't lost the ability. That is the Falklands Factor."[8]

Chapter 6
THE WAR OF JENKINS' MOUTH

Who will rid me of this turbulent priest?

— *attributed to Henry II, c. 1170*

The two middle-aged men kneeling stiffly before an altar in Canterbury Cathedral, on May 30, 1982, might have been figures in a medieval tapestry. Cloaked in white-and-gold robes, they looked like ecclesiastical princes giving thanks for a safe return from the Crusades. After a few moments of silent prayer, they stood up and embraced. An almost audible surge of emotion swept through the congregation.

More than 2,500 people were jammed inside the nation's most important religious shrine that day to witness Pope John Paul II and Archbishop Robert Runcie stage a public act of reconciliation. For some Britons it was one of the most stirring images of the decade. The ceremony performed under hot TV lights meant that Anglicans had taken the first, tentative step toward ending their 400-year-long cold war with Rome.

For centuries, a reunion between the churches had been inconceivable. The Church of England was born out of a sixteenth-century argument between King Henry VIII and Pope Clement VII over divorce, but its subsequent growth was due to a more substantial concern over national sovereignty. Like Parliament and the Crown, the other great preindustrial institutions of the state, the Church of England was to become a cornerstone of British unity for successive generations. The break with Rome was one of the crucial events of British history.

In 1559, Queen Elizabeth I, the daughter of Henry VIII, made the Anglican faith central to the modernizing spirit of the Elizabethan Age when she signed an Act of Supremacy establishing the monarch as governor of the church. The same year, a bishop-elect of London named John Aylmer wrote a letter from France to his parishioners that reflected the strength Elizabethans derived from the church's identification with the secular idea of nationhood. "Oh if thou knewest thou Englishmen in what wealth thou livest, and in how plentiful a country," he wrote, "thou wouldest VII times a day fall flat on [thy] face before God and give him thanks that thou were born an Englishman, and not a French peasant, nor an Italian, nor German."[1]

Aylmer's chauvinism would have found a receptive audience during the 1980s. The Falklands were only the most recent, and most obvious, display of the feelings of cultural superiority that were just below the surface of British nationalism. But any bishop in the 1980s who asked parishioners to give thanks for "how plentiful a country" they inhabited would have been a determined optimist who never read a newspaper.

The Anglican church was deeply affected by Britain's industrial transformation. The one national body that should have been able to exert moral leadership at a time of crisis seemed to be approaching a state of paralysis. A bitter internal argument over the best response to the new currents in British life had been simmering for years. In any other country, such a debate would have been a quiet affair, conducted well away from the theatre of politics. But the church's institutional importance in British life meant that its internal problems were national ones.

The Church of England is one of the few churches in Western democracies with a statutory role in the making of national laws. Its special status, with its overtones of medievalism, looks odd to an outsider. Twenty-six bishops, appointed on the recommendation of the Queen and the prime minister, have the right to vote in the House of Lords. No other religious denomination in Britain has a similar right to be at the centre of the legislative process. However, the authority of the state church rests on what has become a dubious claim to speak for a large segment of the British population. Although more than 60 per cent of Britons call themselves Anglicans, fewer than 50 out of every 1,000 are actually church members. In the 1970s and 1980s, church membership was declining around the country. The traditional parish church, surrounded by crumbling graveyards and increasingly dependent on passing tourists for subsistence, was a fitting symbol of the church's alienation from modern life.[2]

Its diminishing religious importance has had little effect, however, on the Church of England's impregnable position in the British Establishment. The church, which joins the monarchy and the aristocracy as the country's biggest landowners, is worth an estimated £1.6 billion. It earns about £38 million, one-third of its annual income, from its commercial properties alone, and receives large sums in the form of special tax rebates from government.[3]

The bishops and other dignitaries of the Church of England speak and act like an imperial elite, largely because that is exactly what they are. A majority of the bishops have degrees from either Oxford or Cambridge, and more than half have attended one of Britain's privileged public schools. Their motivations and political allegiances have changed very little from the days of England's world ascendancy. Younger sons of the nineteenth-century gentry and nobility who joined the clergy were to be found by the side of their peers in the army and colonial service, administering the Empire. In the 1980s, they were supreme authorities in miniature diocesan empires, a crucial link in Britain's hidden government, and a bulwark of conservative values. "Bishops are custodians of traditional things," the Bishop of Peterborough once explained to a reporter. But their automatic membership in the Establishment had been retained at the price of political independence. "In most matters of real national importance, the Church of England can still be relied upon to be sensible," *The Economist* magazine commented smugly in 1983.[4]

Nevertheless, there were many who believed that the church was no longer performing a useful role. They accused the Anglican hierarchy of having become so devoted to the preservation of its own status that the Church of England had become a bastion of British ethnocentricity in the new postindustrial "Dark Ages." One critic called it a "protective cocoon within which preindustrial Britain stayed strong and safe."[5]

Church leaders have recently struggled hard to become relevant. The Anglican Book of Common Prayer was "modernized" in 1980 to attract worshippers back to the fold, but the move alienated thousands of the faithful who missed the familiar cadences of the old service. There were even rumours of a plan to ordain women priests.[6] Predictably, efforts to give the church a higher profile provoked a backlash from those who saw Anglicanism as the last refuge of "Englishness." Sometimes it seemed as if the more irrelevant the tradition was, the greater the campaign to keep it. The battle inside the Church of England displayed all the contradictory impulses of British life. It was bound to spread beyond the cathedral close and parish hall.

The first hint of the political storm that was to engulf the Anglican leadership in the 1980s came during the papal visit. It was another of the decade's historical ironies that Britain found one of the spurs to her regeneration in a Polish-born Roman Catholic pontiff. The two-week 1982 visit of Pope John Paul II had a powerful impact on Anglicans as well as on British Catholics.

The papal tour occurred just after the first British casualties in the Falklands War were reported; this unfortunate timing nearly led to the cancellation of the trip before it began. With British ships under attack in the

South Atlantic from the Exocet missiles of Catholic Argentina, no one could be sure how the nation's Protestants would react to an ecumenical embrace.[7] As it turned out, British reserve melted under the onslaught of Polish charisma. The visit was judged one of the most successful trips of John Paul's early papacy. But as he travelled around the country that week, by helicopter, train, and "pope-mobile," there were constant reminders of the anxieties caused by the war.

The pope did his best to avoid touching on the political sensitivities of his hosts. He paid a respectful call on the Queen at Buckingham Palace and prayed with her for the safety of her son Prince Andrew, then serving as a Sea King helicopter pilot in the Falklands, but he stayed clear of any formal meetings with the prime minister or members of her war cabinet. However, the pope could not keep completely silent. On a hillside near Glasgow, a city filling important shipping contracts as well as sending many of its young people to the war, the pope prayed for the victims of "both sides" of the conflict. At Coventry, site of massive German bombing during the Second World War, he criticized war as an act of policy. "The scale and horror of modern warfare...makes it totally unacceptable as a means of settling differences," he said. "War should belong to the tragic past, to history; it should find no place on humanity's agenda for the future."

At Canterbury, the friendly reconciliation of pope and archbishop entered the political imagery of the time. If ancient fears and jealousies could be so successfully laid aside, there was hope for those earnestly seeking a new evaluation of their country's suffocating burden of myth and tradition. The most impressive omen of change came in an almost-overlooked incident that occurred during the Canterbury ceremony.

After their prayer and embrace, the two spiritual leaders walked to a small stone slab in the northwest transept of the church, the spot where St. Thomas Becket was murdered in 1170. Becket had annoyed King Henry II with his earnest appeals to an authority higher than the Crown. The King's courtiers misinterpreted one of Henry's temperamental outbursts, "Who will rid me of this turbulent priest?", as a licence for assassination, and turned the scholarly rebel into England's most important religious martyr. Now, 872 years later, Pope John Paul and Dr. Runcie stood together near Becket's shrine to light a series of candles to the martyrs of the twentieth century. It was an intriguing illustration of the day's ecumenical spirit. The two religious traditions had no trouble forming a common bond of support for those who had pitted their faith against the power of the state.

A few months after the pope went home, the archbishop became the central figure in an embarrassing political quarrel between the church and the state. The government had asked for permission to use St. Paul's

Cathedral as the setting for a Falklands memorial service. Permission was granted, of course, but the service was very different from what the government had had in mind. Instead of conducting a celebration of a great Nelsonian victory, Runcie turned the occasion into a sombre requiem. In his sermon to the congregation of assembled ministers, war veterans, and widows of soldiers lost in combat, he asked that the dead of both sides be remembered. It was a surprising, and to the government, untimely, assertion of religious ecumenism. The prime minister was said to feel as exasperated by "her" Canterbury as King Henry had been by Becket. The next day, an atmosphere of national outrage was manufactured by carefully timed leaks to friendly newspapers on Fleet Street. One unidentified minister explained the government's fury this way: "He [Canterbury] seemed to treat the dead of Argentina and Britain as the same." Runcie stood firm. He had intended the St. Paul's service to be a gesture of national reconciliation, and it would have been counterproductive to press the point further. After all, the pope had made similar comments during his visit to Britain. The controversy died down, and the government retreated, still fuming. But the outlines of a new conflict between church and state could already be seen.

The controversy over the Falklands memorial service was not the first time Church of England bishops had found themselves in conflict with the government of the day. An Anglican bishop once tried to offer a "peace plan" to settle the General Strike of 1926, and found himself effectively censored by the fledgling state broadcasting company. During the Depression years, rebellious bishops argued the side of workers and the poor against the Establishment. Their opposition was irritating, but it did not challenge the fundamental compromise worked out over the centuries between the Church of England and the government. While compassion for the poor was acceptable, active political involvement was not.

Bishops and priests in the 1980s found themselves in a new and provocative political environment. British politicians were promoting a "moral revolution" on grounds that religious leaders — particularly those of the state church — had always considered private property. Thatcherism represented an attack on the consensus policies with which the Church of England had traditionally been identified. To receive the "new moralists" in silence was to grant them official approval. "At first, in the Church of England, they would smile and remark that 'politicians do say such things from time to time,'" wrote Clifford Longley, religion editor of *The Times*. "The message has now got through that [Thatcher] means it."[8]

There were many church officials who privately welcomed Thatcherite politics, but those who didn't were faced with extremely unpleasant choices. If they did not speak out, they would lose further credibility with those of their parishioners who were feeling the brunt of the government's harsh economic realism. Many members of the clergy found that by taking a moral stand they were pushed, somewhat reluctantly perhaps, down a more overtly political road.

It took another two years before the skirmish at St. Paul's was translated into a battle for the soul of Britain. By then, the remarkable spirit forged by the Falklands victory had become twisted out of all recognition. A strike by 187,000 coal miners, called in March 1984 to protest government plans to close twenty "uneconomic" pits, was tearing the kingdom apart. The strike was something new in the history of postwar British industrial conflict. Night after night, scenes of pitched battles between striking miners and police forces in Welsh, Scottish, and northern English communities were displayed on the television news like reports from a war front in the third world.

In regions where rebel miners insisted on their right to work, police had to be called in to protect them from angry pickets bussed from all corners of mining country. Both forces, the police and the "flying pickets," grew until parts of northern Britain began to look like armed camps. Police roadblocks turned back drivers suspected of being striking miners. Thousands of constables conscripted from all over the country were billeted outside local towns. The leaders of both sides acted like opposing generals. The prime minister spoke belligerently of defeating "the enemy within." Arthur Scargill, leader of the National Union of Miners (NUM), was perfectly typecast for the "enemy" role. A fiery Yorkshire Marxist who bore an uncanny resemblance to a grown-up choir boy, he claimed that his men were the "shock troops" in a social and industrial Battle of Britain.

A government that had just fought a nineteenth-century war saw no contradiction in its campaign to destroy what it considered the strongest symbol of archaic industrial thinking. The miners, a small tribal community with loyalties to folk memories long since lost to suburban Britons, were the new Falklanders. But this time they were the targets of, rather than those championed by, a government task force.

Thatcher had always believed that her most important struggle — and the one that would legitimize her revolution in Britain — would be waged against the powerful British trade union movement. Shortly after she won a second term in a 1983 landslide election victory, ministers were ordered to build up coal reserves. Not only were the Tories convinced they would face a miners' strike; there were signs they welcomed the opportunity for a showdown. The Falklands success had given the prime minister new strength, as well as confidence in her abilities as a war leader.[9]

But a war at home was not easily susceptible to the "Falklands Factor." The strike sharply escalated the violence that had already begun to erode the fabric of British life in the 1980s. The infantry on the front lines comprised young miners, most of them under the age of 30, who went into battle against the massed ranks of police, singing "Here We Go, Here We Go, Here We Go," the chant of the fearsome British football fans. The counter-reaction was a long time coming, but when it arrived, a white-haired Anglican bishop found himself at its head.

One Saturday in late September 1984, Rt. Rev. David Jenkins climbed to the lectern of Durham Cathedral to deliver his enthronement address as the newly appointed sixty-ninth Bishop of Durham, a post that would make him among the three or four most powerful priests in the Anglican hierarchy.

Jenkins, a 60-year-old former professor of theology who looked like a country vicar in a Jane Austen novel, was about as unlikely a figure of religious resistance as anyone could imagine. But the strike was arousing even the mildest of Britons. Earlier that week, a group of young miners had ambushed a squad of ambulance drivers and police, driving them back with stones and fists. Jenkins took the coal miners' struggle as the text for his sermon. Durham was one of the principal coal-mining regions of Britain, and no Bishop of Durham could have avoided mentioning the strike and its obvious impact on his flock. But he went further than anyone expected. He forced the British to see that they were now facing an enemy more dangerous than the Argies: themselves.

Summing up the national malaise in a new and disturbing way, he charged that the strike was a symptom of the deeper problems of British society. Britain's major problem was the indifference of one section of the population to the poverty and misery of the other, he said, and the miners' dispute had accentuated the growing social divisions. He criticized both sides: the government for its handling of the strike, and the miners for their intransigence. Neither side, he said, deserved to win.

"I am against violence…but I am equally clear that we must understand why ordinary, decent, family-centred working men get involved in violence," the bishop went on. He warned that unless the nation found a way to compromise on industrial issues, it would be unable to tackle the more pressing inequalities of British society, and would suffer irreparable damage in the process. Then, as his listeners held their breath, he moved into political territory where the British clergy had often feared to tread.

Jenkins said the appointment of an "elderly, imported American," as chairman of the National Coal Board made prospects for peace in the coalfields even more difficult. He was referring to Ian MacGregor, a Scottish-born, naturalized U.S. citizen brought in by the Thatcher government to oversee the drastic surgery it prescribed for the British mining industry. MacGregor was a crusty 71-year-old industrialist who had made his name in American coalfields as a manager who knew how to "handle" unions. Not surprisingly, his confrontational techniques increased the atmosphere of hostility in Britain. The new Bishop of Durham said that MacGregor should be fired to give the forces of compromise a new chance.[10] The audience of 2,000 sitting inside Durham Cathedral reacted in a manner surprising for staid Church of England ceremonials. They broke out in applause.

The bishop's speech was the first voice of gentle reason Britons had heard for months, but it did very little to alter the course of the dispute. Another six violent, tense months passed before the miners went back to work in humiliating defeat.[11]

The real significance of Jenkins' contribution was found in the scale of the reaction he triggered in the rest of the country. A leader of the Church of England had broken ranks in public. Most people felt it was about time that someone in authority had delivered a moral opinion. His criticism of the miners, however, was almost forgotten as press attention centred on his critique of government policy.

The government, still smarting from the slight to its authority offered by Dr. Runcie at the St. Paul's memorial service, and aware that religious leaders were murmuring Jenkins-like sentiments in private, decided to launch a pre-emptive attack against the church before the rebellion grew. "I hope before [the bishop] preaches his next sermon on this topic he takes the trouble to study the facts instead of pronouncing on the fiction," snapped Energy Minister Peter Walker. Members of Parliament, encouraged by Walker's example, stood up in the House of Commons to denounce the bishop as a Marxist and a threat to the British way of life. They accused him of "gutter politics" and called him a "walking clerical disaster area."

Leading clergy promptly came to the bishop's defence and even those who disagreed with his remarks defended his right to make them. Derek Worlock, the Roman Catholic Archbishop of Liverpool, moved to cement the alliance struck by the pope two years earlier. During a religious conference on the Isle of Man a few days after Jenkins' remarks, he called the miners' strike "a symptom of the failure of our society to come to terms with the postindustrial age."

"What is to happen to whole communities when the industry about which their lives have been bound up and upon which their livelihood has depended is judged to be no longer profitable, practical, or even the best way of doing things, or serving the wider community?" he asked. "The whole nation needs to take a very clear look about it as we move toward the eleventh hour of the industrial era."

The Archbishop of Canterbury was clearly embarrassed by the furor. He wrote a letter to MacGregor apologizing for any personal offence that might have been caused by his errant bishop. The letter was promptly leaked, and Runcie was forced to make his private views of the struggle public.[12] "We have lost our international reputation for compromise," he said, in remarks seen as providing critical support for Jenkins' message. "We are creating areas of despair and poverty, and mistrust about the future. There will come a time [when] the generality of British people will wake up and say this is not a decent sort of society in which to live."

The Bishop of Durham was soon back in the headlines, complaining in one House of Lords speech about the government's "divisive" monetarist economic policies, and in another, charging it with the creation of a "police state." He infuriated the government again and again. One London head-line writer was inspired to call the endless skirmishing between Durham and his parliamentary critics the "War of Jenkins' Mouth."[13]

"What people want from a bishop is a sort of spiritual anaesthetic, don't they?" Bishop Jenkins said in 1986, when asked to speculate on why his comments had provoked such a strong outcry. "They don't particularly want to be disturbed. But I felt that people needed to hear more than just a statement of principle [at Durham Cathedral]. A friend of mine produced the splendid remark that bishops, generally speaking, are generally speak-ing. That's very good, isn't it?"

Jenkins was the first to break the unwritten code of silence among church officials reluctant to comment on Britain's increasing social ills, but there were soon so many clerical targets for official wrath that it began to seem as if a fifth column had formed behind Establishment front lines. In December 1985, the Church of England sent a bombshell hurtling into gov-ernment ranks that made the Bishop of Durham's sermons seem like bow-and-arrow attacks. *Faith in the City*, a church-commissioned study on conditions in Britain's inner cities, changed forever the church's image as a cozy member of the Establishment. Declaring that the church had a duty to be the "conscience of the nation," the study set about demolishing every aspect of government policy toward urban areas. "We are united in the view that the costs of present policies, with the continuing growth of unemployment, are unacceptable," it said. The report's authors, some of whom had been civil servants under previous governments, charged that current economic policies had "contributed to the blighting of whole dis-tricts" and were likely to "perpetuate . . . human misery."[14]

In the wake of *Faith in the City*, the bishops' benches in the House of Lords came alive with dissent. At the beginning of the decade, few bishops had bothered to perform their parliamentary functions, except during debates on issues with especially religious overtones, such as the death penalty or abortion. Now, they were flailing away at questions ranging from social security problems to sanctions against South Africa. "When there are important social issues we look to see how many bishops are likely to be in the House," commented Labour Party peer Lord Ennals, with undisguised satisfaction, in 1986.

Any timidity government members might have felt about taking on their cassocked opponents soon disappeared. Thatcher accused some of her leading clerical opponents as living in "cloud-cuckooland." A senior cabinet minister, given a courtesy advance copy of the 398-page report, promptly leaked it to the press, with the absurd — and well-publicized — comment that it was a "Marxist" document.

The "War of Jenkins' Mouth" was the final, if not the defining, struggle that helped Britain come to grips with its new status in the world during the 1980s. Jenkins and other rebellious clerics made an essential contribution by pointing out that a spiritual crisis was at the heart of Britain's industrial dilemma. Conscientious members of the clergy no longer took refuge in their privileged status. By their own standards, if they wanted to be relevant, they had to be politically minded and activist. "Politics is too important to be left to politicians," John Gibbs, Bishop of Coventry, had argued even before Jenkins' speech at Durham. "Not to take seriously the great political issues of the day is nonsense. There are great issues on which the church should speak and on which it has a duty to speak."

Much more than the relationship between the church and the government of the day was affected by the clergy's new political outlook. The new clerical activism meant that any future government would have to take the clergy into account in its political strategy. As the vicars of Britain watched their parishioners slide into unemployment and deprivation, there seemed likely to be a long succession of twentieth-century Beckets disturbing the tranquillity of kings.

A crotchety two-carriage train is the only rail link to the northern English mining town of Bishop Auckland, seat of the bishops of Durham for seven centuries. One July afternoon in 1986, a brush salesman and myself were its only passengers. We were deposited on an empty rail platform beside a stretch of track overgrown with weeds.

Four years after the papal tour, and two years after the end of the miners' strike, my journey to see David Jenkins resembled a visit to a landscape that had been ruined by war. "Poxy sort of place, innit?" my companion said cheerfully. I looked around me in dismay. A decrepit station house, its windows covered with boards and graffiti, leaned to our right. There were no taxis. When I looked back, the salesman was already patiently threading his way across a parking lot strewn with broken glass toward a pub.

At first sight, Bishop Auckland's little High Street, crowded with lunchtime shoppers, was an encouraging change from the railway station. But the street's air of prosperity proved deceptive. I passed a shuttered store. Then I passed another, and another. A For Sale sign hung in one shop, which looked as if it had been empty for months. "Closing Down! Last Chance for Bargains," read a splattered piece of cardboard taped across a window. Along five or six blocks, I counted more than ten vacant storefronts. In such a small community, the number indicated an economic collapse of major proportions.

When I turned down a quiet street radiating from the town hall, toward a magnificent arched clock-tower that marked the entrance to the Bishop's Park, I felt an immediate change of atmosphere. A driveway wide enough for Victorian coaches led me past a stone gatehouse and down a tree-lined avenue that seemed to stretch for miles across a rolling landscape. There was a line of forested hills in the distance. The grubby atmosphere of decline was gone: before me was a vision of medieval England. Auckland Castle and its twelfth-century chapel sat in a courtyard, facing the green horizon, their backs stonily turned to the town. I couldn't help wondering whether the man I had come to see took as much comfort from the view as I did.

Even if I had been unaware of his reputation for controversy, the bishop's anteroom would have given it away. Set in a prominent place on an antique wooden table was a bust of Keir Hardie, the radical late-Victorian trade union leader and founder of the British Labour Party. The bust was inscribed with one of Hardie's famous battle-cries: "We are of the workers, they are our kin," it read. "We are part of them. Their battle is our battle. What hurts them hurts us. Where they gain, we gain."

Staring regally across the room at Hardie was the sculpted head of the Right Reverend Herbert Hensley Henson. Bishop of Durham until 1938, Henson was famous, among other things, for having narrowly missed being dunked in the River Wear by local miners infuriated by his opposition to strikes. They had, in a confusion of identity, immersed his dean instead. United in the same room by the present Bishop of Durham, the two busts seemed to have reached some sort of grudging acknowledgement of each other's existence.

The bishop insisted that the Keir Hardie bust, a gift from a local trade union, was not intended to give offence to his more conservative visitors. He explained that he had wanted to make a serious statement about the changes of attitude that he believed were necessary for both the church and his country to survive the industrial crisis. "The Church of England is beginning to see the end of its widespread domestication," he said. "It surprises the average conservative voter to be challenged, for instance, by reports like *Faith in the City*, but if what the church believes has any authentic truth, then the church is called to be one of the independent institutions of society."

The Bishop of Durham had more of a sense of humour than he was given credit for. "The very fact that Mrs. Thatcher signed a letter appointing me must be one of the ironies of history," laughed Jenkins. One of the bishop's heroes is St. Cuthbert, the Celtic founder of the church in the north of England. "I find him very attractive," he said, trying his best not to appear ironic, "because when they decided in the end to make him a bishop, it killed him in two years."

Our conversation revealed a surprising ambivalence on the bishop's part toward his public image as a moral critic of Thatcherism. He was not, for instance, unhappy about the resolution of the miners' dispute. I asked Jenkins whether, following the defeat of the miners, he thought the "best side had won." The bishop appeared hesitant. But he gave, after a pause, a direct answer. "I doubt if society could have borne the victory of the pickets," he said. "Whether one would have chosen the Thatcherite way or not, the first Thatcher administration must be regarded as on balance a good thing for the country, because it drew attention to our economic limits."

Jenkins made no secret of his political sympathies for socialist thought. In one of the many controversial statements he had made over the years, he had advocated a "liberation theology" for Britain, arguing that politicians needed a new framework for action based on the search for social justice rather than jockeying for political advantage. But few socialists would bother trying to recruit him as an organizer. As our conversation proceeded, it was clear that under a radical socialist regime the bishop would be just as much of a dissident. "A good deal of the programs by which right and left always try to sell their policies is based on consumerism — vote for me and we'll redistribute the lolly. Well, this is where the church ought to be able to assert its independent message that man shall not live by bread alone, whether he gets it by market means or Marxist means."

The contrast between the medieval splendour of the bishop's palace and the decay of the town gave him an opportunity to draw an analogy with an earlier era of British history. "In the fourteenth century," he said, "things were so bad that people thought it was the end of the world, but in fact it was the beginning of the Renaissance. What looks like breakdown, you see, is often the beginning of health."

Where, I wondered, did that leave communities like Bishop Auckland? The bishop seemed to be waiting for the question. His reply was chillingly direct. In Bishop Auckland, he pointed out, the closure of the uneconomic mine pits had precipitated an economic chain reaction. The boarded-up businesses I had seen on my way to the bishop's palace were the most obvious casualties. But it was useless, he said, to imagine that the vacant stores could be filled with dozens of new small businesses without changing the economic structure of Britain's north. "You would need in this region, for instance, two thousand small firms and a hundred people employed in each one [to take up the slack in the unemployed]; and for each business you would need five managers, and the money to finance them and their skills," the bishop explained.

But if the government's "private enterprise" dream was unrealistic, so were the arguments made by its critics among the miners and militant left about restoring the industrial relics of the previous century. Artificial stimulation of the economy to rebuild factories and mines that no longer had any economic value could not be a long-term solution, he said. It would only serve to reinforce the resistance to real change.

Jenkins acknowledged that such attitudes would put most politicians in an awkward position with their constituencies. It was easy to see how the benevolent-looking vicar could make a career in the 1980s out of disrupting his compatriots' digestions. He represented an ironic reversal of roles. According to the bishop, it was up to the church to teach politicians not to expect miracles. The country's leaders, he said, needed the courage to let things take a natural course.

"It may make life and tensions sharper, and more worrying, [but] it may actually force a breakthrough," the bishop argued with sudden force. "The present position of the northeast of Britain is the lowest point in the decline of nineteenth-century manufacturing and industrial society. ... People could be forced to see that the only resources we have now got are ourselves. It is not a question of going back to the preindustrial state. We are now, really, the fifth world."

Jenkins said parts of Britain suffered the kind of upheavals associated with the developing societies of the third world, and a few sections were experiencing the poverty and deprivation of the fourth. But the term "fifth world" designated a condition unique to advanced industrial societies. "It affects societies that have been through a particular form of industrialization and been left behind by it," he said.

The bishop maintained that the crisis had already produced some of the new attitudes and more flexible personalities he was hoping for. "We are very thin on the ground," he admitted. "But it's amazing what responses one gets unexpectedly, chatting to a trade union member or even at a church finance meeting. My sense is that things have got to get more sharply and visibly worse before more such people emerge. Clearly, the risk is that it will create such a turbulent, divided, or alienated society that it will more likely fall inward if it doesn't blow outward. But I'm not going to give up some notion of progress; we may happen to be moving through a wilderness, but it doesn't have to be a desert."

After the afternoon's conversation, I was even more reluctant to retrace my path through the desolate High Street. I wandered across the green quadrangle and walked into the chapel. It was empty except for a well-dressed couple admiring the stained-glass windows.

A bored church warden sitting at the door offered me a tour of the castle. I eagerly accepted. "We don't get many tourists," he said. We paused to admire the Great Hall, a vast room lined with portraits of the previous 68 bishops of Durham. I wondered what Britain would be like by the time David Jenkins's portrait had joined theirs. As the elderly warden led me further up a winding staircase to see the rest of the building, I caught glimpses through vaulted windows of sheep grazing along the green river valley of the Wear. I stopped to admire the scene. "It looks as if things haven't changed here for centuries," I said.

The old man studied my face for a moment, as if to see whether I was joking. "Well, actually," he said at last, "it's all changed in the last 20 years. What you're looking at used to be an industrial landscape. The place was dotted with pitheads and slagheaps as far as your eyes could see." He added, unnecessarily, "But of course, they've all gone now."

PART III
Looking-Glass People

Alice laughed. "There's no use
trying," she said: "one *can't*
believe impossible things."

"I dare say you haven't had much
practice," said the Queen.

— Lewis Carroll,
Through the Looking-Glass, *1872*[1]

Chapter 7

THE COALBROOKDALE LEGACY

Almost three centuries ago, the little Shropshire village of Coalbrookdale was the site of an experiment that changed the world. A gruff Quaker named Abraham Darby discovered a new and more efficient way to make iron, by smelting iron ore with coke. His descendants produced the world's first iron wheels, the first iron railway tracks, and the first iron bridge.

Signs of the epochal discovery that transformed the village, and changed the course of Western civilization, are everywhere. Darby's abandoned blast furnaces have the sad, monumental grandeur of the ruins of ancient Athens or Rome; and the iron bridge, reaching one hundred feet across a deep gorge where the River Severn flows through Coalbrookdale, is one of the most moving sights in Britain. But the most significant landmark in the village is not made of iron or brick. It is not even a building, but an ordinary tow-path.

In 1800, the town authorities widened the path along both banks of the Severn to speed up shipments of supplies and coking coal to the Coalbrookdale furnaces. Vessels and barges that had once been guided down the shallow river by men could now be drawn by horses. The "automated" tow-path threw hundreds out of work, but townspeople saw it as a crucially progressive step. "The degrading employment of hauling by men will be done away [with]," boasted the *Salopian Journal*, the local newspaper. "We hope these stout fellows who have heretofore done the work of brutes will find a more honourable employment."

They did, after a fashion. The human "mules" went to work underground in the coal seams or at the blasting furnaces on the river bank, where their descendants followed them over the next 150 years, as Britain became the world's major industrial power. The miners would have regarded the haulers' job as unspeakably barbaric and degrading.

While the ruined furnaces and the iron bridge are reminders of the material accomplishments of the revolution that spread through Britain and the world in the first, confusing decades of the nineteenth century, the towpath recalls its social achievements. The industrial revolution not only created new manufacturing processes; it created new ways of looking at work and, as a matter of course, a new breed of worker equipped to deal with the mental and physical requirements of the dawning age.

Now in the 1980s something similar was underway. If many parts of the British landscape had been transformed by the traumatic events of the decade, so had a large number of Britons. A study commissioned by the National Economic Development Office (NEDO) in 1986 claimed that the industrial crisis had produced a "new" British type, particularly suited to the postindustrial era. Such people were nondogmatic, creative, and, unlike their more reserved compatriots, willing to risk the embarrassment of trying something new. The study, one of several attempting to look at the effects of the country's economic problems on Britons, actually named the emerging group "New People" and suggested that they, more than any other group in British society, possessed the inventiveness and resourcefulness Britain was going to need to survive in the twenty-first century. In order to establish the contrast between the "New Britons" and their compatriots, the study arbitrarily divided British people in the 1980s into three categories.[2]

Traditional Labour and Conservative Party politicians and union leaders were in the first category — all primarily concerned with rebuilding the welfare state and the postwar political consensus — and they were joined by many victims of the industrial crisis, the poor and the unemployed, who sought little else but the material security they had lost. In the second category were those Britons motivated primarily by the urge to material success and power. They were entrepreneurs in the classic sense of the word, interested in finding ways of turning the system to their own advantage. Company directors, middle-class lawyers, and plumbers "on the fiddle" (providing work for cash without reporting their income as tax) belonged equally to this category. People in Category Three, however, marched to the beat of a different drummer. Many of them were comfortably middle-class, and a few had become rich and successful, but there were also large numbers of unemployed and others who would have been considered working class. They were entrepreneurs in a much wider sense, in politics and the arts, as well as in business and the unions, and interested in finding ways of changing the system, rather than simply reforming it. For them, the "new" landscape of postindustrial Britain had changed the rules. Some had achieved success outside the institutions of British life, but material success was not their only goal, nor was it the sole criterion for belonging to this category. Many were simply ordinary people who had begun to think and live differently. The report claimed that Britain already had more Category Three people than any other industrial country except Denmark and the Netherlands. Some 36 per cent of the British were classified in Category Three; of Americans only 19 per cent were, while in Japan, where the majority of people still operated inside a closely controlled traditional culture, the figure was 10 per cent.

The NEDO study was a welcome boost for battered British chauvinism. The idea that Britain was once again at the leading edge of a world phenomenon was therapeutic. "Ironically," crowed the *Guardian* in a comment on the report, "it is today's peak nations — Japan, the United States, West Germany — which cling most solidly to . . . dying disciplines." It was not necessary to swallow the entire argument in order to accept that Category Three people were an intriguing fact of life in contemporary Britain. A number of other studies in the 1980s proudly, and paradoxically, proclaimed the existence of a new "classless" class. In one, Category Three and the New People were called "winners" — a special group of Britons in the arts and business who were regarded as models for the rest. There were even several Category Three political parties. Analyses of the Social Democratic Party, created in 1981 by maverick Labour Party figures to carve a middle way between Labour and Conservative politics (and subsequently linked with the Liberal Party to become the Alliance), suggested that its strength was based on a new group of Britons whose interests and values were no longer met inside the traditional party groupings. But Category Three personalities could be found trying to make headway inside the traditional parties as well.

These "New Britons" were beginning to make themselves felt in the thinking of the country. Their own lives having changed dramatically in the 1980s, they went on to make an impact on the lives of their compatriots. People as different as Joan Ruddock and Margaret Thatcher shared an evangelical commitment to challenging conventional wisdom. The effect of their activities was multiplied at a time when Britons were clearly open to change. "We are very thin on the ground," Rt. Rev. David Jenkins had told me proudly in Durham. I came to believe that there were many more of this new breed than even he suspected. In very different ways, they are heirs to the energy that produced Coalbrookdale. Each of the seven New Britons portrayed here — an unemployed steelworker, an aristocrat, a radical mayor, a pop-music tycoon, a multimillionaire immigrant, an Arctic explorer, and a man who thinks up ways of saving the world — has had a distinctive impact on those around them. Like Alice in *Through the Looking-Glass*, they have stepped out of the roles they would ordinarily have expected to play in British society and begun to consider "impossible things." They were, in a manner of speaking, some of the "looking-glass people" of the 1980s.

i. The Steelworker

Less than 20 miles from Coalbrookdale, the steel town of Bilston sits on the outskirts of what used to be one of the most prosperous industrial conurbations of Britain, and one of the most innovative centres of the industrial world. For generations, the people living in the "Black Country" spanned by the cities of Manchester, Birmingham and Wolverhampton mined the coal, smelted the iron, and produced the machines and cars that gave Britain its pre-eminent position in the West. Even in the mid-twentieth century, the region's engineering works and manufacturing plants drove British prosperity. By the 1980s, however, that prosperity had ended.

Dennis Turner was one of the casualties of the change. He was 37 when he lost his job at the Bilston steel plant in September 1980. More than 2,400 men and women were employed there, along with Turner, when directors of the state-owned British Steel Corporation decided that the mill had become too expensive to keep. The corporate decision, taken hundreds of miles away, amounted to a sentence of death on the town, and on a way of life.

The folk memories of Bilston steelworkers went back to the early days of the industrial revolution. Turner's grandfather had hauled scrap iron with a horse and cart. His father worked for 46 years in the industry. Turner, who first tried to be independent by selling brushes and mops door-to-door after leaving school at 15, eventually followed his father into the mill. The wages were too good to ignore, and being a steelworker in the 1950s was still one of the proudest occupations a working man could have in Britain. Most of the workers and their families had never known another kind of life, and few expected they ever would.

Dennis Turner, however, taught them that a new way of life was possible. He did not merely survive the 1980s. Like the iron and steel that used to pay his wages, he was hammered and reshaped in the fire. In the years since he lost his job, Turner has become one of the area's most successful community organizers. He ran a training centre that found work for hundreds of his former workmates, and he appeared to be heading for a parliamentary seat as a Labour Party candidate in the next general election.

I met him one fal day in 1986, at the site of the abandoned plant itself. Parking my car beside a complex of low buildings, I walked into the New Springvale Social Club. It was similar to many workingmens' clubs I had seen across northern Britain, with a large, parquet-floored ballroom for social events and a well-stocked pub. Turner himself looked identical to hundreds of men I had seen in them.

A large, greying man with a barrel chest and a hint of a beer belly, he did not look prone to sentimentality. But when I met him, the loss of his job six years earlier still called up an affecting mixture of lyricism and pain. "People don't really understand that to be in the steel industry is more than a job," he said as we sat down in his cramped office. "It's a way of life. When you've got a plant going 24 hours a day, where people are having breakfast together and tea together and supper together, you see more of your mates than your family. It's something you can't explain."

Turner was a leader of the Iron and Steel Trades Confederation, one of the largest of the group of unions inside the steelworks. When the plant closed, he felt helpless to prevent the trauma that gripped his fellow union members. Several committed suicide. Others found safer, but no less painful, ways to escape reality. "There was one chap who would start out from home at the same time in the morning, put his bag on his bike, pedal all the way around the Black Country and come back at the time he would usually have gone home from work," Turner recalled. "He did it for four years."

Turner refused to give in to the atmosphere of defeat. Three months after the Bilston closure, he and nine colleagues on the union action committee wrote to the head offices of British Steel with an unusual proposal. They offered to buy the lease on the workers' recreation club on the plant grounds. The club had been built in 1941, in the days when managers and workers shared a common goal of defeating the German war machine. Their solidarity had ended with the closure of the plant, and the club was now scheduled for demolition.

The men offered to contribute £3,000 each from their severance pay as a down payment on the building. "It was a very well-appointed club, like a miniature civic centre," Turner said. "It had facilities that you would never get today: wine stores, a ballroom, kitchen, bars. We felt that it had potential. It could bring back some life into the area, make up for that sense of loss that we all had."

The company agreed, and the men found a bank willing to lend them the rest of the money they needed. One member of the team of new owners was hired to run it as a cooperative. The remodelled social club was never expected to be a money-making operation. It was to be a place where workers could discuss old times and commiserate over their present misfortunes in the shadow of the deserted steel mill that had once filled their working lives.

Moved initially by sullen curiosity, the steelworkers brought their wives and girlfriends to the reopened club, but they quickly became caught up in the spirit of the project. They signed up for day-trips, soccer teams, and snooker contests. Dances and raffles became regular events. Over the next few years, the Springvale Club's success surprised its worker-managers. "It was something that was starting to come to life when so much was dying," marvelled Turner.

The co-op managers had more ideas. When it began to appear they would be able to pay back the loan, they persuaded British Steel to sell them some of the other vacant buildings on the site for use as a skills retraining centre. Soon, with the help of more loans and government grants, parts of the old steel plant were rejuvenated. An old group of offices was converted into classrooms and computer labs. Another building was turned into a barn, where young people on a government-funded youth training program learned how to raise pigs and sheep.

Turner gave me a conducted tour of the enterprise. It seemed to be bursting with energy. In the training centre, groups of young people were learning basic computer-programming skills, knitting, and bookkeeping. Around the back, an old company toolshed had been converted into a welding shop. The manager was a former Bilston steelworks pipefitter, a quiet man who flushed with embarrassment when he spoke about his students. "If you would have told me five years ago that I would be teaching a bunch of kids," he said, "I would have thought you were crazy." Behind a slightly open door down the corridor of another building, I caught a glimpse of elderly men in white shirts and ties, very unlike the blue-collar types around the place. Turner grinned. "Those are unemployed managers," he said. "We help retrain them too."

The Bilston steelworks was not the only victim of the depression that struck the West Midlands. The rising toll of bankruptcies and closures made Turner and his colleagues wonder whether their technique could be duplicated elsewhere in the region. They realized that the area was facing a change as profound as the events that had once turned the agricultural lands of central Britain into the crucible of the industrial revolution.[3] Until then, few had given any thought to what would happen if the manufacturing jobs never returned. The most well-meaning government agencies had no way of coping with the psychological impact of permanent mass unemployment. They preferred to operate as if the problems were temporary. As long-term unemployment began to set in, the former steelworkers and engineers sensed that the factories and assembly lines that had guaranteed them a weekly paycheque were now a thing of the past.

"We began to recognize that there was such a thing as useful work in the community, work which could give pleasure to the person who does it and is worthwhile," recalled Turner. "People have a desperate need to be doing something useful, whether they have a full-time job in a factory or not. They don't want to sit at home, receiving cheques from the state. There are all forms of community service jobs that can provide real, purposeful work for the future. I don't mean in short-term government programs, where people just work for 12 months and then have to go back on the unemployment, but people could be paid for supplying a specific number of hours a week in volunteer labour around town, helping keep the canals free, for example, or ferrying old people to the hospital."

The problem was convincing central and local authorities that this crisis was different from the cyclical economic problems that had often hit British manufacturing in the past, and then showing them that the old solutions would not work. Even a huge amount of public spending would not bring back the full employment British trade unions used to assume was part of the bargain struck in the postwar consensus, Turner said.

Turner's vision of reduced state intervention in the labour marketplace would have pleased the most adamant Thatcherites of the 1980s. But he was opposed to the government's free-market individualism. He believed the sense of community that had mattered so much to himself and his workmates at the steel plant was crucial to any revival of spirit in the region.

The success of the New Springvale complex proved that people who had spent their lives as employees could regain their sense of self-esteem, even when that self-esteem was no longer tied to the industrial occupations around which their lives had been centred for generations. For a committed union man like Turner, it was as radical a departure from the values and habits he knew as the construction of the tow-path had been for the human "mules" of Coalbrookdale. "It's not a question of us being all romantic and sentimental about cottage-type industries and handicrafts," Turner said. "We're all good Black Country yeoman stock here, and we're not going to give up on heavy industry — it's what we know — and I believe there's still potential for those kinds of jobs in the region, especially in companies which are still around. But our policies have to be aimed at the next generation of people who are not likely to get permanent manufacturing jobs. Society will have to change to accommodate a different approach to so-called unemployment."

Turner was persuasive. Undeterred by the prevailing atmosphere of crisis, he went to local city council meetings, banks, and government agencies to lobby for his ideas. The result was the Wolverhampton Enterprise Limited Development Corporation (WELD), an agency designed specifically for working-class people who were otherwise abandoned by the industrial machine. WELD provided loans and advice on starting small businesses for unemployed industrial workers. Between 1982 and 1986, more than 450 new businesses were created. Turner was not surprised that so many of his old workmates who had once seen themselves as part of a permanent struggle between unions and bosses were willing to become bosses. "We had a workforce of 2,400 at the plant, and they had all the skills and crafts that you could ever want — pipefitters, bricklayers, carpenters, people in metal — why shouldn't these people try to have a go for themselves?" Turner said. "We were fighting back, really, against all those old ideas of unions and management which kept us in the same situation for so long."

Hesitantly, I suggested to Turner that the closure of the Bilston plant might someday prove to have been a blessing. After all, it had spurred him and many others along a new and more productive road. He was suddenly cautious. "I'm not sure I want to agree with that," he said, but he added grudgingly, "If you're saying that initiatives like ours had to develop to offset the worst features of this present government's policies, then you're absolutely right." But the "New Briton" in Turner got the better of the traditionalist union and Labour Party stalwart. A pat answer wouldn't do. "It's a paradox," he admitted after a long pause. "A lot of self-help ideas and a lot of new initiatives would never have happened without the pressures we were under."

The guided tour was over. Turner and I walked across a grassy field behind the New Springvale complex toward my car. The walkways were covered over with brush, and an old blue corrugated shed was the only structure left standing from the Bilston plant. It was the first time during my visit that I had come face to face with the fact of the abandoned steelworks. There, in front of me, was a gaping 10.5-acre vacant lot, stretching almost to the horizon, where there had once been a huge plant that had echoed day and night with the roar of furnaces. Turner refused to look directly at the lot. "It gives me an eerie feeling," he said quietly. We walked in silence toward my car. Just before we said goodbye he directed my attention to the sky. Smoke from hundreds of chimneys in the Black Country had once been so thick, Turner recalled, that it had turned day into night. "Now you haven't got a lighter sky anywhere in Britain," he said, smiling.

ii. The Duke

Gerald Grosvenor, 6th Duke of Westminster, 15th Baronet of Eaton, 9th Baron Grosvenor, 9th Viscount Belgrave, 9th Earl Grosvenor, and 8th Marquess of Westminster, never had to worry about getting a job — much less losing one. Nevertheless, the problems of the decade had kindled in him an energy and a sense of communal responsibility not usually associated with members of his class.

I met the slender, 34-year-old duke in his Mayfair office, a few days after I returned from my conversation with Dennis Turner. Indistinguishable from the thousands of well-dressed executives who pour into London every morning from the suburbs, he was amiable, even familiar, and occasionally subject to a hint of a youthful giggle. This nonchalance did not lead me to forget, however, that the duke was one of the richest men in the country. The Grosvenor empire — which embraces London properties, huge tenant-farmed estates in the north of England, and real estate and companies from Canada to Hawaii — is conservatively estimated to be worth £400 million.[4]

Great wealth has gone hand in hand with social power. The duke dines with Britain's and the world's elite. He and his wife, Natasha, the Duchess of Westminster, are godparents to Prince William, eldest son of their close friends, Prince Charles and Diana, Princess of Wales. One of our earlier interviews had been cancelled when the duke spent longer than he expected over lunch with Nancy Reagan at the U.S. embassy. The embassy, down the street from the Grosvenor office, happens to be one of the duke's tenants.

If he chose to, the young Duke of Westminster could lead a life of refined idleness. While trustees managed his financial affairs, he could make the token, face-saving appearances at charity events that are expected of most aristocrats, between skiing trips to Gstäad and Val d'Isères, lunches with the royal family, and grouse-hunting expeditions to Scotland. The duke admitted that it would have been easy for him to ignore Britain's industrial problems, but he has chosen not to. "My generation is infinitely more aware of what's going on than perhaps our predecessors were, and in many respects we are more concerned," he said. "No one likes to see wrongs or injustices being done, and if you've got the energy and indeed, that terrible word, *power*, to do something about it, I think it ought to be exercised. Many of us feel that we have a responsibility to shake people up.

"Most people," he continued, "tend to look inward into their own lives and be satisfied with that, whereas there's a crying need for getting involved with the greater good."

The duke had answered the crying need in an unusual way. In the 1980s, his name had become associated with the development of Britain's inner cities. A substantial portion of the Grosvenor wealth was invested in industrial parks, shopping centres, and land development in some of the most devastated parts of the British landscape. The process began well before the decade opened with a £1 million investment in a new shopping centre in Chester, near the duke's family estate, but by 1986, nearly 50 such schemes were operating in northern Britain.

The Chester project, completed in the mid-1960s, was the first commercial urban redevelopment scheme in Britain, according to the duke. It was praised at the time for keeping the historical character of old buildings. The city's core is made up of medieval shops, with ornate and charming wooden balconies. "What we did was peel back the interior, put a modern shopping centre into it, and then close it up again," the duke said. He added, grinning, "We made a bomb out of it."

The duke's involvement is noteworthy because it runs counter to the image of how traditional wealth is maintained and invested in Britain. Economic power in the United Kingdom is still based to a large extent on ownership of agricultural land. Even after the industrial revolution, the great steel and manufacturing barons poured their new riches into the acquisition of estates and stately homes instead of reinvesting their wealth in the economy. In the twentieth century, the holding of stocks and bonds joined land as a safe and respectable investment. Portfolio managers in London, even those who manage the pension funds of some of Britain's most militant unions, find safe homes for their money in traditional institutions or in investments abroad. Grosvenor — under pressure, by virtue of being both rich in landholdings and a member of the aristocracy, not to gamble away his fortune — took the unorthodox view that the industrial crisis offered an opportunity for investment.

"The traditional attitudes about money people hold here — the sort that think, 'Let's bang it into gilts, or shares' — would make life terribly safe and easy," he said. "I don't subscribe to the theory that Britain is declining. I have historical records leading back to the last industrial revolution, when my ancestors were having exchanges of correspondence right across the social spectrum, and they were using the same phrases we're using today. We're very good at self-criticism, to the extent that we can talk ourselves into decline, but the phrases people use in the Eighties were used in the first industrial revolution.

"In the 1870s and 1880s," he continued, "you had a major industrial shift from the countryside to the towns, and the same phrases have reappeared when we talk about the major shift in the economic basis of the country now taking place. There's a shift in the work ethic, a shift from the big, heavy employer who used to dominate our lives in northwestern England — British Steel, British Leyland, Vauxhall, Ford — who had as many as 20,000 employees. Now you have a lot of small firms in their place. It used to be that if one industry had a hiccup, an entire town went down the tubes. One of those big employers could wake up one morning and say things aren't quite as good as they ought to be and you have 15,000 people on the dole. Now you have a wider spread of the local economy."

The duke believes that his business enterprises, and even his agricultural interests, are part of the shift. "Look at Liverpool, a city that's in the wrong place, at the wrong time, in the wrong century. I live 20 miles from there, and my wheat crops should naturally go out from the port of Liverpool, but they go out through the southeast coast at Felixstowe, because it's cheaper. If it's cheaper for me, what hope is there for Liverpool and people who operate within the 20 mile radius? That's not a product of Thatcherism; that is a product of economics; it's part of our reindustrialization."

The duke refused to say how much his total industrial investment in Britain is worth, and some writers maintain that his investments in North America are growing much faster, but he sounded curiously like Dennis Turner when he talked about the opportunities available in postindustrial Britain. "We all know that the traditions of steel and coal in places like the South Yorkshire coalfields are gone," he said. "It has to be important to give cities the opportunity to invest in new, lower-intensity businesses."

The duke illustrated the new approach when he travelled to the northern municipality of Sheffield in 1982 to negotiate a scheme for an industrial park that was to be built on 100 acres of derelict manufacturing land. Sheffield was under the control of one of the most militant left-wing councils in Britain, and it would not have surprised anyone if the town authorities had complicated the duke's plans with land-use restrictions and onerous taxes. Instead, the encounter between socialist and aristocrat was crisp and businesslike. The project was given the necessary zoning permission, and new businesses were to be attracted to the site with special tax incentives. Socialist worries about dealing with the "class enemy" appeared to have been shelved, at least temporarily. As Grosvenor confessed later, he was surprised to discover how little separated the two sides in their tough-minded approach to the country's economic problems.

"The trip to Sheffield was a leap in the dark," he admitted. "It is one of those towns which is very highly politically motivated, but the [city authorities] knew that no matter how many closures of plants you have, life has to go on in one form or the other. It all hinges around how quickly a community is willing to respond to the winds of change and move out of the industrial-revolution type of thinking into the modern-revolution type of thinking."

Grosvenor said that the most interesting lesson he learned from his trip to Sheffield was that many people in Britain no longer acted according to old assumptions of class and ideology. Sheffield was quicker to pick up the implications of postindustrial change than many Conservative municipalities in southern England had been, he said. "Some people," he mused, "are just quicker to change their attitudes."

Few, apparently, were quicker than a duke who was willing to challenge some of the assumptions of his own class and his fortune. The British aristocracy, representing one of the most powerful concentrations of inherited wealth in Europe, has benefited from the climate of Thatcherism with both tax breaks and, as noted in Chapter 3, from the revived British interest in symbols of the past. But the Duke of Westminster, for all his wealth and position, belongs to the wider class of Britons looking for productive ways of changing society. "You must move with the times," he argued. "You can't just sit back on your heap and watch it diminish. You've got to be aggressive in your outlook, and if you have wealth, it's got to be put back into society and re-created, not only for your own benefit and profit, but for the benefit of the community."

iii. The Mayor

When the Duke of Westminster speaks out on social issues in the accents of the British upper classes, he has the advantage of knowing he will get instant attention. But less-privileged mortals have to work hard to make themselves heard. Political and cultural life in the United Kingdom is still circumscribed by rules of discretion and self-effacement that have their origins in Victorian respectability. When Ken Livingstone became the administrative head of Britain's most important city, and gained titular political control over even the Westminster domains, his victory broke so many of the rules that observers lost count.

The man who met me one morning at the door of a run-down house in West London wore a T-shirt covered by an old bathrobe. His pencil-thin mustache and pallid skin gave him an austere appearance, but his high-pitched voice with its flat nasal tones of South London made him seem as familiar as the corner news vendor. Apologizing for his unorthodox dress — "I've been up all night trying to finish my book, and I've got a cold" — he led me into his kitchen. We sat facing each other across a wooden table piled high with pamphlets and papers. Books on Indian vegetarian cooking sat on a nearby shelf. It was hard to believe that this monastic setting was the private quarters of "Red Ken," the terror of the British Establishment for more than half the decade. He noticed my stare and smiled thinly.

"People were always wide of the mark about me," Livingstone said. "If they had looked at my record, they would have seen that I've always been pragmatic. I'm prepared to lose a lot in popular support for things I believe in, but I was always ready to make concessions."

When Livingstone became leader of the Greater London Council (GLC) in 1981, he was 36, and a self-described "anarcho-syndicalist." Over the next five years, the British media tried to turn him into Public Ogre Number One, often with his cooperation. He pointedly ignored an invitation to the wedding of Prince Charles and Lady Diana Spencer, claiming it would be an insult to London's poor to attend. At the height of the IRA bombing campaign in London, he met publicly with leaders of Sinn Fein, the political wing of the Irish paramilitaries. London was declared a "nuclear-free zone," with Livingstone's support adding weight to nationwide anti-cruise-missile protests. There were other municipalities around the country with similarly radical leaders, but no one else could match the titillating *frisson* of fear and political theatre Livingstone brought to London.

In the words of the *Daily Mail*, once one of his most rabid opponents in the press, he had become "the most effective politician in Britain." When I met him, Livingstone was a genuine political hero in exile, having been removed from office by an administrative reorganization, implemented by the central government, that many saw as a Thatcher ploy to get rid of him. Londoners had once voted him the most popular man after the pope, and were soon likely to send him to Parliament representing a safe Labour seat. "More than any other politician of his generation, he captured the attention of the nation," wrote his biographer.[5] It came as a surprise to discover that Livingstone regarded as one of his political models the prime minister herself.

"Thatcher tapped a ground swell of resentment about being managed by the state," he said approvingly. "Socialists used to be told that the state would wither away, but they never seemed to do anything about it." To Livingstone, the traditional Labour politicians and trade union leaders were as out-of-touch with the realities of postindustrial Britain as the Tory Establishment was. "The left has built its base on what is often the most reactionary section of society, the least liberated and the least tolerant."

Livingstone believed that the only effective national government in a future Britain would be one that allowed local power to flourish. "You can't administer nation-states from their centres any more," he said. "Welfare capitalism has reached the limits of its ability to win the support of the population. The left would be fools not to respond to that." After him, he believed, a new generation of politicians would see the local level as the venue for their most useful service to society.

Livingstone's rise to power and influence was another mark of the sea change that occurred in Britain during the decade. He came out of the radical politics of the 1960s and developed into one of the most effective exponents of a new brand of activism for the 1980s. This new political strain had almost as many elements of grassroots, right-wing decentralism as it did of left-wing militancy. Livingstone's mother was a vaudeville dancer and his father a merchant seaman. Both were Tory voters, but they were, as Livingstone put it, "ahead of their time in sharing relationships." His own constant questioning of accepted values often led him into conflict, but he received parental support for his resistance to taking the safe, ordinary path of working-class Britons, who customarily attempted to move soberly and unobtrusively into the fringes of the middle class. "Their support gave me the ability to stand in the middle of two million people and say you are all wrong and I am right," he said.

His parents' influence also gave him the qualities of a permanent outsider in politics. "Most people attracted to power want to make every decision," he said. "They cannot delegate, and they fail because of that. All my natural instincts are to delegate and devolve. In that sense, I'm sort of the left-wing version of Ronald Reagan. I'd be quite happy to sleep in the afternoon. I didn't see it as my role to get involved in bureaucracy."

Luck and good timing propelled him to the forefront of national affairs. A relatively unknown borough councillor from the wilderness of Irish pubs and faded "bed-sits" in London's Kilbourn area, he was the only left-winger remaining on the London council after a Tory landslide in 1977. Unobtrusively, he built a base of support for himself among his allies in the new left, while allowing the Labour Party machine to regard him as a stalking-horse for more traditional left-wing candidates. Interestingly, the prime minister had used a similar technique in her unexpected climb to the leadership of the Conservative Party.

By the time Livingstone came to power, it was difficult to believe he could make a difference. The era of the great prewar city hall fiefdoms, whose housing, health care, and public works programs had been forerunners of the welfare state, was long gone. Local government authorities had few services under their control, and even less money to spend on them. Central governments, Labour as well as Conservative, had carefully stripped municipalities of any meaningful functions that would make them alternative centres of power.

The economic and political shake-ups of the decade, however, gave the GLC an opening to exert more influence. Livingstone and his cohorts used a loophole in municipal tax regulations, for instance, to get access to funds that they spent on high-profile projects. The most well-known programs were the most controversial — lesbian and gay awareness schemes, minority rights, and feminist education — but they also found £30 million to create a separate policy for job creation. The GLC's flexibility and its high public visibility turned London into an annoying thorn in the side of the Tory government. For the first time since the days of Herbert Morrison, the prewar London boss regarded as the father of municipal socialism (and one of Livingstone's heroes), London was taking on a strongly political identity.

The most effective program the GLC launched struck a typical Livingstonian-Thatcherite populist chord. Soon after they were elected, London's Labour leaders had to decide what to do about a campaign pledge to reduce fares in the London Underground system by 25 per cent. The "Tube" was one of the oldest subway systems in the world. Like most big-city transit systems, it ran at a huge deficit that was offset by government subsidies. Subsidies, however, were anathema to the economic evangelists at Westminster. They left little doubt that there would be no money available to subsidize a fare decrease. In fact, London Transport, told to find ways to trim its workforce and operations, had begun to raise the price of a service whose quality was already declining. The heaviest burden of London transit costs naturally fell on the poor and unemployed. As economic conditions grew worse, those who had the fewest alternatives to getting around the city were doubly punished in the search for jobs. For Livingstone and his allies, it was a clear-cut issue with which to expose the impact of government policies. The council ordered fares to be lowered by 32 per cent, an even greater cut than pledged.

Ironically, the ensuing battle was mostly fought within the middle classes. Several Tory borough councils in the suburbs launched legal action to stop the fare reduction. They claimed, correctly, that municipal taxes collected from the richer suburbs would be used to pay for lower fares. Middle-class homeowners in London were incensed by this protection of privilege and threw their support behind the GLC. The case went to the courts, where the London leaders lost on appeal. Fares were immediately returned to their old levels and then increased again. The episode triggered an unusual coalition of London's middle class, unemployed, and trade unionists. A one-day boycott of the fare increases captured the attention of the city, as a few well-dressed Londoners risked court fines by refusing to pay the new tickets. The boycott fizzled out, but Londoners never forgot the heady experience of identifying with a citywide issue against the surburbs and the central government. The episode fortified Livingstone's concept of a populist, grassroots activism that transcended party politics.

"We had millions of Tory voters who used the Tube each day supporting us," bragged Livingstone. "They had decided that in some instances, public spending was a good thing." The fact that many of his supporters, and nearly all of the GLC leadership, were middle class did not bother him. In the late twentieth century, he explained, "you don't create radicalism out of poverty."

Nothing became Livingstone's period in power as much as the leaving of it. In their decision to end the regional government system, the Tories tried to turn around the grassroots-power arguments of Livingstone and other municipal leaders by pointing out that metropolitan regional governments had become another layer of big bureaucracy, riding roughshod over the old city halls and borough governments. On economic grounds, the argument made little sense. Most big cities around the world had adopted the metropolitan system of government in order to rationalize services. Independent accounting firms pointed out that getting rid of regional governments would probably cost as much money as it purported to save. Few people had any doubt about the real motive of the campaign: it was only the latest attempt by the central government to rid itself of annoying rivals to its power.

With a brilliant billboard and newspaper advertising campaign, the GLC fanned the populist sentiments of Londoners from all political parties. One of the most effective moments of the campaign was unplanned.

Londoners woke up one morning at the height of the abolition struggle to see a startling photograph in their newspaper of Red Ken smiling at the Queen. Had the anarchist who once criticized the lavish public ceremonial devoted to the sovereign's son's marriage reformed? Or was the monarch a closet Livingstone supporter?

The photograph was taken at the inauguration ceremony of the Thames Barrier, an expensive flood-control scheme that had been planned long before Livingstone came into office. The Queen's decision to attend the GLC inauguration ceremony was perceived as an indication of her sympathy with the anxieties of her subjects in London. "She didn't have to come," said Livingstone. "But she let our people know that she would come, even though she was aware that we could have made a public relations breakfast of it." The GLC, of course, never had to make the "breakfast." The intensely competitive British press did the job for them. The monarch's attendance on Red Ken and his court was an arresting example of the coalition-building Livingstone was trying to achieve.

Six months after the GLC disappeared, it was said that Londoners hardly noticed the difference, but such comments missed the point. Livingstone had left a powerful imprint on the way political affairs in Britain had been managed since the war. Looking toward the future, he predicted, "Parliament will be a real pain in the neck — boring, irrelevant — but there is the prospect that the forces which produced the GLC can be brought together to achieve the same transformation nationally."

These "forces" had been a volatile mixture of hard-edged practical politics and consciousness-raising. Only a politician of Livingstone's unorthodox background could have welded them into a political movement. "If I had to choose between challenging sexual discrimination and cutting fares, I would have chosen the former," he explained. "At the end of the day, anybody could have administered a transit system; nobody but a radical socialist could have raised the issues of power relationships between men and women, blacks and whites, gays and straights." As a result of his work in London, Livingstone claimed, blacks, Irish, and other "minorities" in the city had experienced a regeneration. "Changing these power relationships is central to the transformation of Britain," he said. "If you want to see a Britain which breaks away from rigid Establishment loyalty to the past, and concentration of power, the first step is to liberate those groups which are the most enslaved under the present system, and most denied their potential. If you go forward 10 or 15 years, you will find [that] the things we fought for have become the concerns of national leadership in all Western European countries."

THE COALBROOKDALE LEGACY

iv. The Immigrant

It was a bitterly cold day when 12-year-old Bashir Okhai arrived at Edinburgh airport, on a flight from Malawi, in East Africa, but the youngster was too excited to notice the chill. Quickly swept up in the embraces of his elder brother and family, he found himself bundled off to the little city of Dundee, hundreds of miles to the north. For months, Okhai remained in a state of awe at his good fortune in immigrating to the United Kingdom. "Britain was a country one had heard so much about," he recalled more than two decades later. "In Africa, 20 or even 10 years ago, anything made in England was supposed to be the best ever. Now anything made in Japan is the best."

The awestruck boy was now an intensely serious 32-year-old millionaire, and sufficiently at home in his adopted country to be mildly cynical. We were chatting in the offices of his family firm, in an industrial park just outside of Dundee. The tension of being a visible and prosperous member of a minority group had left its mark on the young man's smooth Asian features. The only clue that he ever let down his guard came from a tennis ball that happened to be on his desk. "Sport is a wonderful vehicle for mixing with people," he said somewhat wistfully. "At the end of the day, you're human, whether you're a company director or a machine operator."

Running one of the biggest private business empires in Britain has not erased Bashir Okhai's feeling that he is a stranger in a strange land. "You've always got to keep your eyes open and your mind open here," he said. "I don't understand why people make so much of colour in England." But he concealed a certain amount of bitterness beneath his air of casual sophistication. "I don't think I will ever see Britain becoming a perfect multiracial society in my lifetime," he said, and then added soberly, "but if you asked me 10 years ago whether this society was flexible enough to change, I would have said no. Now I think I would say yes.

"I look at myself as a British citizen, a British subject," insisted Okhai, but when he went on to list the dizzying number of cultural and sports projects he and his brothers have endorsed or sponsored in Dundee, the effort behind their long struggle for acceptance in their community became clear. British attitudes toward race are closely linked with the difficulties of coexistence on a small, crowded island. The large numbers of black and Asian immigrants from all over the Commonwealth who arrived after the Second World War fell in naturally with the British tribal style, settling into their own communities and neighbourhoods, and keeping as much as they could to themselves. There was no question of assimilating into an American-style "melting pot." Nonwhite British were often the victims of systematic, institutional discrimination at school and at work, an ugly reality skilfully hidden beneath the mask of civilized tolerance Britain presents to the world.

It wasn't until 1986, for example, that the British Army conceded it had maintained an unofficial colour bar in its most elite regiments, including the Household Divisions, the traditional protectors of the royal family. In 1985, one reporter conducting an unofficial survey found that there were no black or Asian members of Parliament, only seventeen black journalists on Fleet Street, and fewer than four black or Asian school principals in the entire country.[6] Yet an astonishing number of Britons considered themselves threatened by foreigners. Efforts by Muslims to have classes taught in Hindi or Urdu deeply offended the British tribal integrity. A social attitudes survey in 1986 asked people whether they thought Britons were prejudiced — a clever way of approaching the problem. Some 90 per cent said yes.[7] It has not been any easier for white immigrant groups. Jews in Britain have long been the victims of unofficial discrimination. The Thatcher cabinet was the first to have a substantial number of Jews — perhaps reflecting the prime minister's association with them in Finchley — yet they must still struggle against an ingrained, almost unconscious distrust by the majority. When one Jewish cabinet minister, Leon Brittan, was forced to resign during a government crisis in 1986, a Tory back-bencher commented briskly on television, "Now we can get real British people in there."

But for Britons of Asian and West Indian descent, the economic crisis of the 1980s presented special problems. Their jobs, often the most low-paid and low-skilled in the economy, were the first to go, and they were often the last recruited for job retraining schemes. The most successful, like the Okhais, found themselves the target of unspoken resentment. During our interview, Bashir Okhai provided no specific examples of discrimination, but British journalists who had visited Dundee reported that the family was still under suspicion by some of the local community leaders.[8]

The Okhais, at any rate, were not strangers to adversity. Bashir Okhai's parents had been prosperous traders in Malawi until they ran foul of a wave of persecution against Asians. The oldest of the three brothers, Ibrahim, had been a student politician. He was deported from the country for reasons the family says are still mysterious, and decided to come to Scotland, where the second brother, Azziz, was already studying to be a doctor. When Bashir arrived, he found that his two brothers had decided to follow the family tradition and open a tiny trading company. Operating out of a rented office with one secretary, a telephone, and a telex machine, they bought goods on credit, sold them quickly for cash, and reinvested the capital. Young Bashir was quickly drafted into the Okhai enterprise. Every day, after school, he came downtown to operate some of the machines, do the filing, and even make tea. Bashir was still slightly in awe of his new home and his classmates, but he quickly began to see that his brothers' aggressive business practices easily outpaced their gentler competition.

"Basically, we supplied anything anybody wanted. If they wanted paper, we supplied paper; if they wanted desks, we supplied desks. We had an understanding bank manager, but we could also see that so many of our British competitors were not really interested in supplying what people wanted. It was a matter of, 'We've made this product for the last 50 years, so we'll just continue making it.' "

Their more competitive attitude explained the Okhais' first big success: lollipop sticks. They picked up a shipment of plastic toothpicks that had been rejected by a supplier in Hamburg. None of them can remember now why they thought it might be useful. Ibrahim was on a business trip to Zambia when the manager of a local candy factory complained about the cost of importing wooden lollipop sticks. An idea clicked. Ibrahim invented the world's first hollow plastic stick. Lollipops became cheaper to make and cheaper to ship. Soon the Okhai factory was turning out 35 million sticks a week, and shipping them to clients around the world.

Lollipops made them rich, but marmalade turned them into millionaires. Soon after their candy business had begun to flourish, the Okhais heard through the grapevine that Keelers, one of Scotland's oldest companies, was up for sale. Keelers was practically synonymous with Dundee. The mass-produced jars of marmalade with the trademark small black "golliwog" had appeared on breakfast tables around the world for a century. Nestle, the American multinational, had bought the company years before, but Keelers' old-fashioned techniques and dusty production methods defied the best efforts at rationalization.

The Okhais came up with an offer, sinking nearly all their savings into a scheme to get the marmalade business back on its feet. Pragmatically, they overlooked the racist overtones of the product in the name of brand continuity. The golliwog logo remained. "There was no sales force, no financial team, no purchasing team," recalled Bashir Okhai. "They had all left with Nestle's management. All we had was a factory."

When the brothers finally sold the company to another Scottish firm after four years, its workforce had expanded from 140 to 240, and it was showing a profit. The three brothers believed they had proved an important point. "People say the British workforce is bad," said Okhai. "It was true that all the companies we acquired had union demarcation lines. No one would do what he wasn't supposed to. The attitude was, like they say in Scotland, 'That's not me job.' But the problem has also been management. Very few managers involved their employees in the working of the company, so of course the employees didn't care. We tried to motivate our workers so they saw our companies as their own companies too, and as their future."

Only a trio of innovative Asian brothers in the 1980s, unfazed by the British caste system, could have gotten away with teaching the British a lesson in how to run a business on their home grounds. Unable to afford a full research and development team, they used their own workers. Everyone in their plants was invited to come up with new ideas. They also placed equal value on creating a pleasant, cooperative environment. Employees were offered special bonuses for extra work, and those willing to learn other skills were provided with on-the-job training. The management techniques the Okhais perfected in Scotland soon became a standard for dozens of other Scottish companies struggling to find a way to cope with changes in the economy.

Eventually, the Okhais had one of the most committed, energetic workforces in Scotland's traditional industries. Their workers were capable of moving from one job to another in the plant, and were willing to work the same long hours as the brothers themselves.

"If I go into one of our factories, and I see a dirty floor," said Okhai, "I sweep it myself. The workers say that if it's good enough for the owner of a company to do, it's good enough for them."

He glanced out his office window. In the clear light of northern Scotland, the domain of the Asian brothers stretched across a block of warehouses. "You don't, by any chance," he said, "play tennis?"

v. The Pop Tycoon

The telephone rang in a little houseboat moored in the canal that wanders through Little Venice in West London. A pleasant young woman picked it up, murmured a few words, and then handed it to a casually dressed young man with a reddish goatee who was lying on a sofa. "It's New York again," she said. The conversation that followed was short. The young man spoke softly and authoritatively, put the telephone back on the hook, and sighed. Before he could say anything else, the telephone began to ring again.

Richard Branson's houseboat was one of several dozen odd-looking vessels berthed in the brackish waters behind Paddington railway station. One squat barge nearby had been turned into an art gallery, but most of the other crafts served as floating homes for an eccentric band of drop-outs from urban London life. Few of his nautical neighbours knew, and even fewer cared, that the Branson houseboat was the nerve centre of a global business empire.

The young man on the sofa was founder, chairman, and chief executive officer of one of Britain's 10 largest corporations. When Branson started as a 19-year-old with a mail-order record business, he named his then-tiny firm Virgin as a joke on his own business naiveté. More than 15 years later, the joke no longer rang true. His ventures in film, pop music, airline travel, and record retailing earned nearly £325 million a year, and Virgin was the trademark of a company with interests in 22 countries. The last traces of blushing innocence finally disappeared in 1986, when the Virgin Group went public on the London Stock Exchange.

The idea of using a London houseboat as the headquarters of a major financial corporation seemed pretentious until I stepped aboard Branson's office. The houseboat serves as Branson's refuge as well. He bought it when he was a struggling young counter-culture journalist, and for a long time it was the only living space he could afford in London, a convenient hideout from traffic wardens and bill collectors. Although he had long since bought a country estate where he lived with his girlfriend and two children, the floating office remained essential to his business style. It was an appropriate base for a man who became rich through a shrewd understanding of Britain's leisure-oriented society.

The child of a barrister, Branson grew up in Guildford, a middle-class suburb close to London. He left school at 15 after having had a modest commercial success with a student magazine. In his early twenties, Branson befriended some of the flamboyant young singers in the discos and clubs that spawned the punk movement in the 1970s. A natural entrepreneur, he offered to help manage their careers, and his own was born.

"Tubular Bells," a song by Mike Oldfield, a young composer Branson was promoting, became a runaway success. Others followed soon after. The international popularity of the new wave of singers like Boy George helped Branson ride the crest of the pop music explosion of the late 1970s and 1980s. He soon branched out from promoting singers to selling their records. Virgin opened the largest record outlet in London. Within a few years, the company had expanded into other leisure markets. It bought and financed film properties such as *1984,* and moved into bargain trans-Atlantic charters with the creation of an airline.

Each Branson success was met by disbelief and scorn from the traditional financiers of London. The young entrepreneur was once forced into court to defend Virgin Airlines against the claims of a competitor. His opponent's lawyer asked the judge derisively, "Are you really going to put an airline in the hands of a pop tycoon?" Branson's attorney had a quick reply. The competitor had earned a profit of £1 million the previous year; the Branson companies had earned £12 million. "Is there any choice between the two?" he entreated quietly. Branson won the suit.

But what made Branson different from other entrepreneurs of the 1980s was his interest in playing a role as a one-man venture capital organization. Virgin became a merchant bank for people with ideas. "We get about 15 or 20 project proposals a week," he said. "They come to me because a clearing bank won't take risks on them, and [will finance them] only if they can put up collateral. I only started with four or five thousand pounds. People like me are usually out of luck."

The new companies he takes on are usually connected in some way with the leisure industry. Branson keeps a 75 per cent stake in each business, but his young managers have received experience that would otherwise have been more difficult to get.

Branson still finds himself treated as an outsider in Britain's close-knit business world. When he was preparing to get a listing on the London Stock Exchange, an elderly consultant whispered some advice in his ear. "He told me that he could find a few knighted gentlemen for me to put on my board, and that would soothe a lot of people's fears," Branson grinned. "I thanked him for his advice." His battles with Britain's archaic, traditional business culture gave Branson a missionary drive to educate a new generation. "In the 1960s," he said, "people could afford to protest and not worry about jobs, and be fairly left-wing. But now we are in a competitive world. People are working night and day to beat us."

Branson's genius, like Ken Livingstone's, lay in being able to cross the intellectual divide that separated the 1960s from the 1980s. The radicalism of 20 years earlier had blended lifestyle with politics. In the Eighties, many who thought themselves to be cold realists believed that the flexibility and openness to new ideas of the Sixties were unappealing to a generation that craved job security. But Branson saw British decline as a proving ground for 1960s values. The shift from manufacturing to service industries had given the country a chance to develop some of the skills for living long obscured by the assembly line. Branson proved that ingenuity, inventiveness, and a wry sense of humour — traits the British more often showed in their private leisure-time (or black-economy) activities than on the job — could be profitable.

When I first met him in 1983, Branson was already uncompromisingly, even joyously, rich, and like many rich men, he had developed a streak of evangelism. Radiating equal measures of laid-back charm and predatory cunning, he believed that his own unconventional success was the sign of a major attitudinal change in the business culture of Britain. "Success used to be a dirty word in England — there was a time when you were supposed to be embarrassed to be successful," Branson managed to say between telephone calls. "But now when I walk down the street, I'll get workmen and painters giving me the thumbs-up sign and saying, 'Good on yer, Richard.'"

The Branson houseboat was an equally appropriate metaphor on the nature of success in modern Britain. An urban canal is the last place anyone would expect to find the head office of a great steel corporation or automotive plant, but it suited a new kind of entrepreneurship. In the computer age, most traditional industries in Britain had proved incapable of adjusting to the challenge of foreign competition. Those industries that ran on brainpower and imagination rather than brawn and fossil fuels had the edge.

Branson was a "New Briton" in lifestyle and politics as well as in business. The press was full of his adventures: equipping a powerboat to set a world speed record across the Atlantic (and nearly losing his life in the attempt), attempting to fly a hot-air balloon between Britain and America. Branson seemed to have a compulsion to avoid being pinned down by any label. He was rumoured to be a strong supporter and financial backer of the new Social Democratic Party, but he accepted Thatcher's offer of a post to head a nationwide clean-up campaign that would provide jobs for unemployed teenagers.

Many of his best ideas came from an instinctive grasp of the needs of his contemporaries. When his girlfriend became pregnant, Branson discovered that there were no advisory services for young people who "got into trouble," so he started a youth drop-in centre. Years later, when he discovered how hard it was for people on the move to get good food, he backed a young entrepreneur's idea for a catering service on wheels. Branson found some of his best entrepreneurial managers and market analysts among his youthful workforce of 2,200 employees. An ex-clerk ran the accounting department, and the firm's former switchboard operator was put in charge of one of the music studios.

"It's really astonishing," he said, "how many people think they have such good ideas for making money." He sounded genuinely proud, as if the new generation of would-be alternative millionaires was his own best and most innovative idea. In a roundabout way, it probably was. As he leaned back on the sofa, the telephone was ringing again.

vi. The Expedition Leader

Around midday on August 29, 1982, a weather-beaten red icebreaker nosed around a bend of the Thames River and glided toward a Greenwich pier filled with thousands of cheering, flag-waving people. Prince Charles was at the helm of the ship, at the invitation of the men on board. Three years earlier, the Prince had guided the vessel on its outward journey down the Thames, bound on what was called the "last great adventure on earth."

The two bearded figures who appeared on deck as the SS *Benjamin Bowring* tied up at Greenwich looked dubiously at the crowds. With the help of their royal helmsman, they had just earned the distinction of becoming the first men to circumnavigate the earth via both poles. But after long months of drifting in the Arctic ice, they appeared to wonder what the shouting was all about.

"There were dozens of ships like ours that summer returning from the Falklands, and all met by people waving Union Jacks," remembered Sir Ranulph Twisleton-Wykeham Fiennes. "Ours just happened to come from the north, rather than the south. For Joe Public, it must have been a bit difficult trying to separate the Arctic from the Antarctic, the Falklands from Spitsbergen."

The exploits of Fiennes and Charlie Burton, his fellow explorer on the Transglobe Expedition, did bear a strong resemblance to British adventures in the Falklands. Both were throwbacks to an age when a sense of national mission was the only explanation for taking otherwise foolhardy risks. "It is difficult," wrote the *Daily Telegraph* about the circumpolar trip, "to think of another nation which would undertake it."

But the comparisons to Sir Walter Raleigh, Francis Drake, and the long line of adventurers and buccaneers through British history were off the mark. Although the courage of Fiennes and Burton intensified the sense of vigour and accomplishment that marked Britain in the 1980s, their expedition served as a lesson in the reality of Britain's place in the world. "I don't think expeditions are a national thing any more," explained Fiennes. "Our expedition was full of people from other countries who were just as much into the spirit of our expedition and prepared to sacrifice their funds and salaries and everything for it, as the British members were."

The Transglobe Expedition was an awesome project, and not merely because of the terrain it would have to cross. In an age when only governments can afford the few ambitious adventures left, like trips to outer space, the private explorer is usually priced out of the market. To finance its plans during seven years of preparation, Transglobe secured more than 1,000 commercial sponsors around the world for everything from snowmobiles to copying machines.

From the beginning, Fiennes' team planned to use their trip as the basis of an export sales drive. In return for the tents, food, and equipment they needed to keep themselves alive at the ends of the earth, they offered to serve sponsoring companies as mobile advertisements. Packaging their expedition like a new commercial product, they offered to set up trade fairs along their route. "We found out from commercial attachés the right places to go — Paris, Abidjan on the Ivory Coast, Cape Town, Sydney, Auckland, Los Angeles — and that determined some of our route and our planning." Noted one British trade attaché on the expedition's route: "The Transglobe team gave a positive impression of a young, dynamic Britain, making use of new advanced technologies, displaying initiative and enterprise. There is no doubt that the image of contemporary Britain was given a very good boost from which business prospects ... can only be enhanced."[9]

Appropriately, I met Fiennes in the offices of an international petroleum company that had hired him as a "public relations consultant." He was wearing a suit and tie, having just changed from the jogging suit he used for his daily sprint through Hyde Park. Lanky and dark, he had the peculiarly fixed gleam in his eyes that made me think of the determination of Perry, Scott, Hillary, and other adventurers who had driven themselves to extraordinary feats. "Expeditions," Fiennes said crisply after he'd shaken hands, "are my profession."

Fiennes was 36 the year he set off to reach both poles, the same age as Ken Livingstone when he came to power in London and just a bit younger than Dennis Turner when he was tossed on the scrap-heap by British Steel. All three men shared a drive for achievement that was not tied to the normal goals of postwar society. They did not want money or status; rather, they were enthralled by the prospect of teaching a moral lesson to their compatriots.

Fiennes believed that a strong sense of national identity was as important to a country as a healthy economy. Although his expedition was multinational, he felt Britons could take pride in the knowledge that their compatriots had played the leading role. "What bothered me most of all when I came back was that British people, from the bottom to the top of society, didn't seem to mind whether they were British or not. They just minded about their own status in life," Fiennes said.

"Look, for example, the French are French. They're aware they're French and a lot are very proud they're French. So the French drink Perrier water. But why should the British find it necessary to drink Perrier? We've got perfectly good water of our own."

The traditional roots of British pride had offered Fiennes little. Even his embarrassingly hyphenated name, all that remained of a 700-year-old title, provided small comfort. At 22, he joined the elite Special Air Services team, later to become world-renowned for its lifting of the siege by terrorists of the Iranian embassy in London, but was kicked out for a schoolboyish prank that accidentally blew up a castle. He tried to become a soldier of fortune, linking himself for a time with the Sultan of Oman, but he eventually found war repellent. The only thing he discovered he was good at was organizing "adventure training" expeditions for soldiers in the Alps or northern regions.

He always felt like an outsider, even among the privileged classes into which he had been born. "I was at Eton," he said, "and I hated it. But I think hating a school like that, where you feel one out of the pack, develops individualism. You either go under, or you sort of fight back against the uniformity of the hunting, shooting, fishing mob. The sort of bullying of the unconventional does seem to produce characters who are fairly unsquashable. Because if they haven't been squashed there, they're not likely to get squashed by events subsequently."

Fiennes, who preferred to be called "Ran" by his friends, led expeditions in British Columbia and the Sahara, but until his new wife Ginny made the suggestion of a circumpolar trip one day in 1972, neither of them had been any place colder than northern Scotland. The expedition that sailed from Greenwich in 1979 still bore the imprint of amateurism. Arctic experts had predicted that the leaders' lack of experience would prevent them from reaching the two poles, or kill them, or both. Governments first refused, then reluctantly conceded, permission to use remote bases and facilities as staging points, and scientific establishments bemusedly gave them a number of research tasks along the way.

By the time he planted a Union Jack (as well as a Canadian flag and the flags of their various commercial sponsors) on the North Pole, Fiennes had braved mosquitoes, jungles, polar bears, rapids, and ice crevasses to prove that, for success, Britons needed only flair and imagination. He saw his journey across the polar wastes as part of the political awakening of the decade. "A lot of the good things that have happened to the country come from the fact that Mrs. Thatcher arrived on the scene," he said. "Her voice annoys me intensely, but she believes certain things are necessary, such as making Britain something which the British people can be proud of. She's an expedition leader herself."

For Fiennes there could be no higher compliment.

vii. The Social Inventor

"To be socially inventive, you need to be slightly rebellious and dissatisfied with the status quo, and I think a lot of British people are," declared Nicholas Albery, as we sat in his living room in London one afternoon.

Albery, a tall, gentle Englishman with a talent for inspired lunacy, founded the Institute for Social Inventions in 1985, at the age of 37, to prove his point. Like Richard Branson, Albery was a child of the 1960s. He dropped out of Oxford in 1968 to go to San Francisco. "I was a hippie," he says laughingly now. "It seemed totally irrelevant to me to be studying Milton." He once edited a book of essays called *How to Save the World*. "I suppose we [at the Institute] are keeping the Sixties' spirit alive in a sense. The things that were sort of utopian visions then, we're trying to translate into practical realities."

The Institute for Social Inventions has become one of the most remarkable channels for the ideas of hundreds of "New Britons" around the country. Financed by members' subscriptions and private donations, it is run from Albery's living room and the homes of some of his friends. Every month or so a thick bulletin is mailed to members, with ideas for improving both large and small aspects of British life. It has already had an effect out of proportion to its size. Albery has been given a regular column in the

Guardian to report on members' ideas. A contest for the best socially inno-vative idea was sponsored by major corporate donors, and Albery was planning the first national conference of social inventors. The institute aims to do for British society what the tow-path did for Coalbrookdale.

The bulletin reads like the transcript of conversations on a rural party line. Socially inventive ideas traded and debated around the country range from the whimsical to the profound. In the evidence they provide of the ferment of innovation below the crust of traditional British life, they resemble an Anglo-Saxon version of the Russian *glasnost.*

"Every child while at school should be taught to finger spell the alphabet," suggested Mrs. J.E. Smith of Essex in one bulletin. "Then everyone could make communication with a deaf person without feeling embarrassment."

"We are a group of businessmen and others belonging to an organization called SUBUD," wrote Eustace Wait of Dorset, "[and] we want to imple-ment our idea that selected unemployed youth could be sent overseas to give practice in speaking English to foreign nationals. I have travelled extensively as an English teacher and I am convinced that such 'language ambassadors' would be greatly appreciated."

Fred Allen of Cambridge suggested a "labour tax that you could either fulfil or pay someone else to do, [which would] solve the problem of get-ting nothing from the unemployed."[10]

Some of the "social inventions" have received attention abroad. One idea developed by a member of the institute's Board of Inventors for changing the composition of the South African Parliament was repro-duced in one of that country's most prestigious law journals. Closer to home, Albery reports that many local hospitals have expressed interest in an idea advanced by a reader of the bulletin. During an 18-month stay in hospital, she related, it was only the sight of birds and flowers outside her hospital window that kept her spirits up. She suggested creating miniature "wildlife parks" around hospitals and medical centres as a form of therapy for convalescing patients.

Albery was only moderately surprised by the positive response to the institute. "I was trained as a psychotherapist, but I think that social therapy for society as a whole was what was really required. We don't really need more technological gadgets, like a better vacuum cleaner. What we actually need are more social inventions to help us cope with the technological revolution and, really, to slow it down a bit, even spread its benefits."

Albery's institute raised eyebrows when it first appeared. One socially inventive idea proposed by a mischievous member hit close to home: the construction of a local brick wall in every community against which peo-ple could come and beat their heads. But the directors and members of the institute now include some of the movers and shakers of the "New Britain," as well as fellow travellers around the world. Among them are Guy Dauncey, a "barefoot economist" whose ideas on the regeneration of small towns and local businesses influenced the community business concept used by Linda Echlin in Scotland; Prof. Charles Handy, an expert at the London School of Business; and Prof. Stafford Beer of Toronto, an international consultant in management sciences. Sir Peter Parker, former chairman of British Rail, and head of the British Institute of Management, is a patron. "[We need] nothing less than a cultural revolution to match the...technological revolution that we, and the world, are into already," Sir Peter said during a speech that could have been drafted by Sir Ranulph Fiennes, Bashir Okhai, or any of the other "New Britons" who emerged during the decade.

Albery's own contributions to socially inventive thinking centre on local government and the use of neighbourhood power, echoing some of Ken Livingstone's thoughts. "The neighbourhood is really the blood cell of our civilization," he said. "My vision of Britain is as a number of regional Parliaments, even independent countries, or a federation of countries...a Commonwealth of little nations which wouldn't threaten each other.

"America at the time of Independence could have chosen a confederated system instead of the one they did, which I think has proved an absolute disaster. The best thing America could do to help the world would be to disintegrate and become separate states again. There'd be no danger of another Vietnam."

The most serious work of the institute — Albery calls it his "bread-and-butter work" — is done in the schools. The institute runs weekly brainstorming workshops for youngsters to encourage them to think outside normal patterns. "We get them to try to come up with the most inspired thing they're capable of. They get a £25 budget to carry out a project in a school term, and at the end they get a certificate of applied creativity." One group of eight-year-olds came up with an idea for cleaning up the dog-leavings on the streets with motorized "pooper-scoopers," then organized a march to Richard Branson's houseboat to enlist themselves in his "clean up Britain" drive.

Albery bridles at comments by some critics that the institute is only a band of English eccentrics. "I don't think it's eccentric to go out in society and try changing it in the direction you want to. It's certainly the only sane thing for me to be doing at this stage of life." He preferred to think of institute members as gentle revolutionaries. "Revolutions have a pretty bad record," he admitted. "It's hard to think of one which ended up producing more benefits than dis-benefits. But I think what we're really into [in the 1980s and 1990s] is continuous problem-solving on a social level." Albery pulled a wry face. "I suppose you could call it continuous revolution."

Chapter 8

GOODBYE TO NANNY

Ownership by the state is not the same thing as
ownership by the people.
– *Conservative Party think tank, 1977.*

We are watching… the disintegration of much of
the economic machinery and administrative
apparatus of which the modern state has come to
be composed.

– *David Howell,
former Conservative Energy Minister, 1986.*

A random collection of people was waiting outside the office of Peter Bottomley, MP, in a grey neighbourhood in South London, one afternoon in the summer of 1986: a middle-aged woman in a blue dress, a short man with a jaunty cap and worn-out shoes, an elderly pensioner in a frayed, double-breasted suit and a trimly knotted tie. As they filed into Bottomley's small office, they each had a story to tell about some petty failure of government bureaucracy. A street vendor's permit was being held up because of red tape. An application to move out of a cramped apartment in a public housing estate had disappeared into some official dustbin. A worker's injury compensation cheque was lost. Behind their grimly polite smiles, they seemed unsure as to whether their pleas would do any good.

"You realize, of course, I can't promise to solve your problem," Bottomley, a thin, earnest man in his forties with a disarming smile, repeated to each of his visitors. "I can only bring it up to the proper authorities. I'll do what I can."

By the time their stories were finished, there were many more people waiting to come in. Every Friday, when his office was opened to the voters in the constituency, Bottomley found himself saying the same thing.

The creation of the British welfare state had been one of the outstanding achievements of the century. Yet, 40 years after it began with brilliant visions of social justice, the parade of thwarted hopes in Bottomley's office was a more accurate picture of the condition of the system in the 1980s: a bureaucracy that was remote and unresponsive, and a dependent, humiliated clientele, linked tenuously together by a member of Parliament who could only promise to "do what he can."

The problems of the welfare state in Britain were, in a way, the product of its success. Twenty million people — one out of three Britons — were receiving some kind of state benefit in the middle of the decade.[1] The affluent, the jobless, and the poor were equally eligible to take advantage of the state's largesse. The system had developed far beyond the original conception of its wartime architect, Sir William Beveridge, who wanted to ensure that workers and their families would never again have to be held hostage to the economic depressions that seemed periodically to afflict free-market capitalism. Beveridge and his supporters wanted to use government as a last-ditch guarantor of the basic needs of a civilized society: protection from hunger, assurance of shelter, insurance for unemployment, and the security of knowing that proper medical care would not depend on the ability to pay. However, the idea of a temporary safety net available to every citizen regardless of income evolved over time into a system of permanent subsidies and obligations, forced to keep pace with the rising expectations and changed needs of postwar life in Britain.

An argument could be made that the idea was flawed from the beginning. Prime Minister Winston Churchill had been warned that the price of the ambitious social welfare blueprint mapped out in the early 1940s was more than Britain could afford if it seriously wanted to rebuild its postwar economy. But he approved it as part of the political bargain that had ensured wartime solidarity. The Labour government that soon followed Churchill's into office had no doubts at all. A tiny nation that could mobilize its resources so productively against a fearsome enemy in war ought to be able to solve its peacetime problems. This turned out to be a fatal illusion.[2]

Few recognized at the time the extent of Britain's debt to the U.S. and the Commonwealth for keeping the country afloat and its factories running during the grimmest years of the Second World War. The allocation of millions of pounds for the construction of vast public housing projects, for example, was given equal priority with the reconstruction of the nation's industry. Correlli Barnett, a British academic, suggested the headlong march toward a cradle-to-grave welfare system had ultimately damaged the country. As government services drained away resources needed for rebuilding the economy, he said, Britain was left clinging to the "nipple of state maternalism."[3]

Barnett's view was intentionally provocative, but it was not difficult to sympathize with his outrage over a god that had failed. The welfare system was more likely to be a target of anger than a source of pride in the 1980s. It had become a sluggish, £60-billion-a-year bureaucracy which, despite taking more than 50 per cent of the national budget, was often despised by its clients for the humiliating dependence it exacted from them. Not only had the system grown remote from the people it was designed to help, it was often a source of the inequality and injustice it was supposed to have abolished.[4]

I first met Peter Bottomley soon after I arrived in Britain, at an embassy reception, and I remember being surprised to learn he had been a Conservative MP since 1975. The son of a former British ambassador to South Africa, he had worked in industrial relations and local community development before entering politics. His brother was a Labour Party municipal councillor, and his mother had joined the unemployed shipyard workers on their famous hunger march from Jarrow in the north to London in 1936. He had almost absent-mindedly worked his way up the rung of Conservative politics to become a junior minister responsible for roads and transport.

"I'm the sort of person who could join any political party," he explained when I took up a long-standing invitation to visit his South London constituency of Eltham in 1986. "I'm basically a liberal."

His unConservative leanings did not, however, appear to confound Margaret Thatcher. Shortly after the election of 1979, Bottomley was invited into the prime minister's office for a glass of sherry. As her aides prepared to take notes, she asked a polite question she was routinely putting to every Tory MP: what did he think the new government's priorities should be?

Bottomley needed only a moment to reply. He rattled off several ideas, but one of them made the prime minister's aides raise their eyebrows. Bottomley said he hoped the prime minister would respond to widespread public impatience with a welfare bureaucracy that threatened to destroy family life and individual initiative.

"They all looked at me," Bottomley recalled, "like something the cat brought in."

All of them except Thatcher, that is. The idea of reforming the welfare system was of course close to the prime minister's heart. But the suggestion that government services themselves were eroding the British way of life was political heresy at the time. It ran counter to every assumption about the role of government in British postwar culture. A strong state was assumed to be the only bulwark ordinary people had against the cruelties of the system. This belief was as much a part of the folk-consciousness of modern Britain as the smell of chips wrapped in newspaper.

Nevertheless, Bottomley reflected the changed mood that had brought the government into power. Most of the people who visited his constituency office took it for granted that the "nanny state" would be slow-moving and unfair.

"Why should a mother with four children, for instance, have to go on her knees to a [government] housing department if she needs a new and bigger place on another floor?" Bottomley asked. "People like me have been making those decisions for her for a long time, but now you find her saying, 'I'd prefer to make them myself, thank you very much.' They are tired of white liberal progressives, like me, telling them that we knew what was best. People want to manage their own lives, rather than let it be done by others.

"We used to have a 'death grant' in this country," continued Bottomley. "People got an automatic benefit of £30 to help with the cost of burying a relative. That's a little amount, it costs a lot to administer, and it gives no effective help to anybody. People who can't afford the £300 or £400 for a funeral, for instance, won't be helped at all; and for those who could afford it, it might pay for the flowers. It made no sense to pay all that money for the five per cent of people who could not afford to pay the cost themselves. The welfare state was like a death grant. It didn't help anybody. It was a crazy system. It had to change."

Not yet secure enough to follow Bottomley's recommendation for a sweeping reform, the new government began taking only tiny chips out of the welfare edifice. Conservative rhetoric before Thatcher took office had promised to reduce some of the financial costs of borrowing to pay for public services. Although Britain spent demonstrably less on social welfare in the mid-1970s than other European countries such as the Netherlands, Sweden, and even France and Germany, money — not philosophy — was seen as the principal problem.

Some benefits were separated from cost-of-living increases. Housing allowances, child benefits, and social security payments indexed to the cost of living ended up with net reductions. The government's concentration on the allegedly spendthrift habits of welfare bureaucrats often led to needlessly cruel situations. One such bureaucratic expense-paring led to the reduction of grants to the elderly to pay extra heating bills during a particularly cold winter.

In fact, despite the storm warnings raised by critics, the Thatcher government for the most part left the welfare structure alone. No British administration could have dismantled the network of services that had become as essential to the middle classes as it was to the poor without provoking a political upheaval. Many of the heaviest public spending commitments, such as old age pensions and medical care, were bound to grow as the working generation of the 1940s and 1950s approached retirement age, and these were beyond any single government's control. As Britain moved more deeply into the recession, the Thatcherite welfare reformers found themselves actually increasing social service spending in some areas. At first they tried to conceal this with greater gusts of anti-welfare rhetoric, but eventually they began to claim that their concentration on cost-saving and greater efficiency had actually saved the welfare state from destruction. "From the moment that the Tory party took over responsibility for the welfare state, [we] did it better...because we have a sound financial background," Thatcher bragged to a journalist in 1983.

In its second term, the government proposed major changes in the way the system of benefits was designed and allocated. The "death grant" was eliminated, and the idea of universal entitlement was effectively challenged for the first time. A tax-free maternity grant of £25 to every mother toward the cost of having a baby was replaced in April 1987 by a grant from a new "social fund" that fixed payments according to need. State maternity allowances and paid six-week maternity leave for working mothers was scrapped in favour of a scheme administered by individual employers.

The changes, advertised as a significant overhaul of the welfare system, were still a long way from challenging its philosophy. Nevertheless, critics said the government's so-called welfare review meant the beginning of the end of the principle of universality. A more sober assessment came later. "The worst that can be said by welfare supporters," concluded the *Financial Times* in 1987, "is that the Conservatives have eradicated the generosity of the Sixties and Seventies."[5]

The reforms, however, did have an unforseen result. They cast the inefficiencies and inequalities of the welfare state in a sharper light. Although more money was made available, poor people simply got poorer. It was true that the economic downturn had increased the pressure on welfare services, but it only underlined the fundamental problem: a system based on simple redistribution of wealth could ensure neither justice nor basic needs.

Despite a complex arrangement of supplementary benefits for people whose living standards could not keep up with the majority, the number of those estimated to be living below a government-measured poverty line rose from six million in 1979 to nearly nine million in 1983. Some analysts put the number even higher, at over 11 million. More than half the couples receiving benefits, according to one study, had used up all their weekly state allowances before the end of the following week just to keep up with the cost of food and basic services. Some three million people in 1986 could not afford to heat the living areas of their homes, and 3.5 million could not afford gifts that Christmas.[6]

The National Health Service, once one of the world's finest systems of medical care, had begun to deteriorate long before Thatcher came to power. But under the pressure of demand from growing numbers of people affected by the economic crisis, the NHS was visibly overwhelmed. Huge waiting lists and inattentive, often inefficient support services frustrated doctors, nurses, and managers as much as they did the patients.

The goal of good public housing for all had become similarly flawed. Many public housing estates were deadening, soulless places, where repairs failed to keep up with the pace of deterioration. The gap between those who needed space and the space available reminded some observers of housing shortages in Eastern Europe. In 1984, 14 per cent of the people on the list for new council housing had been waiting nine years or more.[7]

It was natural, politically speaking, for Thatcher to get the brunt of the blame, and it was possible to detect among some Tory ministers an unseemly eagerness to take credit for what they considered a long overdue rationalization of the system. But both the critics and defenders of welfare reforms in the 1980s usually preferred to blur the link between the decline of welfare services and the state's inability to satisfy a population whose needs had changed dramatically since the war.

The link was also blurred by welfare casualty "horror stories" that filled newspapers in Britain and overseas. I admit I wrote some myself. In one section of South London stood an aging but excellent medical facility, Guys Hospital, that ran a special intensive care unit for children. In 1983, Dr. George Haycock, one of the physicians there, told me 70 children had to be turned away the year before because there wasn't enough money to treat them. "We call it the heartbreak log," he said. "Every time I look at it, it reminds me of the disastrous state of the health service."

Much later, a different story emerged. Although it was true that funds for many London hospitals had been cut, forcing them to close down wards, the health service as a whole had received a steady increase in government aid through the 1980s. The extra money, however, had usually gone to medical facilities in the north of England, to hospitals that served entire regions. It was argued, with some justification, that there were enough medical services in London and the affluent southeast to make up for the loss of individual wards. Under the economic conditions of the time, hard choices had to be made about how to divide a shrinking pie. Even more to the point, it was not clear that extra money alone could improve the level of medical services.

International attention focused on the struggle between Thatcherite cost-cutting conservatives and their liberal opponents. Like most struggles, this one was never as clear-cut as the headlines suggested. It wasn't necessary to be a Conservative in order to have serious doubts about the intrusive presence of government in Britain. Since the war, the country had been managed by an interlocking directorate of government departments, quasi-government organizations (usually abbreviated as "quangos"), state-controlled industries, and trade unions. Despite the myth — cherished as much by Britons as by tourists — that the country was a network of small villages and shopkeepers interrupted by the occasional city or industrial plant, the United Kingdom was a massive corporate welfare state, underpinned by a steadily enlarging bureaucracy.

Margaret Thatcher had risen to power as a right-wing anti-government crusader, but it was no accident that her program attracted many Labour Party supporters and beneficiaries of the welfare state. Most people could see the problems, and as the majority of Britons grew more affluent, they were more likely to resist the simple nostrum of spending more of their taxes to keep the system stumbling along. Thatcher believed the problems were inextricably linked to the failure of liberal welfare capitalism and to the legacy of the other major architect of postwar British culture, the Cambridge economist John Maynard Keynes. Forty years after the issue had been swept under the rug by the Churchill government, Thatcher asked whether Britain could continue to support a welfare state superstructure erected on a crumbling economic base. She argued that the country could only meet its welfare obligations out of its earnings, and she maintained that the revival of the industrial base from which those earnings came had to be the first priority of a humane society.

The welfare state, in effect, had been forced to bear most of the burden of Britons' inability to decide what kind of nation they wanted to be: a society resting comfortably on the achievements of its past, or one that would risk social inequality to find a new place for itself in the world. As the economy went further into decline, the welfare state was bound to reveal its inbuilt weaknesses. Sounding almost like a Thatcherite himself, former Labour Prime Minister James Callaghan was explicit about the problem. "You cannot carry a first-class welfare system on the back of a second-class economy," he said in 1986. The ultimate goal of the welfare architects, the just distribution of wealth, was impossible to achieve if there was little wealth left to distribute.

While Thatcher stopped short of directly challenging the philosophic contradictions of the system, she was able to respond to those who advocated wider reform, like Peter Bottomley, with measures that, on the surface, were not directly linked to welfare services at all. The measures went to the heart of the problem posed by centralized government in the late twentieth century: how do you rescue individual initiative and dignity from a state bureaucracy that always professes to know best?

During the Conservatives' first term, public housing tenants were given the right to buy their homes at discounts of up to 50 per cent off the market price. Local housing authorities complained that the sale of public-housing accommodation, along with cutbacks in housing construction funds, constricted the market and made it impossible for thousands of people to find good living quarters. The response to the scheme, nevertheless, astonished even the government. More than 500,000 publicly-owned houses and flats were sold between 1979 and 1983, accelerating a trend toward a home-owning society. Less than 29 per cent of Britons owned their homes in 1951. By the mid-1980s, more than 60 per cent did.[8]

The popularity of the program made even opponents in the Labour Party think twice before criticizing it too harshly. Given the option to choose, people preferred not to live up to some theoretical egalitarian ideal, especially if it meant a chance to reduce their own dependence on the state.

The Thatcher government was not the only Western administration during the decade to challenge the orthodoxy of liberal welfare capitalism, but the Thatcher experiment came to be seen as either a warning or a model (depending on the political philosophy of the observer) for the troubled economies of Europe and North America.

Under Thatcher's leadership, the United Kingdom became the least Keynesian country in the West. Overall public spending on capital programs was held to tight financial limits, and the national budget actually shrank by six per cent. By 1983, Britain's deficit had been reduced more than in almost any other major industrial country. The cost-cutting and budget-slashing lowered government borrowing by four times the average for the members of the Organization for Economic Cooperation and Development (OECD), the "club" of major industrial economies.[9]

Thatcherism's approach to the state and its welfare obligations was often misunderstood by the right as well as the left. Thatcher, echoing Karl Marx's comment on Marxism, sometimes found the need to insist she was not necessarily a Thatcherite. She never identified herself with extreme right-wing ideas that envisaged doing away with the welfare structure altogether. Instead, she saw herself as paving the way for a new British "enterprise society" in which individuals would have the freedom to redefine their relationship with the nanny state. "The essence of communism and extreme left-wingism is the desire to control people's lives," she said in 1986. "They want this first because it gives them enormous power, and second because they think they can do it better. They forget that what happens in every society is that it will dwarf and diminish people, and if you come to a nation which dwarfs its citizens you will find that, with small people, no great things can be accomplished."

A substantial number of Britons evidently agreed with the prime minister, and still do. Few of those who voted Conservative in 1979 and 1983, and again in 1987, would have considered they were casting a vote to dismantle Britain's cradle-to-grave welfare system. They wanted, however, to see it managed better. Backed by public clamour for change, more fundamental reforms were set in motion. What had begun as an effort to reduce government spending accelerated, because of economic stress, the breakdown of an entire set of assumptions about the role of government in an age of scarce resources.

David Howell was a director of the Conservative Political Centre during the mid-1960s, when much of the intellectual framework for Thatcherism was worked out. He went on to become energy minister in the first Thatcher cabinet, only to find himself eased out as a "wet." His bullish views on government spending marked him as unsound. In 1986, he wrote a book that turned out to be one of the most engrossing political analyses published during the decade, although — being neither bitter nor partisan, nor the revelations of an "insider" — it received only cursory attention. The book's title, *Blind Victory*, pithily summed up his assessment of the Thatcher experiment.

Thatcher's problems began with her victory, he observed. "[There was] a confusion in the minds of the victors of 1979 about the real causes of their electoral success, and the true forces at work eroding the foundations of collectivism. Those who thought that they were simply returning to the market economy and the world of classical economics, on a rebound from Keynesianism, were inclined to the view that not much further intellectual debate was necessary...."[10]

"The Great Hope of 1979 in Britain," he wrote in another section, "was... that the party and government policy-makers who had been given power would recognize [the] newly emerging and wholly different landscape, would accept it rather than obstruct it, and reshape both policies and... style accordingly....

"In effect we are watching, although not always seeing, the disintegration of much of the economic machinery and administrative apparatus of which the modern state has come to be composed, and of the intellectual beliefs on which it was founded."[11]

The "newly emerging landscape," in Howell's phrase, was how the welfare state in the 1980s really looked and not as its detractors or supporters wished to see it: "A whole structure of state activity, of central institutions and procedures which has grown up over a period of between 60 and 70 years, roughly from the birth of modern macro-economic thinking and advice, and which has expanded massively...is now becoming obsolete," claimed Howell.[12]

Howell's most illuminating example of how the government set in motion changes it did not always understand was the plan to sell off state assets to the private sector. The idea of "privatizing" state-owned industries had been an insignificant part of the Tory campaign manifesto in 1979. It was then regarded as a useful tool for raising cash to finance government cutbacks. Almost accidentally, the Thatcher government had found itself at the cutting edge of one of the most radical of all the postwar changes in British government policy.

Howell, who claims to have coined the word "privatization," said few government officials believed the corporate might wielded by massive public utilities and state-run enterprises could ever be weakened. When he became Secretary of State for Energy in 1979, he inherited a giant national monopoly of electricity and power with one of the largest work forces in Europe. Plans were then underway for even more empire-building, with an enlargement of the energy grid through the construction of several new nuclear power stations costing £2 billion each. "I can recall no one inside or outside Whitehall ever suggesting to me that electricity investment could be considered in a less massive and therefore less hair-raisingly inflexible way," he said.[13]

Most of the other basic state industries, from steel to cars to telephones, were administered in the same "hair-raisingly inflexible" manner. The concentration of industrial power and national resources in a few central agencies and centrally organized industries reflected the Keynesian philosophy that government needed to occupy the "commanding heights" of the economy to protect its citizens against the price-fixing practices of private monopolies.

The nationalization of key industries was, like the welfare state, a response to the trauma and uncertainty of the 1930s. Trade unions (similarly organized on a national scale) and government planners valued state concentration for its ability to smooth out the fluctuations of the economic cycle. But by the late 1970s, the industries propped up by industrial welfare had as little to show for the money poured into them as the social welfare system. "Ownership by the state is not the same as ownership by the people," said a Tory think tank in 1977. People in all political parties could easily find themselves nodding their heads in agreement.

In its first term, the Thatcher government found it hard to resist the temptation to bail out crippled public firms. However, a new consensus developed among both new right monetarists, who believed that in order to create a climate of risk-taking and entrepreneurship the state needed to contract instead of expand, and new left economists, who believed that smaller units of industrial power would respond better to the needs of communities and regions. "The old consensus about the role of the state in industry has disappeared," concluded the *Economist*.[14]

By 1983, what had started as a tiny privatization program had become the nexus of Thatcherism's approach to economic management. Britain was now "the biggest and most advanced laboratory" for rolling back the frontiers of state power.[15]

The government raised more than £8 billion between 1979 and 1986, in what amounted to the largest sell-off of state-supported industries in the

West. From the "hiving-off" of small segments of nationalized corporations like British Steel, to the wholesale disposal of British Gas and British
Telecom, the Thatcher government began to fragment elements of the corporate state that had once been considered untouchable. The government's supporters could claim with some justification that privatization
was the start of an historic "world-wide movement."

"Britain, so recently known as the 'sick man of Europe,' is leading the
world," crowed the Adam Smith Institute, a right-wing Tory think tank, in
a 1986 booklet. "Other countries are turning to privatization precisely
because of the success achieved [here]...." The institute went on to claim
that the preponderance of the state in British life gave the government's
success in tackling "statism" a global significance. "Britain, which experienced the problem at its most severe, has had the first experience of the
solution," it said, a boast that beautifully captured the nationalistic sentiments of the reformers on the right.[16]

The exposure to the world of "free-market" competition did turn some
government enterprises that were previously mired in red tape into sleek
and powerful competitors on the international market. In other cases, the
government merely replaced public monopolies with private ones. But the
privatization program led to another development with an effect beyond
that which its architects had planned.

Some of the largest state enterprises were turned into "limited companies" and were floated on the stock exchange, enabling the government for
the first time to sell blocks of shares to employees and customers on prefer-
ential terms, and to individual investors. Although it was nominally a case
of offering for sale to the public what the public already "owned" in principle, the sales struck a populist nerve. Spurred by high-power advertising
campaigns, they were as popular as the council house sales had been.
Theoreticians of the Labour movement, who assumed that the enmity
between the working class and the bosses, between wages and capital, was
a permanent element in the British social structure, were as taken aback as
the government. When some of the large, state-owned utilities and commercial enterprises went on the auction block, more than six million
Britons became shareholders for the first time in their lives.

The sales of British Telecom in 1984 and of British Gas in 1986 were
among the largest placements on the stock exchange markets in the world.
The excitement and interest they generated were phenomenal. The Great
British Public blithely ignored critics who argued that the government was
selling them what they already owned as taxpayers and mailed in their
applications for shares. Thousands of people sold their British Telecom or
British Gas shares at a profit a few days afterwards, but millions more held
on to them, justifying government predictions that the long-term ownership of shares, sweetened by the promise of discounts in gas and telephone

bills, would be as attractive as the lure of instant profits. Architects of the scheme believed it would also give investors the feeling that they had a measure of control for the first time over the state monopolies that had run things in their name for so long.

The sales of council houses and the creation of a new class of shareholders represented a challenge to the corporatism of the welfare state. The establishment of a classless, property-owning and shareholding democracy was seen by Thatcherites as the way to create new wealth, and it also changed assumptions about the limits of radical change in British society.

"Much of what occurred [in the 1980s] was in line with what people wanted to do anyway," Peter Bottomley said. "It was not Mrs. Thatcher who imposed the change. The things she achieved came about because conditions were such that they could happen." Others nevertheless argued that the political culture had not changed and that any attempt to move it in new directions was dangerous, or impossible, or both.

Ralf Dahrendorf, director of the London School of Economics during the 1960s, called it "totally absurd to try to change a society 180 degrees." He disputed comparisons between Thatcher and the "anti-government" crusaders in Reagan's White House. "The point about Ronald Reagan's success is that he is reviving traditional American values and virtues," he said. "Mrs. Thatcher is trying to do just the opposite: fight all the traditional English values and virtues, and in my view, she is doomed to failure.... Britain is a society of many solidarities, totally averse to the spirit of competition between individuals. If you try to set one against the other, you get nowhere in Britain. America is exactly the opposite. There is a great tradition of trying to get somewhere on your own. In Britain, you always pretend you are not trying."[17]

Yet indisputably, something had happened. "There was a major change in intellectual attitudes [in the 1980s]," said Conservative philosopher Roger Scruton, who went on to assert that the sense of liberation extended well beyond his colleagues in the new right. "People could see that Britain's illness was a chronic self-indulgence, and that they had been too willing to depend on the state for help, rather than take responsibility for their own lives."

Despite the inconsistencies of Thatcherism and its occasionally brutal impact, it had provided the first voice to a new political culture. By the mid-1980s, Thatcherite and non-Thatcherite ideas about changing the role of government were competing in an invigoratingly free market. Few topics were considered closed for discussion. Very often it was hard to distinguish who was proposing what.

A Tory think-tank paper in 1983, for example, called a "vigorous voluntary sector the sign of a healthy society," and suggested channelling many of the activities of the state welfare system into locally administered and financed benefits. Some saw in these advocates of "volunteerism" the signs of a campaign to drag Britain back to the era of the poorhouse and the charity box. But the concept was strikingly similar to arguments advanced on the other side of the political spectrum.

"In a situation of failed dependency such as we are living in today, it becomes increasingly fruitless to make claims on institutions which are becoming increasingly incapable of meeting them," argued left-wing critic James Robertson. "The energy spent on demanding that other people should organize socially useful work — or, for that matter, almost anything else — for us is likely to be more effectively spent organizing it for ourselves."[18]

Michael Ignatieff, a Canadian-born philosopher living in England, similarly tried to redefine the aims of a post-welfare society from the perspective of the left. In *The Needs of Strangers*, a book published in 1984, Ignatieff movingly described pensioners scrabbling in a monger's barrow for old clothes. Like the people lining up at Peter Bottomley's office, they were as much the victims as the beneficiaries of modern state welfare. While their immediate needs of food and shelter were taken care of, they had somehow been disconnected from the society that supported them.

"The political arguments between right and left over the future of the welfare state which rage over these old people's heads almost always take their needs entirely for granted," Ignatieff wrote. "Both sides assume that what they need is income, food, clothing, shelter and medical care, then debate whether they are entitled to these goods as a matter of right, and whether there are adequate resources to provide them if they are. What almost never gets asked is whether they might need something more than the means of survival."[19]

Where that "something more" could be found was beginning to be clear in the late 1980s. Peter Bottomley, like Dennis Turner in Bilston, was convinced that encouraging the ethic of self-help was an essential part of regaining British self-respect. "The more I can do for myself, the more I am likely to do for others," he said simply. "The more I do for others, the more I am likely to have the competence and confidence to do things for myself."

The debate stirred by Howell, Robertson, Scruton, and many other Britons pointed the country toward a reshaping of the role of government in national life, not necessarily its emasculation. On June 11, 1987, British voters effectively delivered their approval of the direction the debate was taking. Thatcher's decisive election to a third term in office made it clear that the old methods of curing the ills of the welfare state by applying a bandage here or adding a dose of public money there — remedies repeated in the Labour Party program of 1987 — were no longer satisfactory to substantial numbers of Britons. Thatcherism, in effect, broke through a crucial psychological barrier.

Resting on a shaky new foundation of right-wing individualism and left-wing social conscience, the 1980s represented a start toward redrafting the social contract between the state and the citizen. But changing the rules of the welfare state was not the only component needed for the "enterprise society."

Chapter 9

ELECTRONIC CAPITALISTS

There must be something wrong with this country
if it's so easy to make money out of it.

*— Roy Thomson, Lord Thomson of Fleet,
Canadian press baron.* [1]

Above the noise of Mayfair traffic, Sir Clive Sinclair sat thinking in his third-floor office. Thinking has made Sir Clive a millionaire several times over. The world's first pocket televisions, digital watches, home computers, and electric cars all sprang from his hyperactive mind. The revolutionary pocket calculator he developed in 1972 transcended simple gadgetry to earn a place in New York's Museum of Modern Art. The calculator, like its balding, monkish-looking inventor, is a true icon of the electronic age.

However, icons are not immune to the insults of time and fashion. The 1980s were difficult for Sir Clive. A series of bad management decisions sent his business career plummeting, and his electronic wizardry did not always save him. When his electric car proved unmarketable, he became a figure of scorn in the British press. Critics said the car was dangerous as well as impractical. The inventor responded angrily that he had become a victim of the nation's "anti-industrial culture." Only in Britain, he complained, were there so many people waiting to pounce on an entrepreneur who had had a run of bad luck.

Sir Clive might have responded to his hard luck in business by finding himself a research sinecure in a university — or perhaps, like other British scientists, he might have opted for the more lucrative climate of the United States. The fact that he remained at home to compete as a businessman underlined the special place he occupied in contemporary British life. The electronics revolution pioneered by Sir Clive represented more than a revival of British scientific genius. Thanks to him, his imitators, and his

141

successors, Britain's image as a nation of brilliant but impractical amateurs slowly began to change.

My notes from a conversation with the shy inventor in his Mayfair office demonstrated the link between British scientific innovation and the "enterprise culture" of the 1980s. "Britain is the best place in the world for inventors," said Sir Clive, whose latest project involved figuring out a way to make robot-computers do the routine work of lawyers and accountants. "There are fewer obstacles here than almost anywhere." The successful commercial exploitation of research in advanced science and electronics finally broke down some of the barriers that had artificially stunted the roots of the British economy in other fields, Sinclair said. He had proven long before the decade began that scientific enterprise could be both respectable and profitable.

"People used to be afraid of computers, afraid that they would impinge on their lives, but they were also thrilled by the idea of them," he said. "I knew that if you could get one out at the right price, and say to people, look, we'll send you one in a brown paper envelope if we have to, it would work. This country has always tended to be the lead consumer."

He was right. The Sinclair computer was a success story of the 1970s. Relatively cheap to buy and easy to operate, it made the benefits of advanced electronics and the microchip accessible for the first time to laymen. It was marketed to schools as a teaching device, and its storehouse of games and simple word processing programs made it an absorbing device for hobbyists. Like the early stereo hi-fi, the computer became a status symbol in ordinary homes. Britons, as Sinclair predicted, went computer-mad. A decade after Sinclair first tested the market, nearly one in four Britons owned a home computer. "The acceptance of an idea, once proven, is swift," Sir Clive added. "When you've got something new, it's not Japan that succeeds — they've had the most appalling disasters — it's been America and Britain. One reason is that we've stopped being a country where there was a feeling of lack of hope."

Eliminating obstacles to creative entrepreneurship is still one of the most contentious achievements of the Thatcher government. Just as its moves to widen share ownership and home ownership challenged the assumptions of the corporate welfare state, its legislation promoting business initiative transformed the postwar consensus on the relationship between government and private enterprise.

When she came to power, Thatcher turned private enterprise into a national ideology. She made the entrepreneur a model for the rest of Britain and, by peeling away the layers of protective regulations around business, she doused Britain in a cold shower of self-interest. The government slashed the tax rate on the highest levels of income from 98 per cent to 60 per cent. Currency exchange controls put in place by previous Labour governments were ended. While the government reluctantly came to the rescue of some large public companies in its first term, its refusal to help a manufacturing industry suffering from the effects of competition abroad and recession forced factory managers to look seriously for the first time at new technology and new methods of marketing and organization.

A surprising number of businessmen and entrepreneurs, regardless of their political affiliation, date the beginning of their success to the change of government. Entrepreneurial activity in science and leisure-related fields accounted for much of the new wealth created in the 1980s. In the first six years of the Thatcher government, more than 140,000 new businesses came into operation. It was a remarkable rate of business formation at a time when so many other companies in more traditional fields of British industry were failing. According to Her Majesty's Treasury, Britain accounted for two-thirds of all venture capital raised in the European Community during 1985.[2]

It was a dramatic change in a country that appeared to be congenitally afraid to take business risks. The making of wealth in Britain had been associated in the public mind for so long with distasteful and occasionally exploitive "trade" that it had been easy to tar all capitalists with the same brush. In 1971 the Tory reform committee pronounced itself "horrified at the damage done to this country by individualistic businessmen." Quintin Hogg, a prominent Conservative who later became Lord Chancellor, called capitalism an "ungodly and rapacious scramble for ill gotten gains."[3]

The Labour Party had been equally wary of an unregulated capital market. Even the technological revolution promoted by Harold Wilson's Labour government in the 1960s, which was intended to bring Britain into the "white heat" of the electronic age, was circumscribed by red tape and government regulations. The climate created by the Thatcher government's hard-edged attitude toward business was ultimately more significant than the new legislation promoting individual enterprise.

"The tougher government became, the more people were forced to take their future into their own hands," said Sir Clive Sinclair. "Developments like the change in the basic tax rate created a new investment climate. We now have a venture capital market which didn't exist 20 years ago, and the effect of that in ten years' time will be stunning, because all that money is going into businesses which are going to be very big in ten years' time."

Sir Clive's career was a symbolic bridge between the 1970s and 1980s. His success marked a change in national attitudes toward wealth and the making of it. Lord Thomson of Fleet, the Canadian newspaper tycoon who became owner of the *Sunday Times,* once observed dryly, "There must be something wrong with this country, if it's so easy to make money out of it." The comment perfectly reflected his frustrations at dealing with the guilt-ridden attitudes of the British toward wealth and success.

In contrast, the scientific and commercial entrepreneurs of the 1980s pursued routes to success that were once dismissed as being of little significance to Britain's industrial future. Neither old-fashioned capitalists nor smooth-talking corporation men, they made an impact on their country's economy without changing the industrial landscape. Their millions were not earned by gouging mines out of the countryside nor by erecting glass skyscrapers. In the sense that they were prime movers in Britain's invisible economy of service exports and brain power, they were electronic capitalists. Why they flourished, what their stories suggested about the future health of the country, are key questions for anyone attempting to understand what the 1980s meant to Britain.

"What matters now is technology and brains. Natural resources aren't very important," said Dr. John Bradfield, bursar of Cambridge University's Trinity College and a noted mathematician, as he sat in an office overlooking the Trinity quadrangle.

No hint of the computer age interrupted the musty tranquillity of Bradfield's cubbyhole office. The desks and chairs were worn-out antiques, and framed prints of old English scenes hung on the walls. Just outside the quadrangle, languid young men in candy-striped blazers idled on the banks of the Cam, and staff were stringing paper lanterns through the trees in preparation for the college's annual May Balls. Only the antiquated telephone system threatened to strain Bradfield's donnish reserve. As he found himself persistently connected with the wrong number, he puffed at his pipe with irritation.

The air of detachment and reflection hanging over the Trinity bursar's office was a product of history. But like most such British images of the past, it was illusory. The university has played a central role in the nation's scientific life since the days of Isaac Newton, but the new spirit of scientific innovation had transformed it. Computer labs and successful electronic entrepreneurs associated with the university attracted the kind of fervent supporters associated with football clubs in other parts of the country. Commercial electronics was now as much a part of Cambridge life as the May Balls.

In 1969, a planning committee chaired by Sir Nevill Mott, a professor of physics and a Nobel Prize winner, recommended the establishment of a science park on 130 derelict acres owned by the university on the outskirts of the city of Cambridge. The introduction of a private enterprise ethic represented a departure for the sheltered, government-funded research centre Cambridge had become in the postwar years. Anticipating the temper of the 1980s, the committee suggested that the link between commerce and academe would profit both sides. Technology, the report's authors pointed out, was moving so quickly that businessmen needed to stay abreast of the latest developments in order to have an edge in the market-place; university scientists would benefit from participating in the development of practical uses for their own research. "We saw the park as a seedbed in which ideas fall, germinate, and prosper," Bradfield recalled.

A remarkable group of advanced engineering and computer-related companies came to life in the region over the next 20 years. The science park created what became known in Britain as the "Cambridge Phenomenon." In 1961, there were fewer than 30 small firms involved in the fledgling electronics industry in Cambridge. The figure climbed to 100 in 1974. By 1986, 322 "high-tech" companies, employing 13,700 people, poured about £890 million a year into the regional economy. Many of the firms became household names in Britain and around the world. Sir Clive Sinclair formed his first company here. Acorn, a tiny firm created by ex-Cambridge students and researchers, pioneered the use of home computers as educational tools. Developments in bio-technology and computer software design begun in the Cambridge area won — and lost — international fortunes. The phenomenon showed no sign of abating. An average of nearly three new firms a month opened in the area through the middle part of the decade. "The Cambridge phenomenon...represents one of the very few spontaneous growth centres in a national economy that has been depressed for all of a decade," said a firm of Cambridge consultants in 1986. "[It is] certainly the only one where growth is being led by high technology industry, and indigenous and small companies at that."[4]

It would have been easy to miss the turn-off to the science park. The area was marked by a tiny sign, as if it resolutely refused to call attention to itself. Once inside, the visitor finds himself in a Disney-like landscape of rural tranquillity. Sheep graze before a complex of low bunker-like buildings surrounded by trees and hawthorn shrubs. Swans and ducks swim in a tiny man-made lake.

"It's another world here," admitted Peter O'Keeffe, managing director of QUDOS Ltd., a computer software company. "If you go to many other places in England, certainly in the north...Sheffield or Leeds, for instance, or even Manchester, it's like going back into the Dark Ages." The people who work in the computer labs and electronic workshops scattered around the park may be painfully conscious of the contrast between their surroundings and the depressed industrial heartland of the country, but they also appear grateful for having been liberated from the constraints of the old industrial culture.

The most exhilarating period in chemical researcher Bill McCrae's life, for instance, was between 1979 and 1981, when people wouldn't listen to him. During those years, he and a colleague knocked on the doors of government offices and bankers in London in what seemed a fruitless search for backers for a bio-tech company they planned to establish in Cambridge Science Park. "Those people, to a man, didn't even know how to spell bio-technology," he remembered. "To them, we were simply scientists with a small 's'; they didn't understand what we were saying. They only wanted to put their money in safe houses. It was always, 'Sorry old chap, what about a cup of tea.' I never got reasons for why they turned us down. You sit down with a 21-year-old, a classics graduate who has become an investment manager, how can he know anything about bio-tech or high tech?"

The constant refusals made McCrae and his partner only try harder. McCrae was the first person in his family to finish school. His father was a bricklayer and his grandfather a farmer. With a pearl in his pink tie and a dapper white beard, he looked more like an actor than a 52-year-old high-tech businessman. He had the energy of a man half his age. McCrae was so confident that their technique for producing the diagnostic serums used in human and veterinary medicine would make them a lot of money that he had already given up his job as a consultant for an international firm. The market was then almost completely dominated by American pharmaceutical companies. Few British scientists believed they could compete with America's industrial muscle, even when they faced U.S. companies on English turf. "The British mentality is ahead in being creative and innovative, but not in seeing the commercial applications," McCrae said. "You offer an idea to an American scientist, and he'll look for ways to make money out of it. Offer an idea to a British scientist and he'll look for ways to make a research paper on it." McCrae and his associate managed to raise a flicker of interest from civil servants operating a new business start-up scheme. They raised £1 million and then found additional help from a new government-backed venture capital organization. Within a year, their company, Cambridge Life Sciences, was thriving with more orders than it could handle. A few years later, the company was on its way to becoming one of the world leaders of commercial bio-technology.

Only two other areas of the country besides Cambridge experienced the kind of dynamic growth in electronics or computer-related industry usually associated with California's Silicon Valley; the corridor along the M4 motorway running west from London to Bristol, and a triangle formed by Edinburgh, Glasgow, and Dundee in Scotland called Silicon Glen. The one factor all three regions shared was the absence of a dominant heavy manufacturing industry. Neither the M4 corridor nor Cambridge were ever major manufacturing centres; in Scotland, most of the old coal and steel mills and shipyards had shut down. The story of Silicon Glen, in fact, was the most instructive of all for understanding the culture of British scientific enterprise in the 1980s. The decline of an industrial infrastructure there was directly responsible for allowing a new kind of business enterprise to take root.

Silicon Glen is not really a glen at all. The image it calls up of a stark, peaceful valley peopled by kilt-clad Scots falls to pieces when you drive through the industrial triangle of southern Scotland, where more than 80 per cent of the 5.5 million Scots live. The landscape is pockmarked with empty shipyards, abandoned mills, and grim factory towns. The reminders of Scotland's slide from industrial prominence make the presence of a burgeoning electronics industry even more remarkable. "We've been the ones who've been hard hit," Ian McLennan, a tall, quiet Scot who works for the Scottish Development Agency (SDA), told me almost proudly in his Glasgow office. "A father will say to his son, there's no point in you going into the shipyard because it's not going to be there soon, so why don't you try and get into one of these new companies, these electronics companies?"

The special capacity of the Scots to adjust to economic change, along with funding from the government-sponsored SDA strengthened the capacity of the Scots to adjust to economic change. Beginning with the arrival of the first semi-conductor company in 1960, Scotland's industrial belt witnessed an electronics explosion. The country now produces about 70 per cent of Britain's output in silicon wafers, which contain the microchips essential for the new information technology. Of the 400 companies in the area, at least 100 were formed in 1985-1986 alone, attesting to the industry's continuing health, despite a temporary world slump. The majority of the firms was small. Most had fewer than 50 employees, and hardly any were involved in large-scale production. Orders were usually farmed out to sub-contractors, and unions played only a small role.[5]

John Gahagan, managing director of a tiny company called EKC Technology Ltd. in the town of East Kilbride, moved from marine engineering to electronics, in a rite of passage that became familiar in the decade. Despite its formidable name, EKC Technology Ltd. was little more than a warehouse and a few offices located in an industrial park when I saw it in 1986. EKC, which sells the chemicals used to strip photo-resistant material off the silicon wafer, is owned by a California firm. It had started up only a few months before, but Gahagan could already imagine the orders coming in. "This is a fickle industry," the gruff 52-year-old Scot told me, "with product life-cycles lasting as little as two years. The way to success is to continually think ahead."

Foresight was a quality Gahagan exhibited in his own life. He entered electronics after a series of timely career switches that mirrored the twisting path taken by the Scottish economy since the war. Trained as a marine engineer in the 1950s, at a time when Scotland was a powerful force in world shipping, he went to sea for five years. He was only 26, however, when he sensed that the marine industry was beginning to slide, as he put it, "down the slippery slopes." He retrained himself as a machine drafts-man and went to work for a large company, working himself up to chief engineer. Once again, he suspected that his future prospects would be limited by the slump in Scottish industry. So he changed again and formed his own company, which employed, by the time he sold it, more than 1,000 people. Gahagan believed his story was not unusual — at least in Scot-land. There is a drive for survival there, he said, that isn't readily visible in other parts of England. "Perhaps it's our folk memories of trouble and hardship," he speculated.

"If people like me can go into technology, what the hell is wrong with British people?" Gahagan asked. "They can adapt as well as I can. It's the ability to look at the horizon. Maybe all these problems are what we needed to get off the backside. In the Fifties and Sixties we became a very cushioned society, with large conglomerates, national health service, cra-dle-to-the-grave stuff. You're looked after, cossetted, the winds weren't allowed to blow on you. Maybe that wasn't too good for the British atti-tude, maybe the fact that Maggie said, 'Yeah, we'll still look after you, but not quite as well, you're going to have to do more for yourself', maybe that was the key thing." Gahagan was very far from being a Conservative sup-porter, but he said approvingly that government policies had done what he had been trying to do in his own life. "If somebody writes this 50 years hence, and that's probably the perspective one's got to get it into, the thing that'll be written about Thatcher is that she brought stability. Okay, she carved up an awful lot of people in the process, she cut an awful lot of deadwood, but she forced industry to do an awful lot of things they didn't want to do."

Computers and silicon chips were not the only area of British enterprise where new 'winds' were blowing. Revenues of British public relations firms went from £7.4 million to over £50 million between 1979 and 1986, a period when more Britons could not afford enough to eat than at any time since the 1930s. Advertising and public relations were two of the "few areas where an enterprising man or woman can create a billion-pound business from absolutely nothing," according to the *Spectator* magazine. Like the entrepreneurs in Cambridge and Silicon Glen, the admen had to fight against a business culture and ethic that was opposed to their product.

"At the beginning, we had to convince financiers and banks in the city to back us," said Simon Mellor, who, while still in his thirties, rose to become one of the senior executives of the Saatchi and Saatchi advertising agency. "They couldn't understand backing a company that had no assets except brains, but why should we be a factory making things that people don't want to buy?" The Saatchi company was one of the most notable British success stories of the 1980s. A small, struggling agency operated by two immigrant brothers who set up shop in Hampstead, North London, Saatchi and Saatchi was taken on as "volunteer" PR consultants by the Thatcher team when she became leader of the opposition in 1975. The agency went on to mastermind her winning campaign of 1979. Its good fortune could be traced directly to the Thatcher government, though some Britons would say it was just as true the other way around. The purchase in 1986 of an American company made Saatchi and Saatchi the biggest ad agency in the world, with more than $3 billion in annual billings and a controlling stake in a global communications business.

Another electronic capitalist, Eddie Shah, the owner of a provincial advertising weekly, became a national figure when he successfully defied a union attempt to prevent him from automating his production processes. The notoriety helped him challenge the power of the newspaper barons on London's Fleet Street by creating a newspaper called *Today*. Using computerized, fully automated equipment, Shah underspent his rivals; *Today* had only a fraction of the huge production staffs of the big dailies. However, his drive for better, more economical production was made at the expense of good journalism. The newspaper produced by his tiny, overworked editorial staff failed to meet its circulation targets. The paper was floundering in mid-1986 after less than six months of operation, and in 1987, it was bought out by press tycoon Rupert Murdoch. Shah's "failure," like Sinclair's before him, attracted mockery and scorn from those who said, "I told you so," but he had triggered a revolution in British newspaper production. With the power of newspaper unions steadily diminishing, the barons of Fleet Street soon followed Shah into computerized production.

The special qualities of people like Sir Clive Sinclair, the Saatchis, Eddie Shah, and John Gahagan would probably have brought them success in any culture. But the best evidence that the electronic revolution had caused a major shift in British attitudes could be found in the financial bedrock of old England: the banks and investment houses that have underwritten Britain's worldwide influence and prestige for centuries.

A pretentious old building in the City of London, with wooden panelled doors and gaslights outside, is the centre of the London International Financial Futures Market. Shortened to the acronym "LIFFE," this new offshoot of the traditional stock market is a visible sign of what has happened to Britain's financial culture in the decade. LIFFE did not exist before the 1980s. Today, a visitor inside sees a blur of colour, a littered floor, a small rectangular room with partitions and blinking computers. Young men and women in various coloured uniforms that identify their employers race back and forth with electric energy. Some are dressed like hotel doormen with gold braid. Others wear blazers with flashy red linings; one sported a lime-green coat with yellow frills. The scene is like a send-up of an old movie about British public schools.

Most of them are young, between 18 and 25. They stand around joking, flirting, gossiping or reading newspapers. There are few chairs. A sudden burst of energy brings a knot together, and they motion to colleagues sitting by computers, who in turn shout into a perpetually open phone. The young, gaily dressed characters are part of London's newest market. They are trading in futures for their respective investment houses. Between them the young brokers are responsible for 25,000 contracts a day. Few last past the age of 30. The lightning-quick reflexes are gone by then, but they retire rich.

The City of London, which still holds the monetary life of Britain within its square mile of ancient, narrow streets, experienced a cultural shock in the mid-1980s at least as staggering as any experienced in other parts of the country. George Nissen, former deputy chairman of the London Stock Exchange, was present at the beginning. An imposing, red-faced, pin-stripe-suited Englishman of the old school, he is not a person given to hyperbole, but he talks about the roots of the City's transformation with boyish amazement. "I remember sitting in a room at the Stock Exchange Council, when it first became clear that there should be major changes in the way the stock exchange was organized. We debated whether we should do it gradually or at once. We had asked for five years, and were given three, to the end of 1986, to plan. Someone said, 'Well, we'd have to do it all in one big bang.' "

The Big Bang, as it soon became called in the British press and in financial centres around the world, happened on October 27, 1986, with the announcement of major changes in the way investment capital, stocks, and shares were to be traded in the City. The announcement ended forever the image of British high finance as a cosy gentlemen's club and, in one stroke, moved the world of bowler hats and umbrellas into high-tech.

The compelling reason for change was the threat to the City's position as a global financial centre. The computer revolution liberated markets from the limits of geography and time. At the touch of a button, a broker could make decisions on the movements of capital around the world. Money and financial power naturally flowed to those markets able to master the new technology. City men were nervously studying the increased prominence of other European financial markets such as Amsterdam. "What we were trying to do was create a new market, not one just oriented toward the U.K., but one that can become international," said Nissen. "Some people might have regarded us as a Rolls-Royce system, but we weren't in line with the approach to trading in other centres."

However, domestic political considerations were equally important. The cosy, closed world of City firms contradicted the most fundamental Thatcherian axioms. If powerful trade unions were to be regarded as an unhealthy restriction on the free movement of labour, how could Thatcher's ideologists avoid tackling the restrictive City practices that impeded the flow of capital? A complex set of rules governing who deals in securities and how much commission could be paid had effectively kept the City a closed shop. The argument, in fact, met few objections among those financiers who recognized that a deregulation of City practices would strengthen their hand in the competition for international influence.

The City of London's atmosphere of stuffy conservativism had always masked a determination to keep its distance from industrial Britain. The first part of London to be settled, it was always a special country. Here, the English sense of propriety sends itself up, with tongue firmly in cheek. The East India Arms, a pub on Fenchurch Street, has a sign in its window warning, "We regret that we will refuse to serve anyone wearing dirty clothing." City police have to be two inches taller than London bobbies (five feet, two inches) and even the royals cannot cross the boundaries marked by statues of sedate griffins without "permission."

But recently the ancient buildings and evocative street names, like Mincing Lane, have been joined by new shapes and accents. The new Lloyd's Insurance building, eerily resembling an oil refinery, overwhelms the Wren churches. Glass and concrete towers are everywhere, and instead of bowler hats, it's more common to see blue pinstripes, cotton and polyester. Reality reflects the image. Of nearly 500 banks operating in the Square Mile, just under half are actually British. This fact was one of the chief reasons British bankers took action. Under the new regulations, 48 of the merchant and investment banks found partners in banks, stockbroker firms, commodity dealers, and insurance houses, in order to be able to compete with the capital flooding in from overseas. "You can imagine the kind of trauma it caused," said Nissen. As new financial expertise was needed to keep track of the technology that connected London instantly with other financial centres, a premium on sharp, young securities traders like the ones in LIFFE pushed salaries in the City to astronomical levels.

Its denizens have already begun to think of how the Square Mile will look in the future. The City, says Peter Tann, a young investment analyst, could become a financial supermarket. "There may not even be banks, but a new financial culture, that can do anything from trade to make markets. London is becoming more important, not less important." But even Tann feels a twinge of guilt. "The City is an island in terms of rewards in relation to those elsewhere in the country."[6]

Every success story and cultural transformation in the 1980s aroused as much scepticism as praise. The rise of silicon-chip firms, said critics, rarely provided a significant benefit to local economies. The industry usually employed low-paid labour, including many women, and there was little security for a town when the investment ended or failed. The strengthening of London's position in the world of international finance raised questions as to whether there would be less domestic capital investment available for struggling British industry. The electronic capitalists, in their drive to cut through the international barriers that had kept Britain reasonably stable, offered little comfort to the unskilled, uneducated, or unorganized. These criticisms were valid, but they were secondary to the main point. Financial deregulation and the promotion of high-technology entrepreneurship infused traditional British industrial culture with an energy that had not been visible for decades. The challenge was to harness that energy for the profit of the entire nation.

Even John Gahagan admitted that the electronics industry could never take up the loss created by the dying of Scotland's traditional industries. He felt keenly what had happened to his generation in the 1980s, the men who once had worked alongside him in the shipyards along the Clyde. "People brought up in heavy engineering are gradually becoming dinosaurs," he said. "The sad thing is that a lot of people who are 50, 55 today, in engineering, or the coal industry, or the steel industry, will probably never work again .... But something's happened this decade. Maybe you need three million people unemployed to have people start looking after themselves."

According to the accepted view, Britain in the 1980s was in the final stages of "deindustrialization." The collapse of huge corporations employing thousands of workers and exporting a range of finished industrial products abroad seemed the final proof of British decline, which attracted the lion's share of attention at home and abroad. The flexible, innovative companies making waves in fields like entertainment, leisure, and electronics were usually regarded as diversions on the path back to industrial success. The fact that many had become so closely associated with Thatcherism was further evidence to critics of their unreliability as models for the future.

The alternative view regarded such companies, and the innovative personalities who started them, as Britain's only real hope of survival in the twenty-first century. "They represent the leading edge of structural change," wrote Tom Lloyd, a British financial journalist who examined many of the new electronics and computer businesses developing in Britain. "In the long-term the health and vigour of these young shoots now emerging from the corporate undergrowth are much more important than the ailments that beset the larger, more well-established companies."[7]

Lloyd offered a tongue-in-cheek suggestion for an enlightened industrial strategy of the future: instead of propping up the dying manufacturing sectors of Britain, governments and VIPs should allow natural selection to take its course. They could attend corporate funerals in the same way as they attended ribbon-cutting ceremonies for new plants. "Such ceremonies would be sombre, but they need not lack dignity," he wrote. "There would be a sense of gratitude for services rendered and for a job well done — a feeling of sadness perhaps but also one of inevitability."

In a more serious vein, he compared the problems of the older companies to the death throes of dinosaurs: "The closure of a shipyard or a steel mill can rip the heart out of a community, and the billions of pounds spent on subsidies for our ailing motor industry visibly impoverish all of us," he wrote. "We see, hear and feel the process of deindustrialization taking place all around us. The parallel process of reindustrialization is, for the time being, below the threshold of normal perception."[8]

Chapter 10

A JOB IS A JOB

A job is a job. I am surprised to find
Mr. Wainwright adhering to the rigorous
Stakhanovite doctrine that male employees
should be fully working the entire time.

— Alan Clark,
Under Secretary of State for Employment.

A few years ago, the Hitachi television plant at Hirwaun, Mid-Glamorgan, Wales, offered £1,800 to any worker over the age of 35 who wanted to take voluntary retirement. The offer was sweetened with a promise that anyone accepting it could nominate an unemployed 16-year-old fresh out of school to take his place. Japanese managers saw no contradiction in the fact that their own company chairman was then a vital 73. Older employees, they argued, were prone to sickness and were slower on the job. They had poorer eyesight than their younger workmates, a worrisome hindrance to the delicate work involved in assembling micro-electronic circuits. But the explanations failed to disguise the most telling point: the Japanese evidently considered anyone over the age of 35 in Britain resistant to change. Their remedy was drastic and not likely to win more than laughter from the average British worker. (Only 15 of the plant's 800 workers took up the offer, of whom five requested that their sons or daughters take over their jobs.)[1]

The Japanese were only underlining perceptions already shared by executives of many British companies. The trouble was, few British managers cared to be as provocative. The experience of one British firm that bought new machines for its assembly line was typical of the prevailing approach to technological change. The company knew the machines meant 160 workers would no longer be needed; but instead of receiving help in retraining or in finding new employment, the men were paid to come to work every day and do nothing — until they grew bored and left on their own. In this way, appearances were preserved. No one was hurt or offended. Yet the money and time wasted could have been spent more productively.

Even before the decade began, the impact of new technology and automation presented a challenge to the organization and composition of the British industrial workforce as great as that posed by the industrial revolution more than two centuries earlier. But until the economic crisis of the 1980s, the challenge was slow to be taken up. "Most companies took a big stick and few carrots," said Dr. Michael Cross. "People who didn't bleed to death got the carrots. It was awful."

Cross was one of the growing number of British experts who made the study of industrial change central to British life in the 1980s. I met him at the offices of the Technical Change Society on a busy West London street. The organization offered a kind of industrial first-aid for companies likely to be hit by future shock. As far as Cross was concerned, all of British industrial society was a patient in need of help. "You are not dealing simply with a job, but with emotions, attitudes, and a way of life," he said. "Every time a new plant is opened, it puts pressure on everyone to match the new technology, and it's now [starting to hurt] people in their thirties and forties."

Circumstances eventually proved that the Japanese assumptions about British inability to change were incorrect. A significant body of innovative industrial management techniques accumulated over the decade, sufficient in fact to become a new British export industry in itself. Many of the techniques were refinements of ideas used in North America and Japan; nevertheless, the British experience in refining those ideas became critically important. Britain, once a model of government administration for generations of native-born civil servants around the Empire, became a source of expert management training for would-be business managers of the developing world. During the latter part of the 1980s, managers and management trainees flocked to Britain from Commonwealth and Third-World countries, joining business consultants already there to investigate British privatization schemes.

Some of the most interesting techniques of business reorganization were rooted in much older concepts of work and workplace relations that had been eclipsed by the industrial revolution. Co-ops, for instance, had been early building blocks of British working-class movements. By the mid-1980s, there were over 900 new co-ops, many funded by local cooperative development agencies, compared with 100 in 1977. They employed 10,000 workers.

New breath invigorated the old ideals of industrial democracy such as worker participation and control. Often, the new ideas came from abroad. Quality circles, a Japanese method of inspiring teamwork among employees, were adopted in 250 companies. For British workers, the technique came close to restoring the preindustrial pride of a craftsman in his product. At the Duracell battery plant in Crawley, for instance, workers at one quality circle designed a new factory bench. For the first time that managers could remember, workers on the traditional British tea-break were actually talking about their jobs. It was not always a comfortable sensation for executives used to the stratified organization of the British factory. "There's a thin line between ordering people about and involving them, which our culture finds hard to tread," said Maurice Jones of Duracell.

A quality circle at one British textile plant decided to investigate the company's security measures. Over a period of five months, they accumulated a roomful of knitwear without anyone knowing. Finally, they stole the director's Rolls-Royce. When they presented it to him with a flourish, they submitted 78 recommendations for improving security.

Profit-sharing, once regarded as a threat to worker solidarity, crept in through the back door of privatization schemes. The sell-off of nationalized industries on the stock market made it possible for many employees to buy shares, sometimes at discounted prices. With almost 800 worker-share schemes in place in 1984, there were new attitudes visible on the shop floor. "There's a tremendous attitude to cost saving," said Harry Batty, workers-shareholder director of the recently sold-off National Freight Company. "In the past, drivers kept engines running in the depots, but not now." There were obvious limits to the schemes. Sharing of profits did not necessarily mean sharing of responsibility or control. British Jaguar's share program, for instance, did not prevent a strike for higher pay, and worker-shareholders in another plant in Jersey returned from their summer holiday to find that the managers had dismantled the factory.

However, the decade witnessed a change not only in the organization of the workplace, but in the kinds of people who were working. Under the pressure of economic change, the composition of the British workforce was transformed. The number of self-employed increased from 1.8 million in 1979 to 2.2 million in 1984. Although the main increases came in the "soft" service industries, not in manufacturing, and although many people were forced into self-employment because of job layoffs, the transformation was profound. Many companies began to contract out for the people they needed, instead of maintaining traditional large staffs that were idle for long, unproductive periods. Self-employment in the construction industry rose by 70,000 in the four years up to 1983, while employment in the same sector fell by 200,000. Most of those construction firms found the idea of temporary hire attractive for economic reasons. So did employees. The number of part-time and temporary workers steadily rose throughout the 1980s. Private employment agencies and contractors filled over one million temporary slots in 1984. Only about seven per cent of the work force at any one time were "temporaries" in Britain, but there were signs that a "temporary" class of professionals was growing in size. Doctors, nurses, paramedics, dental hygienists, accountants, and even managers, under a program called "executive leasing," found it suited their lifestyles to contract out their services.[2]

The changes gave people new options in managing their time. In some firms, employees could arrange with their bosses at the beginning of the year the amount of hours they would work over the next 12 months. Others shared their jobs. The traditional concepts of working time and the working year became irrelevant, especially in industries using new technology. Personal computers equipped with telephone modems allowed more people to work at home and reflected a return to some of the preindustrial methods of organizing work. "Scotland used to be full of crofter-fishermen and crofter-blacksmiths," said Alex Macrae, who moved to a tiny Scottish island to produce software programs. "There's no reason why it could not be full of crofter-programmers."

It was no accident that many of the techniques for reorganization of the workplace were most successfully implanted in the new electronic "knowledge" industries. Change in the more traditional sectors of the British economy usually meant eliminating craft demarcation lines, and consequently it threatened the foundations of security for many workers. Yet more than 50 leading British companies during the decade did just that.

Pilkington, one of the world's leading glass makers, was a notable example. In 1980, it decided to build a new automated plant on a "greenfield" site at its headquarters outside Liverpool. The greenfield concept, in which companies opened up new facilities on rezoned urban land, allowed managers to by-pass many of the constraints previously imposed on them by unions and local authorities. Pilkington could make a good case for itself. The recession had forced it to lay off many workers, and managers believed that unless they could install competitive new technology, Pilkington would be forced to move a large part of its operations outside Britain and throw even more workers onto the dole queues. The managers negotiated with unions the elimination of 21 separate skill categories some of which dated back to the early years of the industrial revolution when the company was first established. "We even had a guy who brushed away broken glass with a long stick. It was one of the most dangerous and boring jobs in the plant, and it was completely unnecessary," Allan McKendrick, assistant works manager, told me during a visit I paid to the plant in 1984. "We had one man listed on the books as 'belt splicer' even though there were no belts to splice. Our idea was to organize the work force into three major craft areas — mechanical, electrical, and building. It was a question of survival and the unions agreed.

"When people realize the need is there, they cooperate. We didn't have a monopoly of the market any more. We had to change our operations."

The new Pilkington production line was virtually run by a computer the size of a typewriter. Eight people, including a computer programmer, oversaw the mixing of sand, soda ash, and limestone to make glass in a process that once required the backbreaking labour of hundreds of men. The ending of craft distinctions transformed life on the Pilkington factory floor. Employees all worked the same numbers of hours a week, and they were no longer confined by union rules to the same monotonous task day after day. Once they received proper training, they could move to different jobs around the plant every three months. To help persuade its workers of the benefits of change, management offered the carrot of a higher-than-average salary for the area, about £10,000 a year. Pay differentials were abolished, along with standard working shifts. Under the new agreements worked out with unions, an employee could arrange with his supervisor how he wanted to fill his working week. He could, for instance, decide to come into work three mornings in a row, then come back to the plant for three night shifts.

Automation did mean job loss. It also provided security for those workers who remained. "Two years ago, management-labour relations were so bad around here that you waited for meetings to break up before you knew whether you still had a job," said Mick Webster, a 31-year-old former shop steward at Pilkington who had become a management trainee. At Westland Helicopters in Milton Keynes, conventional lathe operators who were retrained as computer programmers talked as if they had a new lease on life. "There's no way I would go back to operating conventional machines," remarked Peter Willis, a 20-year veteran of the lathe. "This job makes you feel like an electronic wizard." But the central question for many workers in the traditional industries of Britain during the decade was whether the new organizational techniques were an iron fist or a velvet glove. Would they be forced to give up all the protection their unions had struggled so hard over the decades to obtain?

Unions were the only institutions in British society able to persuade the mass of the workforce to make the adjustment to industrial change. Consequently, the most important battles occurred in their ranks. A survey of companies conducted in 1984 graphically illustrated the strength of trade union resistance. Eighty-six per cent of the firms surveyed reported they had made major changes in working practices over the previous five years, but nearly the same percentage said trade unionism was a big or fairly big factor in preventing more changes.

The power of trade unions in Britain was beginning to weaken in the 1980s, but their considerable clout persisted. Although the number of days lost through strikes had begun to drop in the 1980s, several studies indicated that the recession had not fundamentally changed industrial relations in Britain. While many British unions had learned the lessons of the winters of discontent and appeared to acquiesce in the rule changes demanded by employers, their tranquillity was relative. Many of their members were conscious of the lengthening dole queues outside the factory. When a group of car workers began to stage familiar walkouts after several years of labour peace, *The Times* warned: "The message from the more militant . . . unions appears to be that, as soon as the fear of immediate job losses has abated, you can forget . . . about [worries of] competitiveness and pricing people out of jobs. That is clearly a depressing message for those on the dole queues who have paid the heaviest price for industrial restructuring and the drive to improve productivity."

The Electrical, Electronic Telecommunications and Plumbers Union (EETPU) stood out as one of the few trade organizations willing to accept the imperatives of postindustrial change. It risked ostracism from the union movement when it signed no-strike agreements with Japanese companies establishing themselves in Britain. Under the agreements, management and unions pledged to "avoid any action which interrupted the continuity of production." Roy Sanderson, an EETPU official, said his union had made the decision to break new ground in labour-management relations after a painful self-examination. "In 1980, we took a survey of strikes by our members over two years, and we discovered that our members were coming back after the strike was settled with so little difference that it made the whole thing nonsense," he said. "We decided to stop fighting yesterday's battles." The EETPU went even further. It became a promoter of new industry, actively wooing Japanese and other once-reluctant foreign firms to invest in Britain with the promise of labour stability. "I'll guarantee that by the end of the 1980s everyone will be trying to do what we're doing," predicted Sanderson. "We've proved that we can use our power in a way that's not damaging to our members. Sure, there's a culture shock. Shop stewards and a lot of other union officials don't really know what to do in a situation where the idea of conflict is not built in. But if we can't work our problems out, we're finished as a movement."[3]

It was a significant change of gear for a union that had once been in the front ranks of the militants. Frank Chapple, former head of the union, once boasted to a cabinet minister, "I could stop the country in 48 hours." For many of the old union barons, that kind of power was not easy to relinquish. In a long conversation one afternoon at London's Savoy Hotel, a retired and contrite Chapple admitted that the unions needed to rethink how they used their power if they wanted to survive. "Trade union leaders have been sorcerers' apprentices in Britain," he said. "They called into being forces they didn't understand. Unions ended up being organizations established for their own sake, rather than the old ideal of being instruments for changing society."

The Thatcher government no doubt helped many unions — forcibly — to see the light. Trade union leaders saw Thatcherism, often quite justifiably, as their enemy. Some Tory ministers made no secret of their belief that trade unions were the single obstacle to accomplishing the Thatcherite vision of an enterprise society. "Trade unions are the most significant, unreformed institution in our system," said Norman Tebbit, the dry-witted former airline pilot (and union member) who became infamous for his shock tactics against the unions as employment secretary. Three major pieces of legislation — the Employment Act of 1980, the Employment Act of 1982, and the Trade Union Act of 1984 — put British unions on the defensive, a position from which they have never completely recovered. The 1980 law outlawed secondary picketing. The 1982 act allowed a closed shop only when 80 per cent of union members voted for it by secret ballot. The 1984 act required unions to hold secret ballots before taking strike action and during elections for executive posts, as well as ensuring that union members could vote on where they wanted their political contributions to be sent — an unsubtle attempt to undermine one of the cornerstones of Labour Party financing.

Thatcher may have done more to push British unions into the twenty-first century than any other force in the country. Some Britons believe she did it with a single event, the 18-month-long miners' strike of 1983-84. The defeat of Arthur Scargill and the coal miners was undoubtedly a watershed in British labour history. According to one editorial of the time, it ended "30 years of dominant union power which had consigned this country to third-rate industrial status. Scargill's failure achieved what decades of exhortation did not. It enabled the labour movement to sever its atrophied link with the tribal loyalties of the 1920s, and with the 'them' and 'us' mentality of class-war slogans. In splitting his own union, losing its funds, and sending strikers back to work with nothing, Scargill opened the way to a new unionism based on the ballot box, free of ideological claptrap."[4]

But it took even more heated struggles than the miners' strike to force unions into acknowledging the necessity for reforms. The painful, year-long battle in 1985-86 between printers' unions and the management of *The Times* over the newspaper's move from central London to a new computerized plant in Wapping near the old London docks was a classic struggle of wills in the enterprise society. For months, unions tried their time-tested tactics of mass demonstrations and pickets, pitting themselves against mounted policemen. But British public opinion was no longer on their side. Significantly, the printers' opposition to what they considered management's use of new technology as an antiunion weapon was perceived as an attempt to preserve an old and irrational form of industrial organization.

"In our own union, militants were reinforcing the natural conservativism of our members," said Bill Jordan, the boyish-looking leader of the Amalgamated Union of Engineering Workers (AUEW). During the 1950s and 1960s, Jordan worked in the fastening industry in the West Midlands. "In those days, everything was expanding," he said. "We were comfortable, and we all resisted change, particularly the introduction of new technology." Brisk, lean and a non-drinker, Jordan challenges most stereotypes of British labour bosses. About all he shares with Arthur Scargill is his working class origins. "Fear of change is as natural as breathing with us, but by reinforcing the idea of class war, the (militant miners) were only making the situation worse." Jordan believed the rhetoric of Scargill and other militant trade unionists gave a misleading picture of the postindustrial labour movement in Britain. "The lesson of the failure to change had been learned by the vast majority of trade unions," he said, adding pointedly, "I wish it had been learned by some other institutions in society."

For all their power, the unions' responsibility for industrial change inevitably stopped at the factory gate. Finding new ways of working and living in a country where unemployment had become the norm for millions was beyond the power of any trade union. Even the most enlightened union bosses refused to address the problem of redefining what a "job" should be in an era when the nature of work itself was clearly changing. Dr. George Matthewson, chief executive of the Scottish Development Agency, said British prejudices about work had set back the country in international competition: "prejudices like the British macho ... notion that no job is a man's job unless you have to do it deafened and stripped to the waist." Matthewson spoke hopefully about "a future of people doing less work, different work, and a lot of that work being involved with helping other people rest and play."

Professor Charles Handy, a former oil executive who became a business school professor and one of the country's prominent thinkers on management, is the progenitor of many of the new ideas about work explored in the decade. His 1985 book, *The Future of Work*, captured the issue, behind the ferment both on the shop floor and in the office. He argued that Britain could not expect to assure a decent life for all its people, much less a successful place in the world economy, unless she re-examined the nature, as well as the patterns, of work. "We have, to put it crudely, made the job the only legitimate form of work and then priced many jobs so high that we have effectively priced them out of existence," he wrote.

One solution was to allow work to follow the patterns of change already at work in postindustrial society, rather than trying to fit management and production techniques into the artificial constraints of traditional jobs. Many people, he said, had already found the kind of work that best suited them, at home and in the community, even if it could not necessarily be called a "job." Why not encourage their resourcefulness with government help? He described the new patterns as a lifetime "portfolio of activities and relationships" that no longer fit classic concepts of a working career. By the time Handy's book was published, the definition of a "proper" job was already under attack. During the decade, for the first time in British history, white-collar workers outnumbered blue-collar workers. Between 1973 and 1983, the number of people employed in "non-manual" work grew from 43 per cent to 52 per cent of the British workforce.[5] But mass unemployment in Britain added a new dimension to a trend already at work throughout the West. The number of blue-collar workers was not just diminishing. They were disappearing; and with them was going an entire culture.

In 1986, two unemployed men living in a poverty-stricken public housing estate in Glasgow unsuccessfully applied for jobs at a new factory that was taking on workers. Later, one of the men moved out of the estate into a middle-class neighbourhood. When he went back to the factory, giving his new address, he got the job. Did his new location make the difference — or did he somehow present himself differently? Colin Roxburgh, a 34-year-old Glasgow development worker and the person who told me the story, believed that the traditional culture of being an employee had prevented most jobless people from finding new opportunities. "Most of them are people who until they lost their jobs were purely employees, living in houses that were publicly owned," he said. "Their ability to do things for themselves was taken from them. The culture of living close to your neighbours, of having your prospects determined by who you are and where you come from, is ingrained deep in the working-class soul of Britain. Going out on your own isn't a real choice for someone who's been unemployed for eight or nine years."

But it was possible to break through those barriers. Roxburgh took me in his car to a pub on the south side of Glasgow, at the edge of Barrowfield, a bleak public housing estate infamous in the city for its high crime rate and the gangs of young unemployed men who fought openly in the streets. Row on row of terraced cottages stretched into the Scottish urban mist. We parked near a huge, vacant lot that, until 18 months before, had housed a steel foundry employing 12,000 people. A feeling of menacing frustration seemed embedded in the sidewalks. As we parked, a passerby warned me, "You ought to be careful of your car round here."

It was the middle of the day, but the pub was already crowded with men playing snooker, nursing a drink, or simply staring at their reflections in the large mirror above the bar. The most noticeable aspect of the scene was the virtual absence of the cigarette smoke that usually hangs in wreaths in British pubs. Here, cigarettes were a sign of affluence. Only a few men had them in their hands. Colin took me into a back room, where a group of men and women were sitting around a table. When we walked in, conversation stopped. "We were just finishing our board of directors' meeting," one of the men volunteered with a grin.

It was not a joke. This board of directors' meeting may have had a more unorthodox setting than any in the City, but it was no less serious. We had walked in on the regular monthly meeting of the Barrowfield Estate's community service board. The members of the board were all unemployed and receiving state welfare, but they ran a business worth £250,000 a year. Several small companies were under their control — a caretakers' association, a window-cleaning firm, a printing shop, a welding and glazing operation, and even community transport service.

The last item of business on the agenda that day was a farewell lunch for Colin Roxburgh, who was about to go off to Canada and the United States for three months on a special fellowship. The young, blond, university-educated Roxburgh somehow did not look out of place in the company of the men in rough work clothes. They welcomed him as an equal, with no evidence of the usual smouldering resentment of working-class Britons.

I sat next to the chairman of the board, a former foundry worker in his fifties named Jimmy McDowall. "Barrowfield used to be a good place when everybody was working," he said. "At the end of the war, anybody who wanted work could get it. They didn't ask you what skills you had; they just took you on. Everybody helped everybody else." Sitting across the table was Willy Murray, 31, the company secretary. "What we have here now," he said, "is what I call the giro [unemployment cheque] syndrome. This community lives for Friday, when the cheques come in to the post office. If the postman is late, or he doesn't come, at 8:30 in the morning, there's 20 people walking in the streets, looking terrible. You wouldn't understand unless you lived through it."

Murray had been a bus driver for the local council until he was laid off. He found work as a tire fitter, a glazier and a barman. Each time, the job disappeared from under him. The experience could have confirmed Murray's bitterness at life. In his earlier working career, he had been a militant union shop steward prone to blame all the problems on management, but any bitterness he felt now was reserved for his old union comrades-in-arms. "They should have seen what was coming," he said. "Let's say you have a steel mill at Sheffield, where the workers demand a wage rise. When they get it, Glasgow steelworkers ask for it, too. But they have to fight for it, even though the company can't afford it. So they go on strike. The company closes down, and then everyone is out of a job, all because of workers competing with workers. As a result, a lot of people's faith in unions was shattered. I think we've gone beyond unions now."

Murray said the board of unemployed people had been conducting its own successful experiment in industrial relations since 1981 among the 210 employees working in their scattered businesses. All the people on the community business payroll had been, like the board directors, unemployed. Not only had they changed their approach to work, but they had worked out a system of management-employee relations that rivalled any of the systems in operation at factories and high-tech electronic workshops around Britain. "No one has gone out on strike," said Murray with a note of real triumph in his voice. "I think it's because we're all socially minded people. The kind of management we need in this country is the one that rolls up its shirtsleeves and goes to work, instead of sitting by itself in the office. That's what we've been doing here. We think in terms of worker participation. Everyone around here knows that if they can think of a better way to do something, all they have to do is come to see us, and we will listen."

On the face of it, the new relationship between management and labour had not made any difference to Murray's situation. He continued to be unemployed. The conflict-of-interest rules governing boards of directors prevented him from taking advantage of any of the new jobs started by the board. But Murray in fact has a job. The notion still startles him. Murray's expenses and living costs are paid in effect by the state, through his weekly unemployment cheques. But he is as productive a member of his community and his society as anyone on an assembly line. He has never found himself so active or involved with work. "When I worked eight hours a day, I just wanted to get paid and go home. If you said to me five years ago I would be a company secretary of a firm turning over this much money, I wouldn't have believed it."

Neither, he might have added, would anyone else in Britain.

Chapter 11

GREEN AND PLEASANT LAND

Wherever men have tried to
imagine a perfect life,
they have imagined a life where
men plough and sow,
not a place where there are great
wheels turning
and great chimneys vomiting
smoke.

— *William Butler Yeats.*

Peter and Jean Rix live in a fourteenth-century thatched cottage on a wind-ing country lane near Boxstead, two hours' drive from the metropolitan sprawl of London. Approaching the cottage in the stillness of an English country morning, I half-expected to see medieval peasants emerge from the old oak doors, yawn, and begin a day's work for their feudal lord. Instead, the very unmedieval figure of Peter Rix, a powerfully built man in his late fifties, with greying, curly hair, bright blue eyes, and a sun-red-dened face, invited me in for tea. The interior of the cottage dispelled any illusions I held about dirt floors and smoking hearths. Here was the very comfortable home of a prosperous farmer, well-endowed with indoor plumbing, pictures of grandchildren on the cabinet, and fox-hunting prints on the walls. The long wooden roof beams, painted black, were all that remained to suggest the cottage's centuries-old origins. Rix seemed to enjoy my surprise. Directly behind the cottage, he said, were a swimming pool and a tennis court. "I don't believe in false preservation," he declared. No sentence could have summed up his philosophy better.

The Rix cottage was the headquarters of a family farm that earned £1 million a year. Rix seemed genuinely amazed when I asked him if he ever tried to imagine how the people who occupied his house in the 1300s had thought and lived. "I'm just glad I'm not them," he said after a thought-ful pause. "Think how hard their lives must have been."

Rix has very little time for flights of historical fancy. With his two sons and a full-time workforce of 12, he farms 1,300 acres of onions, potatoes, and wheat. His unsentimentality is a refreshing contrast to the standard British approach to the countryside.

Britons believe they have a special and mystical affinity with the land, a belief that has not been affected by the fact that they are one of the world's most urbanized peoples. Although more than 80 per cent of the British live in towns with a population of at least 50,000, they still like to picture themselves as a rural nation. Civil servants and trade union leaders putter about in their gardens. Rock stars and politicians enjoy the fruits of their success in country estates. The Queen herself seems most in tune with the feelings of her subjects when she appears in public with the head scarf, sensible shoes, and shapeless coat of a country matron.

The rural myth has been central to the British national identity since the dawn of the industrial age. It has usually been associated with nostalgia for a golden, preindustrial past, and if Britons themselves have fallen victim to it, it is not hard to see why millions of tourists each year are similarly seduced by the moors, heaths, and forests of Albion. The literature of the industrial revolution, from Blake to Dickens, is filled with wistful praise for the "green and pleasant land" and with nostalgia for the close-knit village communities that were buried by urban sprawl. The decline of Empire and international prestige in the postwar era further intensified Britons' distrust of the Americanized urban culture that spread across Europe in the 1950s. The hunger for the pastoral is palpable, often satisfied by providing "country" names to public housing estates or building mock-Tudor cottages in the suburbs. Campaigns for "real ale" or "real bread" aim to recapture the lost qualities of village life, and environmental preservationists grow in numbers and strength. In the 1980s, ruralism has been an attractive antidote for industrial despair. Between the 1970s and mid-1980s, the National Trust — an organization devoted to saving Britain's large country houses — quadrupled in membership from 315,000 to 1.3 million. Other groups devoted to wildlife and nature have enjoyed similar success. Friends of the Earth increased its membership from 1,000 to 27,000 in 1986, and the Royal Society for the Protection of Birds grew from 98,000 to 466,000. Nearly every British town has a society dedicated to protecting monuments, country walks, or old crafts.[1]

Both the myths and the realities of the countryside have inevitably influenced the political debate in Britain's most trying decade. Thinkers and politicians on the right and the left borrowed essentially rural-based values in their efforts to rescue the country from its industrial malaise. The spirit of self-reliance and the traditional cohesion of the rural community formed an integral part of the appeal of Margaret Thatcher, as well as of the alternative thinkers like the "barefoot economists" who stressed the rejuvenation of local communities through self-help projects. Such appeals made a great deal of sense. Silicon Glen and the Cambridge

Science Park illustrated the advantages of a rural environment for some of the new patterns of life and work in postindustrial Britain. However, "false preservation," in Peter Rix's phrase, appealed to those who still had a stake in the values and conflicts of an earlier era. As long as the countryside was left intact and immaculate, a snapshot of fourteenth-century or seventeenth-century Britain, the entire nation was condemned to the status of a quaint museum exhibit. In fact, it was often easier to find real change in the countryside than in the cities, where the ruins of abandoned factories made it much more daunting to begin anew. A visitor was as likely to run across a well-run modern farm as an efficient factory in the 1980s — perhaps more likely.

Rix is as innovative and entrepreneurial as an electronic capitalist. The Rix agri-enterprise combines modern methods of land management with a willingness to use foreign goods and techniques. After tea, we drove in Rix's pickup truck to see one of his latest innovations for the automated farm. A German-made "cropper" machine was making quick work of a 50-acre field of onions. As I watched through streaming eyes, a lone driver operating the machine snapped the stalks across three parallel rows. Another machine gathered the onions lying on the field and shot them into a waiting pickup truck. It was a smartly efficient operation. Rix said it would take just three days to complete an onion harvest that had once taken weeks. Then they would begin planting wheat. Variety is part of the Rix approach. "Growing corn year after year," said Rix with his customary directness, "would be infinitely boring."

Automation has similarly transformed the storage process. Rix has installed special storehouses to keep the onions at uniform temperatures, allowing him to put them on the market only when the price is right. In one storehouse, 600 tonnes of onions were drying on huge platforms so that their skins could be attractively browned for the market. A complicated cooling and heating system kept the warehouse temperatures controlled. Three men stood by a conveyor belt picking out stones, while a man working a robot arm directed a continuous spray of onions to the other side of the shed.

But Rix's operation is not the large-scale industrial farming of North America. The devotion to high productivity and perpetual expansion typical of multimillion-dollar agri-businesses on the other side of the Atlantic fill him with a characteristically British dread. "The farmer in North America spends too much time making things bigger and better. He never enjoys life or has fun. You have to have fun at what you do." Rix was living up to his principles. When I met him, he was just back from a fishing holiday in Scotland. Earlier in the year, he had spent three weeks in the Seychelles. Some of his trips abroad were working holidays. In the previous five years, he had visited farmers in Canada, the U.S., New Zealand, and

Australia to check up, so to speak, on the competition. He explained, "It's what any good corporation should be doing."

Why shouldn't a farm be managed like an innovative, high-tech business in Silicon Glen — and be judged by the same standards? Rix's eldest son, John, 28, half-jokingly referred to the Boxstead land as "factory floor space." The notion was light years away from traditional British attitudes towards the land and its symbols. But, with reason, Britain's farmer-entrepreneurs felt the nation's manufacturing industry could learn something from them. Rix was as harsh as any of the social critics writing in London. "It makes me weep sometimes when I go to some firm and see separate loos [toilets] for directors and workers," said Rix. "I feel like ripping the nameplate off the door. It's the kind of thing that establishes the 'we and they' syndrome which has ruined industry in this country. This morning, I swept out our barn with three other people, because I wanted the job done before breakfast time. If I hadn't been there, a job like that would have taken twice as long. People tell me, 'Rixie, you don't have to do that.' But they're wrong; I have to do that."

In his travels, Rix was amazed to discover that Britain was not the only country in which a system of hierarchy operates in the workplace. When he asked a farmer in North Dakota how many employees he had, Rix was stunned at the reply. "He told me, 'There's just three of us, my wife, me and my son, and oh yes, there's the hired hands.' Hired hands! He didn't even count them as workers. How can you think of them as hired hands and expect them to feel part of your operation?"

Rix has introduced a limited form of worker participation on the farm. There is a twice-yearly meeting of staff and members of the Rix board of directors (made up of Rix, his wife, his two sons, a daughter, and their spouses). The system is less encompassing than the worker-control schemes operating in some progressive industries, but on a family farm, it is still revolutionary to think of farm labourers as members of the enterprise. "We tend to involve them as much as possible," said Rix, though he was vague about what such involvement amounted to. At the semiannual meetings, bonuses that sometimes amounted to 25 per cent of the basic wage were awarded as a rudimentary form of profit sharing. The basic wage on the Rix farm reflected the typically low pay scale in the agriculture sector — £110 for a 40 hour week — but Rix claimed his workers could average £8,000 a year. With rent-free accommodation and no commuting cost, it compared favourably with the income of a skilled manufacturing worker. And it was also well above the average farming income of approximately £4,000 after taxes.[2]

The unpredictability of farm income, caused by the vagaries of the weather and the market, is usually cited by farmers as the reason they cannot compete with industrial wages, but it is also one of the factors that have forced farmers like Rix into becoming innovative. By giving workers even a small stake in the operations, the enlightened farmer can assure himself of a stable workforce. In 1985, a hailstorm ruined crops in that part of the country. Rix stood up at the general meeting and told the assembled staff there would be no bonus that year. He and the family waited nervously for complaints, but they never came. Finally, as Rix told it, "Someone got up and said that they rather expected that, but if it happens next year, we shall expect a change of management." Rix was candid about his motivations. "We would rather make less money in a congenial atmosphere. But you don't, of course." He paused for effect with a grin. "You make more money."

Not all British farmers could follow Rix's example even if they wanted to. British agriculture has not escaped the economic crisis. Average farm income dropped 43 per cent in 1985.[3] Small farm units in particular were affected by the application of monetarist policies that raised the cost of farm equipment and loans. Rix, however, believed uneconomic farms, like inefficient factories, needed to be driven to the wall. "The small family farm is almost a social evil," he said. The farmer who clings to his unprofitable parcels of land is setting a bad example for his children, as well as giving them very little opportunity in the world, Rix argued. "There are some very good agricultural people in this country — I wish we had as good industrial people — [but] a lot of farmers, maybe as much as 50 per cent, should be out now. They're not really keen on farming. It's a stupid thing to spend your life doing something you don't like. I think they should sell out and invest the proceeds. In farming or anything, you can't have preconceived ideas, I learned that in the Navy; there are no excuses. You just have to find a way of doing the job."

Like most British farmers, Rix got his early lessons in modern economic realities from the Common Market. When Britain joined the European Economic Community in 1973, the resulting jolt in attitudes had the same impact on agriculture as the manufacturing crisis was to have on British industry over the next decade. The European dimension widened the outlook of most farmers, while it deepened the gulf between them and the rest of Britain. Common Market subsidies created the "Eurofarmer," an extraordinary protected class of producers who no longer needed to depend on the unpredictable domestic market to sell their crops. Across Europe, they piled up controversial grain mountains and wine lakes. In Britain, their special status not only insulated them from the problems other sectors of the economy were having in selling their high-priced goods abroad, but constituted a threat to national sovereignty. Decisions about production quotas and prices were more likely to be made in Brussels, where the Common Market agricultural policy was formed, than in Whitehall.

The economic crisis of the 1980s sharpened the conflict in the countryside. The prosperous farmer became a target of censure in the press. From a folk figure who was the repository of Britain's most cherished myths about the purity of the land, he turned into a threat to the country's green heritage. A 1987 report to the European Parliament claimed that 40 per cent of British farmland was threatened by erosion because of intensive farming. Nearly five million acres were at risk from erosion of a "higher than acceptable degree," the report charged, leading one newspaper to say Britain was "one of the worst examples of an environment being despoiled by modern industrial farming techniques."[4]

The following comment, published in 1980, was typical of the fears aroused in the middle classes by the activities of the Eurofarmer. Between the lines, it was possible to read a note of mute accusation that the farmer had somehow betrayed his role as keeper of the national identity. "The English landscape is under sentence of death," wrote Marion Shoard, a former assistant secretary of the Council for the Preservation of Rural England. "The executioner is not the industrialist or the property speculator, whose activities have touched only the fringes of our countryside. Instead, it is the figure traditionally viewed as the custodian of the rural scene — the farmer."[5]

Such comments were received by Rix with a fatalistic shrug. "We farmers are a minority," he said. "When people are desperate for food, then we're important. When there's no desperation, and they can get their food anywhere, then we just disappear."

Nevertheless, he has not been able to escape the debate. His neighbours have accused him of destroying land contours and cutting down irreplaceable hedgerows. Rix took one elderly, upper-class gentleman who complained that too many trees were being cut down to a stand of new trees he had just planted elsewhere. "I don't want to preserve a tree just because it's old," Rix told him, "especially if I can plant a dozen trees like it. We can only preserve the countryside out of profits, not out of losses." But he made little headway. In the 1980s, Rix found himself the target of a curious alliance of the old landed establishment and the new middle-class "squirearchy." Boxstead's proximity to London made it a nesting ground for middle-class city-dwellers, eager for country living. Having profited from Thatcherite policies that increased competition in insurance, banking, and the stock market, they nevertheless become anti-Thatcherists when the same policies were applied to the land.

In a private joke between themselves, Peter and Jean Rix divided their new neighbours into "strivers and thrivers." Thrivers were willing to accept the changes in the countryside as part of the price to be paid for their ability to enjoy it. Strivers wanted the countryside to remain as they always had imagined it, pretty and unsullied, for their personal enjoyment — even if it ignored the needs of those who must earn their living from it.

The strivers are easy to spot in Boxstead, Rix said. They are on the train to London first thing in the morning in their pinstripe suits and bowler hats, and they return at the end of the day looking shattered, with three or four drinks already inside them. On Saturdays and Sundays, they dress up in Wellington boots and windbreakers and try their best to be "agricultural." Local farmers usually shun them like the plague. Rix knew one wealthy would-be country squire, with whom he would go out for an afternoon's "shooting" in the man's new Range Rover, but the acquaintance didn't last. The man kept trying to persuade Rix to cut the afternoon short because he had to return home to make phone calls. "That man won't make old bones." Rix shook his head sympathetically.

The thrivers, on the other hand, are more relaxed. They are better adjusted to the evolving traditions of country life. Rix felt thrivers were closest to his own coolly unsentimental ideas of how to rebuild the countryside. "It should be a part of farming to provide leisure as well as food," said Rix. "On our farm, we let people fish in our reservoirs, and we allow people public access to walking paths. It's also good business."

One drizzly summer day, on a hike in Cornwall, I came upon a crowd of men and women staring intently at a patch of shrubbery in a muddy clearing. They were motionless, like figures in a medieval frieze, and when they had to say anything they acted as if they were in church, speaking in soft whispers. As I edged closer, I discovered the object of their attention. A tiny bird was busily hopping back and forth in a gully, apparently oblivious of its rapt audience. A man in Wellington boots, noticing my puzzled expression, said the bird belonged to a species rarely seen in Britain. "The word got around that it was here, and we all dropped what we were doing and came over," he said. "Some people even came up from London."

No matter who they are, or to what class they belong, the British seem happiest in the countryside. On any Sunday, outside any major town, Britons can be seen walking, bird-watching, playing cricket, or simply spending hours in a roadside country pub. Any notion that the British were defeated by the industrial trauma of the 1980s could be put to rest by a walk in the countryside — or even a drive through the suburbs.

"This country is a mass of dedicated gardeners," said Professor Charles Handy. "You might not notice it, but if you got off the motorways, and took the byways through Suffolk, for instance, you would see the most wonderful gardens. They aren't the gardens of middle-class people. They're working-class homes. Gardening requires initiative, hard work — and those qualities have obviously not disappeared in Britain. What we have been bad at is putting it into our large workplaces."

Professor Handy is an example of the healthy "thriver" who takes advantage of the changes in the countryside. Following his own advice about making room for younger people, he gave up a tenured teaching post in the London Business School long before he had to retire. He found himself spending more and more time in his summer cottage in East Anglia. The sense of community and the willingness to take risks, both congenial to his philosophy about the necessary conditions for a new work ethic, were rarely to be found in the dying manufacturing culture of Britain. Like the Bishop of Durham, Handy found in nature an analogy for Britain's contemporary condition. "You are constantly reminded in the country that there is no possibility of evolution without death," Handy said.

Handy's East Anglia is a vivid illustration of his point. A lovely area of salt marshes and pleasant farms, it was a rural backwater for decades. The road to Handy's cottage twists through fields by the North Sea, past ancient Norman churches, and the sites of forgotten battles between Saxon chieftains and Scandinavian invaders. The coast is dotted with the remains of small villages, that were once great centres of medieval commerce and politics, now swallowed up by the tides. East Anglia was bypassed during the development boom of the 1960s and 1970s, but in the 1980s, it became one of the most dynamic areas of the country. The Common Market, new technology and, in a larger sense, Britain's decline as a major Atlantic trading power were the factors responsible for East Anglia's regeneration. Deepwater North Sea ports like Felixstowe, which has always been privately operated, have been turned into thriving centres of business, in contrast to the atmosphere of decay that oppressed the British Ports Authority-operated ports of Liverpool and Glasgow in the early years of the decade. For most farmers in the north of England, it was cheaper to send their goods over longer distances to Britain's east coast for shipment to Europe on the large container ships. The evolving east-west axis of England is certain to become even more pronounced in the 1990s with the construction of a Channel tunnel linking Britain and France. The changes are visible in the brisk, efficient attitudes of businessmen and the traffic-clogged streets in most eastern towns; but there is also a type of "new Briton" who has begun to thrive there, anxious in typical British fashion not to let progress destroy the special quality of the community.

In the old seaside resort of Southwold, an eighteenth-century inn called The Crown was reopened in 1985 as a gathering place, with weekend theatre, chamber music concerts, wine-tastings, and cultural meetings. Few expected a project that catered obviously to young urban professionals to succeed so far from London, but it rapidly became one of the most attractive centres on the Norfolk coast. Significantly the presence of regular visitors from London did not drive away the locals.

"We wanted to build up a sort of on-going life in the place by creating activities which should go on at every small town, and naturally should be focused on this sort of inn," said Simon Loftus, the man responsible for rehabilitating the Crown. "There isn't naturally within most English country towns anything like the equivalent of a simple, French country hotel-restaurant which is the natural focus of life and activity, and where everything happens, whether it's weddings, political meetings, or concerts."

I met Loftus, a forceful, articulate 40-year-old, in the Groucho Club in London. It was a fitting venue. Groucho started in the 1980s as an alternative to London's stuffy club circuit, a place where the new entrepreneurial and artistic elite of the city could feel at home. We sat in an upstairs room, looking out at the bookstores and restaurants which were beginning to crowd out the district's infamous massage parlours. In any previous decade since the war, someone like Loftus would have made a successful career in London's urban environment — perhaps retreating to a countryside estate for peace and quiet. But he was happy to be a visitor to the city, and a "thriver" in the countryside. Already a successful entrepreneur when he started the Crown, he had established a prosperous, "up-market" wine retail business in his family brewery in East Anglia. He had never been tempted to move his operations to London. "We are already selling internationally, so it doesn't matter where we are based. I love living in the country, and I'm determined that we should not regard country living as a backwater [existence], where you are deprived of town activities. The way of doing that of course is to create more life and activity in the country."

Over coffee, Loftus tried to explain his motivations. "I was brought up within a Catholic family, with a very strong sense of moral responsibilities," he said. "It wasn't a strict morality, but a sort of social attitude. I have always felt it would be inconceivable to leave the world without having made it a better place. I know that sounds rather pretentious, but my family is Anglo-Irish; we weren't absolutely part of the genteel English environment."

Loftus's strong sense of moral obligation, as he suggested, makes him different from most urban-oriented Britons. It also illustrates another aspect of the countryside's impact on British life in the 1980s. Older conservative values, joined with the newer innovative attitudes, can be expected to provide fresh spiritual strength to handle the problems of the decade. "We think the strength of a community is in the family," said Peter Rix, "and the strength of a nation is in the community."

Peter Rix, like most people in Britain, has not completely managed to get out from under the dead hand of history. Despite the farmer's disdain for the medieval "romance" of his house, he was himself locked into a feudal situation. More than half his 1,300 acres belong to a local baronet, Sir Joshua Rowley, whose family has owned the land for centuries. Under the antiquated system of land tenure, Rix's freedom of operation was as limited as that of the tenants on other estates. The relationship with his landlord has sometimes been as irritating as the separate "loos" for directors and employees Rix saw in industrial plants. "I've only got Sir Joshua to see me as an equal in the past five years," Rix admitted, "but that's when we go out shooting together. Twice a year, it's 'Joshua and Pete', but the rest of the time, it's Sir Joshua."

The hierarchical relationship extended to the economics of running the farm. Although Rix approached his work as a private farming entrepreneur he was still legally a tenant on someone else's land. Sir Joshua's agents can tell him what to plant. The storehouses and other farm buildings constructed by Rix are officially the property of his landlord. Sir Joshua's daughter, who lives in town, will inherit the land when the baronet dies. If she decides to sell out, particularly to meet the steep British inheritance taxes, the inherent limitations of Rix's position would be clear. "As far as I'm concerned," he said with his customary stoicism, "it is a business arrangement, and we are contractors." Rix believed Sir Joshua's daughter wouldn't sell. "Land prices are not what they used to be," he said. "Even if she does (sell), we'll probably get the first option to buy." However, Rix is prepared to accept what fate, and the British land tenure system, deal out to him. "If we lose out, we'll just go somewhere else," he said.

Rix and his wife were building a retirement bungalow nearby. His younger son would soon move into the medieval cottage with his family. It would mean, he confessed, his effective eclipse as farm manager. "Whoever lives in this house is the boss," Rix said. I was nonplussed. "You mean you'll give up this beautiful old house?" I asked. He smiled without bothering to answer.

Chapter 12

DISTURBERS OF THE PEACE

Dear George, let me have the honour and glory of
marrying a man who has gained a seat in the
Parliament of Great Britain! Of all positions
which a man may attain that, to me, is
the grandest . . .

— Anthony Trollope,
in his novel Can You Forgive Her?, *1864.*

Former Prime Minister James Callaghan could barely contain his rage. He stalked to the platform of the cavernous Brighton Conference Centre like a boxer about to enter the ring. It was October 1983, and the British Labour Party was holding its annual political conference in the seaside resort of Brighton, a few months after it had suffered one of the worst defeats in a national election in its history. Sitting with the delegates, Callaghan had heard himself named as one of the men responsible for the catastrophe. While "Sunny Jim" simmered, speakers attacked him for criticizing the Labour Party's campaign plank of unilateral disarmament. Virtually branded a traitor to the party he had served all his adult life, Callaghan had finally had enough.

"What the [disarmament] movement has failed to understand," he said in the ringing tones he once used from the front benches of Parliament, "is that it reversed the traditional policy of the Labour Party, on which we had fought eleven succeeding elections, without any real attempt to convince the British people that what we were doing was right." As the clamour in the hall grew louder, the 71-year-old Callaghan's voice strengthened. "You made a fundamental mistake in believing that by going on marches and passing resolutions without any attempt to tell the British people what the consequences were, that you could carry their votes," he said. "You lost millions of votes and you will continue to lose millions of votes." The rest of his speech was drowned out. Hundreds of delegates rose from their seats to give him a thumbs-down signal. *"You* lost the votes! *You* lost the votes!" they chanted.

That poignant moment captured the distinctive temper of British politics in the 1980s. Public life was characterized by a belligerence that startled many Britons. Striking miners and printworkers, the protesting antinuclear women of Greenham Common, minority rights activists, animal rights crusaders, and environmentalists, among many others, brought the tactics of confrontation onto the centre stage of national politics. Operating in a "grey area" between legitimate political lobbying and radical protest, they tried to shock the British public out of what they considered its moral neutrality. The 1960s and 1970s had also been a time of unsettling activism, but the 1980s introduced an apocalyptic tone that matched many protesters' perceptions of the threat posed to Britain's future by the industrial crisis. "We had to articulate our concerns in a way appropriate to the Eighties," explained Joan Ruddock, chairwoman of the Campaign for Nuclear Disarmament (CND). "In the Sixties, we were constantly being told, 'You didn't go through the war; you don't know what it was like.' But now we've been through a kind of war, where kids went hungry and people were fighting for jobs."

However, as for everything else in British life, it was possible to find historical precedents for this explosion of crusading energy. The mid-Victorian novelist Anthony Trollope, who wrote at a time of great changes in technology and the distribution of wealth, portrayed the new middle classes' frustration with a nineteenth-century political establishment whose approach to Britain's problems had the cautious inoffensiveness of mild beer drawn from a pub tap. "All our political offences against civilization have come from men drawing it mild," declared a character in the 1864 novel *Can You Forgive Her?*. "Why is it that Englishmen can't read and write as Americans do? Why can't they vote as they do even in Imperial France? Why are they serfs, less free than those whose chains were broken ... in Russia? Why is the Spaniard more happy, and the Italian more contented? Because men in power have been drawing it mild!"[1]

A new, self-assertive middle class of white-collar trade unionists, entrepreneurs, computer technicians, teachers, and lawyers similarly considered "drawing it mild" an affliction of political life in the 1980s. They often justified their challenge to public decorum by pointing to established British institutions that, by failing to reflect the needs of the country, were helping to accelerate its decline.

The parliamentary system was an easy target. For most of its venerable history, the Parliament at Westminster was able to institutionalize, and in some ways anaesthetize, the conflict between classes and economic interests; but as Britain slipped in international prestige and economic strength, Parliament appeared stagnant and impotent — a talking shop that even its members did not take seriously. The House of Commons' leather-lined

gentlemen's-club atmosphere and arcane rules made it a Victorian ana-
chronism in twentieth-century Britain. It reflected only dimly the changes
in British complexion and attitudes since the war. There were almost no
non-whites and relatively few women serving in the chamber as sitting
MPs. The caucuses of the principal political parties were composed of people of similar educational backgrounds and similar lifestyles who flung
ritual insults at each other with little conviction.

If Parliament provided a one-dimensional picture of Britain, the bureaucracy and civil service were even less equipped to face up to the challenges
of a modern, postindustrial state. Pinstripe-suited mandarins with the
accents of Oxford and Cambridge ran the Whitehall establishment as if it
were the last relic of Empire. The government was among the most secretive in the West. The country's newspapers were still subject to censorship
rules left over from the Second World War, and a disturbing number of
decisions taken by unelected and unaccountable civil servants governed
the daily lives of millions.[2] Britain's government resembled one of the
medieval castles that dotted the countryside: a beautiful structure wonder-
fully arranged for a function it could no longer fulfil. Jonathan Porritt, the
mild-mannered, Eton-educated scion of an aristocratic family, who led
Britain's Ecology Party from the mid-1970s to the mid-1980s, said: "To
those of us who live in the middle of it, our class-based politics is a nightmare. It has led to the paralysis of the political system in this country in a
most damaging way."

Nevertheless, many in the tolerant, quiet middle of British politics felt
the cure for paralysis was as bad as the disease. They had no trouble trac-
ing the blame for the pugnacious climate of the 1980s. According to them,
the arrival of a radical female prime minister raised confrontation to a
political norm. There was a great deal of truth to the charge. In setting out
to shake up British society, Margaret Thatcher reawakened the natural
quarrelsomeness Britons had spent much of their political history trying to
tame. She made little secret of her intent to destroy the consensus politics
she had inherited from her predecessors. The prime minister was more
successful than even she had dared to imagine. It was small wonder that
both her admirers and her detractors regarded that success as one of her
principal contributions to British politics.

A writer in the left-of-centre newspaper the *Guardian* once suggested
that Thatcher was different from previous British leaders in that she was
not afraid to make her moral convictions a basis of policy. "Margaret
Thatcher knows that there is no spiritual peacetime," said Elizabeth
Cottrell. "Life is a constant battle between good and evil, in which neutrality serves only Satan. She has therefore made morality, and especially
political morality respectable again. ... To the British, fed on the opium
of the welfare state, and secure in the knowledge that someone else

will pay, she often seems a disturber of the peace. . . ."[3]

"Disturber of the peace" managed to describe both Thatcher and the activist-politicians who arose during the 1980s in her shadow. The prime minister's impatience with the status quo was shared by a variety of special interest groups campaigning for change in the 1980s. "We are part of a new politics in Britain," Iltydd Harrington, deputy leader of Ken Livingstone's Greater London Council, once told me proudly. "It's getting hard to ignore us."

Jim Callaghan would have agreed. By the time the new politics had drowned him out in Brighton, the forces that had transformed political debate during the decade were already changing the structure of the Labour Party. The revolution inside what was once one of the most powerful and stable left-wing political parties in the West represented as much of a watershed in British postwar history as the rise of Thatcherism.

The roots of Labour's problems could be traced to the same intellectual ferment and impatience with Britain's declining status that had produced the leadership of Margaret Thatcher. But the final cataclysm was triggered by Thatcher herself. Her victory in 1979 inflicted a wound from which the party did not seem likely to recover. Labour did not merely lose that election. It was humiliated by it. The party's share of the vote dropped to 37 per cent, its lowest since 1931. The election raised, not for the first time, the possibility that Labour might drift into political obscurity. The party's fortunes were to sink even lower in the election of 1983. It would recover only some of its former support in 1987, but at the beginning of the 1980s, it was already clear that Labour needed a long-overdue reassessment.[4]

The party of the British working class had outgrown the slogans and dreams of its founders. Britain's economic prosperity in the 1960s had diminished Labour's traditional constituency. Trade unions continued to supply the majority of funds to the party, but rank-and-file members were deserting Labour in droves. At the beginning of the decade, the party had drifted into a kind of middle-class welfare corporatism.[5]

"The Labour Party was no longer the party of change; that was the Conservative Party. The Labour Party was the party of the Establishment, the party of steady-as-we-go, leave it to Jim," said Chris Mullin, one of a growing vocal group of young Labour Party members who were already challenging the monopoly control of Labour MPs over the party line.[6]

With the election of Michael Foot as party leader and successor to Callaghan in 1980, a showdown between the emerging new intellectual forces inside Labour became inevitable. The white-haired Foot was a talented journalist and public speaker with roots in the party's left wing. A prominent antinuclear campaigner during the 1950s, he had served in minor cabinet posts, but he had never been considered leadership material during the years when Labour was building its image as a responsible government of the centre. It was a measure of how much things had changed that the party turned to him at the beginning of the decade as a moderate who could work in the ruins left by the Thatcher victory.

The critical dividing issue between Callaghan and those who rudely shouted him down was Clause Four of the original Labour manifesto, which called for public ownership of the major sectors of the economy. Labour governments had long since ignored the clause, preferring to blend nationalization with private enterprise. The mixed economy, tacitly accepted by all the major parties, was the key compromise of postwar British politics. It had allowed the country to create a successful welfare state without seriously disturbing the principles of free-market capitalism; but a new generation of idealistic reformers believed the abandonment of Clause Four had made Labour an accomplice to Britain's political and economic stagnation.

Many disillusioned young people, eschewing traditional party politics in disgust, took up the fringe politics that were to have such a destabilizing effect during the decade. Many others — not all of them young — saw in the Labour Party's 1979 defeat a chance to recall it to its roots. "Our failure to win has always been that we are not able to mobilize our natural constituency," said Tony Benn, a former Labour minister who had been making a name for himself as a radical in the 1970s. "Power just slipped through our fingers, because we were saying nothing very useful to people."[7]

The eloquent, aristocratic Benn became the lightning rod for disenchantment. His outspoken criticism of policies with which he had once been identified and his call for greater democracy inside the party inspired numerous groups of radical reformers. The first stirrings of rebellion occurred in the mid-1970s, when a small group of left-wing intellectuals and MPs began plotting to cleanse Labour's ranks of "right-wing" accommodationism, in much the same way the band of right-wing thinkers and MPs that was to coalesce around Margaret Thatcher aimed to purify their party of the taint of welfarism. By the beginning of the decade, the "hard left" was an active, unmistakable force with adherents among the young and well-educated. The Militant Tendency, as one of the most well-organized Labour splinter groups was called, joined radical white-collar trade union leaders and socialist and activist groups to advocate changes in the rules by which the party had been governed. Militant Tendency advocated a "mandatory" reselection of MPs, in which the parliamentarian had to submit his voting record and his activities for the approval of his constituency party once a year, and it campaigned to give rank-and-file party members and trade unions an explicit role in the election of a party leader.

More democracy was something everyone in the party could accept, but the proposed reforms were developed in a self-consciously clandestine way that fitted the climate of mutual suspicion in the party. The reformers operated out of "cells" that infiltrated local constituency organizations. Labour Party members had been a relaxed, jovial lot, retiring to the local pub after a few hours of passing resolutions. The radicals stayed later and worked harder than anyone else, managing in the end to elect their own people to party associations. Few people realized what was happening until radical calls for workers' rights and class struggle began to be sounded from the pleasant garden suburbs and sleepy industrial towns that had been Labour strongholds for years.

The highly politicized middle-class "Bennite" was soon an ineradicable presence in Labour and trade union conferences around the country. Benn offered his own explanation of why the militants began to take on an almost sinister aspect within the party. "What frightened people was the thought that the Labour Party might be being serious," he said. "If I were to sum up the real critique of what we were doing, it wasn't that we were hard left, or extreme or revolutionary, it was that we were serious. The heart of the analysis ... has been the understanding that however revolutionary a speech may sound at conference, you go and have a chat [in] the lobby afterwards, and laugh about it. ... We weren't playing games."[8]

Michael Foot was both intellectually and politically incapable of controlling the hard left. Under his leadership, the party reorganized itself, giving trade unions and constituency organizations 70 per cent of the block votes in a new "electoral college." Parliamentary MPs who were supposed to have been the flag-carriers of Labour now had reduced power to elect the party leader. While the electoral college appeared to broaden party democracy, it in fact handed authority to a well-organized group in constituency and union organizations who had no mandate from their members to remake the party in Militant Tendency's idealized image. The rule changes represented the last straw for a group of equally determined opponents of Militant Tendency.

Many moderate Labour MPs, privately disturbed by the strength of the hard left, had already been involved with plans to create a new centre-left grouping in the party. They were predominantly MPs and ministers from the Callaghan and Wilson governments who had led the successful campaign to bring Britain into the Common Market. This "European" group despaired of the party's future as much as Militant Tendency did, but for different reasons. The polarization of British politics between left and right perpetuated the notion of a class struggle that was no longer relevant to Britain, they said. Philosophical relics of another age, like Clause Four, should not only be ignored but torpedoed. The moderates believed they had proof they were on the right track. One poll in 1980 found more than 55 per cent of Britons would welcome the creation of a real party of the "centre."

On January 25, 1981, the civil war inside Labour assumed its final, irrevocable shape. Four leading members of the Labour Party, Roy Jenkins, William Rodgers, Shirley Williams, and David Owen, announced the formation of a Council for Social Democracy that would work toward defeating the hard left. Meeting in Owen's home in the Limehouse section of the East London docklands area, they issued a statement to the press setting out in all but name the principles of a new party. "We recognize that for those people who have given much of their lives to the Labour Party, the choice that lies ahead will be deeply painful. But we believe the need for a realignment of British politics must now be faced," they said. The Limehouse Declaration, as it came to be called, sent a fresh wind blowing through British politics. Within two months, the same four people, backed by thousands of new supporters, announced the formation of the Social Democratic Party.

Although the SDP was explicitly intended to rescue Britain from the extremes of politics, it was itself an extreme step. The founding members, popularly dubbed "The Gang of Four," described in language that called up images of personal crisis, in the hurt tones of abandoned children, their decision to break ranks with the party that had nurtured their intellectual faith. "We had no consciousness of anywhere to go [at first]," remembered Shirley Williams, a former education minister and the most volatile member of the group. "We just saw ourselves as unable to continue." (Only a few months before, she had publicly dismissed the idea of a new party of the centre as having "no roots, no principles, no philosophy, and no values.") William Rodgers, a former minister of transport, confessed, "I'd reached a crisis that nobody could resolve but myself."[9]

Roy Jenkins, the oldest member of the group and in many ways its spiritual leader, had also originally doubted a centre party could succeed. But his conversion was total. Aged 60 in 1981, Jenkins had been a Chancellor of the Exchequer and president of the European Economic Commission. He once admitted that he began searching for a new political home when he realized he was no longer a socialist. Traditional socialism was too hidebound to respond to the needs of British society, he said. "We cannot successfully survive unless we can make our society more adaptable, and an unadaptable political system works heavily against this," he said in a famous 1979 BBC lecture that presented the idea of a new party for the first time. "Politicians cannot cling defensively to their present somewhat ossified party and political system while convincingly advocating the acceptance of change everywhere else in industry and society."[10] Jenkins envisioned a streamlined Labour Party that could take its place alongside the other modernizing social democratic parties in Europe.

David Owen, a former foreign secretary, was the most fascinating figure of all. A medical doctor who represented the Royal Navy town of

Portsmouth in Parliament, he disliked the "soft left" almost as much as the militants did. He was a frank admirer of Thatcher, often praising her resolution and forcefulness. In return, he was said to be one of the few parliamentary opponents Thatcher took seriously. Owen had his own solution to Britain's political paralysis, espousing a radical democratic socialism which combined an attack on monopoly power with a strong defence of the profit motive. Married to an American literary agent, Owen was closer to being an American-style politician than a British one. He had the glowering good looks of a matinée idol and a talent for direct and cutting oratory that set him apart from traditional parliamentary obfuscation. Some of his admirers said that his magnetism recalled the young John F. Kennedy, but there were even more striking similarities with Thatcher (who some also accused of being in the American mould). However, his Thatcherite impatience with British postindustrial defeatism was tempered by a concern for the social implications of her policies. "Our basic problem is that we have been in relative economic decline for 10 or 20 years," he told me in his office in 1984. "We were the victims of many things beyond our control, but we still needed to become more efficient, more modern. If we were more entrepreneurial, more risk-taking, and maintained our social consciousness, we might have a more attractive country to live in."

The formation of the SDP disturbed the peace of the other major parties. Several Labour MPs immediately announced they would sit as SDP members, and the worldwide publicity generated by the party's birth both shocked and infuriated those who stayed within the Labour Party. Years later, Michael Meacher, a member of the moderate left, said that no one had understood the depth of the split at the time: "Had I realized that it was going to be as damaging as that, perhaps we would have made more effort to prevent it occurring." Although the Conservatives at first hoped the new party would produce the long-awaited disintegration of Labour, it soon became clear the SDP was equally attractive to Tories put off by hard-right Thatcherism. One Tory MP even crossed the parliamentary floor to join the SDP ranks, and there were many others who admitted privately that they found the SDP approach congenial. The party membership grew to 80,000 within the first few months. The volunteers who poured in to help stuff envelopes and answer phones came from the progressive and newly affluent layer of British society: professionals, workers in the media and publishing worlds, entrepreneurs. In the cutting phrase of Roy Hattersley, another moderate Labour leader who stayed on, the SDP's principal aim appeared to be making Britain a safe place for "credit card holders."

Like most stereotypes, the picture of the SDP as a group of middle-class yuppies concentrated in England's southern counties contained an element of fact, but the point was often overlooked that this group remained the least represented in the British political scene. Unable to accept Thatcherism, they also found the combination of old Labour nineteenth-century rhetoric and the new left indigestible. Many of them were sympathetic to the Liberal Party, once the champion of the rising middle class of industrial England. But the Liberal tradition of strong individualism represented too much of a break with their collectivist past.

David Steel, the boyish-looking and sharp-witted Liberal leader, was one of the most popular politicians in the country. Although he had never held national office, he had skilfully deployed the tiny force of Liberals in Parliament to occupy the centre ground until the SDP arrived. He lost little time in proposing talks with Social Democratic leaders on running candidates jointly in future elections. It was a natural alliance. The Liberals had a strong, battle-hardened campaign organization in the field, and the SDP had the glamour and air of seriousness long missing in the party of Lloyd George. The compact was made official following a Liberal Party conference in Llandudno, North Wales, in 1982. Together, the two parties hoped to take advantage of polls showing early disenchantment with both Thatcher and Foot — and in the process short-circuit the lengthy growing pains of most new political coalitions. It was an uneasy alliance from the start. Many Liberals suspected that the SDP harboured a secret admiration for Thatcher, and the SDP in turn distrusted the Liberals' "left-wing," which was showing a disturbing inclination to support policies such as nuclear disarmament.[11]

The first two years of the SDP-Liberal Alliance proved a surprising success. Roy Jenkins decided to risk running in a by-election in Warrington, a staunch Labour seat in the heart of England. To the amazement of most observers, and the shock of the other major parties, he came close to winning. SDP or Liberal candidates won majorities on a number of municipal councils around the country, and parliamentary by-elections established the coalition's growing strength. Polls repeatedly gave them up to 30 per cent of the national vote. If the Warrington results had been translated nationally, the SDP-Liberal Alliance would have gathered 501 seats in the next Parliament.

Such statistical sleight-of-hand only revealed the main obstacle to an Alliance breakthrough. As long as Britain retained a parliamentary constituency system in which the candidate with the largest number of votes gained the seat, the Alliance's support across the country would never be reflected in the number of seats it won. Only a form of proportional representation that allocated parties seats in Parliament according to their share of the national vote, as used in many European countries, would make the Alliance a serious contender for power in Britain. Accordingly, the Liberals and the SDP made electoral reform a key plank of their party manifestoes. Their arguments, not surprisingly, were ignored by other parties, but the point was hard to ignore after the 1983 election. Although the Alliance picked up almost as many popular votes in the country as the Labour Party, it won only 23 seats in 1983. It was an important break-through in an election that finally jarred loose most of the assumptions of British political life.

In May 1983, Margaret Thatcher won a sweeping parliamentary majority of 130 seats, the largest won by a Tory prime minister this century. Politi-cal analysts found themselves groping to explain the apparent popularity of a government that presided over one of the country's most catastrophic economic eras. They compared Michael Foot's campaign across the coun-try, a series of old-style barnstorming meetings, to the slick, media-orches-trated tour of the prime minister; and they pointed out that Foot had been hamstrung by one of the most explicitly left-wing party platforms Labour had ever presented. The memories of the Falklands triumph were also said to have given Thatcher an aura of invincibility. As we have already seen at Brighton, ideologues inside the Labour Party found their own scapegoats.

The truth was more prosaic. Thatcher won less of the popular vote than she had won in 1979, but she captured the support of those areas of the country, and those sectors of the population, that had no vested interests in the old power struggles of British politics. The Thatcherian vision of liberation from the state had made a direct impact on their lives. Cuts in interest rates and income taxes had put more money in their pockets; the beginnings of the assault on bureaucracy and red tape were giving them new choices.[12] Conservative "wets" had warned the prime minister to moderate her image of radicalism if she wanted to succeed. They were proved wrong. To a certain extent, the Thatcher victory in 1983 justified the arguments of the militant Labour left who had urged similar radical visions of the future. But Labour needed more than structural reform to prove that it could generate new ideas. The Conservatives were still clearly the party of change.

One evening in 1980, Geoff Edge, a defeated Labour MP, invited a group of friends to his home for a discussion of the losses suffered by Labour the previous year. His guests were fellow university lecturers and employees of local government in the Birmingham area who, like him, were also searching for a way to respond to the manufacturing crisis in the Mid-lands. The discussion in Edge's living room produced the West Midlands Enterprise Board, one of the most intriguing responses to the 1980s' indus-trial crisis. The WMEB combined the functions of an investment bank and regional development body, and it soon became the most successful exam-ple of local initiative across the country. Since 1982, it has pumped more than £10 million in public funds into struggling business enterprises around the region. It filled the vacuum left by municipalities, who no longer had the money or authority to act, and the central government, which plainly refused to act.

The WMEB, with Edge as director, chose its investments carefully. They had to be small or medium-sized companies, owned locally, which were willing to give the board a share of management control. The "hands-on" approach, a phrase Edge uses often, ensured the investment would be carefully monitored and also that it would fulfil its founders' principal goal: to develop new skills and jobs in a region where manufacturing had reached a dead end. The enterprise board established a crucial link between industrial and political responses to British decline, as it found itself getting involved in the complete process of industrial revival, by funding training centres and courses to provide the workers for the new industrial technology. One such WMEB-funded project was the training complex started by Dennis Turner, the unemployed welder, in Bilston.

The WMEB was one of a number of projects in the mid-1980s that revived municipal activism. "Cities have always played a vital role in development in Britain," Edge said. "Birmingham, for instance, had the first municipal bank; but when government, and I mean a Labour government, took responsibility for full employment, it all ended. Municipalities didn't need to do anything more. When we were prosperous, it didn't matter. Suddenly, it was different."

Edge and his friends did not find the going easy. Grants to industry were controlled by the central government or the central banking system in the City, and a regional municipal bank was a departure from established rules. "We flushed one legal opinion down the toilet on a train between London and Birmingham," Edge said proudly. The enterprise board illustrated another alternative to the hard-left approach. "Our concept of socialism recognizes the need for partnership between the centre and the regions and the local communities," Edge said. "The old socialism, where you had nice nationalized industries of coal and steel, is dead as a doornail, and the last thing we want is the hard-left politics of the gesture."

Edge was not the only one to recognize new political opportunities in the disintegration of traditional politics. "We are in a flood tide," said David Blunkett. "We either fight the battles of the future or the battles of the past." Blunkett, the blind, soft-spoken leader of Sheffield City Council, had been considered a hard-left militant, but his growing reputation as a conciliator between the old and new left established him as a different kind of Labour activist.

He was part of the 1960s generation that had campaigned for what was then fashionably called grass-roots democracy. Labour's election defeats in 1979 and 1983 provoked a new look at community initiative and neighbourhood organization. "What we saw in 1983 was a rejection of collectivism," said Blunkett. "In the Labour Party, we allowed democracy to be taken over by welfarism. People just hadn't been involved with their society. Thatcher has made us, or ought to make us, go back to our own roots." The day I met Blunkett at Sheffield City Hall, dozens of municipal workers were picketing the building. They had been on strike for the previous 12 weeks, protesting the introduction of job-threatening "new technology." It was the kind of cause the orthodox hard left would have leapt to the picket lines to defend — as it did so often in the decade — and it was the kind of issue that represented the real dividing line in the "new politics" of the decade. While the militants regarded automation and industrial rationalization as forced unemployment, the municipal socialists felt the Labour Party ought to explore the best ways of using new technology before it was too late.

"I have to ask myself what's going to happen in ten years' time," said Blunkett. "We could have George Orwell's nightmare society, with half the population in a drone economy, doing the gardens for the other half — or we could share the wealth and productivity, create shorter work weeks, and develop new skills. The energy we put into the first industrial revolution we will have to harness for the second."

It was no accident that the energies of people like Blunkett and Edge were focused on municipal or regional politics. With Thatcher firmly controlling the central government machinery and dominating Parliament, there were few other political forums open for young and ambitious people on the left to make their ideas felt. Ken Livingstone was able to exert a disproportionate influence on the debate from his base in London's metropolitan council. His concept of a "rainbow coalition", formed from the urban disadvantaged and minority groups, galvanized the capital's political climate. (The GLC also ran a successful enterprise-board.) The hard left gained control in several northern British cities, such as Liverpool, where they tried to put into effect the policies they wanted to impose on the Labour Party. The municipal reformers infused British regional politics with an excitement it hadn't experienced for generations — and a local city hall was a perfect place from which to attack Thatcherism at its most vulnerable point. Despite Thatcher's populist sympathies, she had contributed to the concentration of executive and bureaucratic power in Whitehall. "Sheffield used to operate and build its own trams and buses, it organized its own telephone and electric systems," said Blunkett. "Thatcher has taken away more and more local control." As the ideas of the municipal-based "disturbers of the peace" trickled into the national debate, the stage was set for a realignment of British party politics.

The same Labour conference that jeered James Callaghan gave itself an intriguing new leader. Neil Kinnock, a freckled, ginger-haired Welshman who had never held government office, was, at 41, one of the youngest leaders ever to be elected to head a major Western political party. He was also the first to be elected under the new rules. The huge block votes of trade unions and constituency parties ensured his victory over Roy Hattersley, the private choice of most of the front-bench Labour MPs.[13] Like his mentor Michael Foot, Kinnock had strong roots on the left, but there were significant differences of style between the two men. Although Kinnock had kept his higher political ambitions to himself, knowledgeable people on both sides of the Atlantic had singled him out years before as a possible future prime minister.[14] Bright and inventive, Kinnock was another member of the generation restless with the smugness of old Labour policies. He had been president of the Cardiff University Student Union and a long-time activist against nuclear weapons and South African apartheid. Soon after he was elected to Parliament in 1970, he quickly joined the "Tribune" group of left-wing MPs who were lobbying for rule changes in the Labour Party. Yet both he and his wife Glenys were more comfortable with their friends from the days of university protest, like Joan Ruddock, than staid parliamentarians.

Kinnock made headlines during the 1983 campaign with a clumsy assault on Thatcher's conduct of the Falklands War, accusing her of taking political advantage of soldiers who had left their "guts" on Goose Green. Despite the occasional outburst of rhetoric, he was human and self-deprecating in a way that few political leaders had been for generations in Britain, once telling an interviewer from a police journal that he saw himself as a "witty, pipe-smoking, ruminative detective inspector." He had charm and a disarming vulnerability, both put to early effect when he accidentally fell into the sea at Brighton before a battery of newspaper photographers. In his more thoughtful moments, he appeared conscious of the need to change the Labour message. "The idea that there is a model Labour voter, a blue-collar council-house tenant who belongs to a union and has 2.4 children, a five-year-old car, and a holiday in Blackpool is patronizing and pathetically inaccurate," he told a conference in London in 1986. "The idea that a vague coalition of have-nots can be built as an adequate base for Labour support and that therefore no effort is needed to secure the backing of the 'haves' and the 'haven't-got-enoughs' is a betrayal of the very people that we most want to help by gaining and using democratic power."

But the conflicts in the party drove Kinnock into a corner. In order to present himself as a credible leader, he had to restrain the hard left, who immediately branded him a traitor to his early ideals. Militant Tendency, interpreting the 1983 election defeat as proof of the party's ideological weaknesses, redoubled its efforts. Hard-line miners and pseudo-Marxist city councillors refused to accept Kinnock's argument that regaining power took precedence over all other items on the party agenda. Even though Kinnock conveyed an impression of tough realism, it was hard to tell precisely whether he stood for anything more than a spruced-up version of Labour's old centralist, interventionist policies. When he earned praise from Callaghan himself, it appeared to be the final proof of Kinnock's estrangement from the new left. In the fog of Labour's internal battles, the genuine re-examination of traditional socialism begun by people like Blunkett and Edge was lost to view. "You just wait for the next election," Edge told me in 1986. "It will be a complete reversal of 1983." But it seemed only a half-hearted conviction.

The Thatcher government called an election for June 1987. At the time, the two opposition parties appeared to be gaining strength. Polls showed the Conservatives losing support, the result of several years of government scandals and ineptly handled policies. Thatcher for the first time seemed weak and indecisive, and her own radicalism appeared to have been dulled by power.[15]

The 1987 election campaign promised to be the definitive struggle for the future of Britain. So it turned out to be, but not quite in the way the moral crusaders on both sides had imagined. Thatcher won a 102-seat majority, an historical benchmark second only to her 1983 landslide. Her popular vote, however, had slipped once more. The Conservatives were still the most successful political party of the decade, but a new, stronger opposition had ended their monopoly on the rhetoric of change.

Parliament began to reflect the new British realities of the Eighties. There were now four non-whites in Westminster, the first visible sign in national politics of the country's multi-ethnic character. The number of women MPs went from 28 to 41. The new left, which now outnumbered the centre and right wings of the Labour Party, was in a position of unaccustomed influence. "Rainbow coalition" leaders as well as hard left reformers joined municipal socialists on Labour's benches: Ken Livingstone, David Blunkett, and Joan Ruddock were all new MPs. And in the Conservative Party, "new Britons" were also amply represented. Peter Bottomley, for instance, won re-election. Meanwhile, the older Labour and Conservative guard was either retiring or defeated. Roy Jenkins had lost his seat in the Scottish constituency of Glasgow-Hillhead. Voters in Northern Ireland had ended Enoch Powell's stormy political career.

The most original product of the 1980s had, however, also been destroyed. The SDP-Liberal Alliance share of the vote had dropped three points from 1983. After the promise of their early years, the decline represented a stunning setback. The Liberals had outperformed their partners again, gaining twelve seats to the SDP's five. David Owen, who had led the SDP campaign in tandem with David Steel, was the only member of the original Gang of Four to remain in the House of Commons.[16]

Despite the respect Owen enjoyed among the voters, the weaknesses of coalition politics had proved his undoing. The "two Davids" campaigning together under the Alliance banner managed to blur their differences without offering a coherent image. They never made clear whether they were running as an alternative to Thatcher or to Kinnock. Much of the SDP's middle-class left-of-centre constituency returned, at least temporarily, to the Labour Party in order to register its disapproval of the government. "It's hard to sell a combination of parties," Owen had admitted prophetically in 1984. Owen had always resisted suggestions for a merger, convinced the identity of the SDP would be lost inside the older Liberals. He was overruled after the election. The members of the party he had helped to create voted by a narrow margin in August 1987 to begin negotiations with the Liberals to form a single political unit. Owen, isolated even from his former Gang of Four colleagues who were in favour of a merger, promptly quit as SDP leader. Meanwhile, Steel, who had broached the idea of a "democratic fusion" publicly a few days after the vote — thereby infuriating his Alliance partner — confessed his own days in politics were probably numbered. It would be difficult for him to lead a party that could no longer be considered exclusively Liberal. What would such a merged party stand for? The politicians who had tried to "break the mould" of British politics seemed headed for the thorny ideological minefield they supposedly had left behind.

Labour's own internal conflicts were far from resolved. It had won a crucial victory over the SDP as a result of the most impressive public relations campaign in its history. Kinnock was sold like an American presidential candidate. Television commercials showed him smiling warmly at children and old age pensioners, or at home with his family, a man of the "caring left." Yet for all the money and energy spent on brushing up the party image, Kinnock improved Labour's national vote by only three percentage points over 1983. Political columnist Peter Jenkins wrote in the *Independent*, "It looks as if there has been a permanent shift of allegiance away from the Labour Party as the spread of property and wealth has widened...." Perhaps more significantly, there had also been a permanent shift away from the politics of centralism. "The argument over [public] ownership is dead," declared Labour MP Austin Mitchell. "Our real job is to make capitalism work better than our pathetic British capitalists have ever been able to."

Those might have been comforting words to Margaret Thatcher, whose avowed aim in politics was to make British socialism irrelevant. In fact, she was partly responsible for its renewal. Her refusal to compromise her principles, at least rhetorically, had set the pace for a decade that was hungry for new ideas. After its own bruising experience at her hands, British socialism was beginning to show signs of the European approach so ardently desired by the founders of the SDP. "Among West European socialists there is a growing acceptance that centralist answers are not always best for economic democracy or efficiency," noted the *Economist* in 1985. "Most socialists will now agree that the generosity of the welfare state can often be bureaucratic and inhuman; and they are seeking answers to the broad conservative charge that, however well-intentioned, reform-minded social engineering normally leads in the end either to unantici-pated failures or to the unacceptable infringement of people's liberty."[17]

Margaret Thatcher, now acclaimed as the true "mould-breaker" in British politics and the most successful radical politician of the postwar world, faced a challenge in her third term of office quite different from that which she had faced in her previous two. A majority of her political oppo-nents who shared her urge to disturb and restructure British society were now well-placed to argue with her on her own grounds. "We will work with [Thatcher] over the next four years because we have no choice," said David Blunkett, in an interview published after the election. But he added that the prime minister would also have to work with those who wanted more fundamental changes in areas of British life so far untouched by Thatcherism. Such an "alliance," if it happened, promised to make the 1990s even more turbulent than the previous decade.

Chapter 13
SMOKE AND MIRRORS

...From the year of coronation date the first steps
towards Britain's recovery. At long last the
nation's pride, the nation's will to leadership
asserted themselves. The second Elizabethan age
was to witness, like the first, a far-reaching
renaissance of the spirit.

– Advertisement in Punch *magazine, 1953.* [1]

On the morning of April 29, 1986, Queen Elizabeth II and 13 other members of the British royal family went to St. George's Chapel, on the grounds of Windsor Castle, to attend a funeral. Most of the country seemed to be watching. David Runcie, Archbishop of Canterbury, led the prayers, and Prime Minister Margaret Thatcher was among the official mourners. But despite the trappings of a great occasion of state, there was something awkward about this funeral. The royal family sat stiffly on wooden benches in the choir, hidden from the view of most of the congregation, facing a casket of dark English oak. A solitary wreath of spring flowers lay on the coffin. Inside the historic sixteenth-century chapel, final resting place of 10 English kings, there was an air of prim embarrassment.

One of the psalms chosen for the funeral service seemed to sum up the mood. "Thou has set our misdeeds before thee and our secret sins," it read. "We bring our years to an end, as it were a tale that is told." To Britons of a certain age, the words were delicious irony. The funeral was the closing act in a scandal that had nearly destroyed the British monarchy 50 years earlier. The "misdeeds" and "secret sins" of the woman the congregation came to mourn had stamped the lives of every royal person in the chapel that morning, and the ceremony made it painfully obvious how hard it was to forgive her. Not once in the strained service was she ever mentioned by name.

Even in death, Wallis Simpson, the American-born Duchess of Windsor and the widow of the former King Edward VIII, had an uncanny power to complicate the fortunes of the British throne. The news of her death in Paris a few days earlier had unleashed a torrent of words in the British press. They were still printing excerpts from her letters and diaries when the funeral began. A 90-year-old recluse, nursed to the end by a few loyal retainers, she managed, posthumously, to cloud the feeling of goodwill left by the festivities held just nine days before in honour of the Queen's sixtieth birthday. Most Britons had joined those festivities in a national mood of self-congratulation — but the ceremony at St. George's Chapel was a jolt back to reality. The ultimate symbol of British nationhood, the monarchy, appeared as vulnerable as ever.

Mrs. Simpson's affair with the Prince of Wales, who became King Edward VIII only to give up his crown in 1936 for "the woman I love," had threatened the House of Windsor with the fate of the other great European thrones that had faded into obscurity after the First World War. In a national opinion poll taken that year, some 50 per cent of those surveyed admitted they would not have minded terribly if Britain were to become a republic.[2]

Wallis Simpson's funeral buzzed with the coded meanings and hidden messages that Britons love. Was the service an apology — long-overdue — for the cool treatment her royal relatives had given the Duchess and her husband when they were alive? Or did it represent a kind of reluctant tribute? "Nobody is going to admit it, but she [the Duchess] did the monarchy a favour," wrote Alastair Burnett, a television "presenter" who had earned a certain notoriety (and sniggers from British journalists) for his ingratiating interviews with the royal family. Burnett suggested that the abdication crisis had been a healthy shock to an institution that had temporarily forgotten it was supposed to be the nation's guardian of "old-fashioned...family virtues." He added, in what sounded like a polite warning, "The surviving monarchy was reminded of what the country expected of it." The association of the royal family with the morals of the land actually had very little to do with the traditions of the British throne. Royal domestic virtue was largely a creation of Victorian image-making. But Burnett's meaning was unmistakable: what the people wanted, the people's sovereign had to deliver.

No one could doubt that, over the next half-century, the House of Windsor had grasped the message. The throne not only regained its popularity, it emerged as the one British institution with the strength to unify the country during the 1980s. Yet even before the Simpson funeral, many Britons were asking themselves whether it had been *too* successful.

"Monarchy shields us from reality," suggested Charles Mosley, a former editor of *Debrett's Peerage*, the bible of the British upper class, in a television discussion in 1985. "It lends us as a nation an aura of glamour and success which is both undeserved and misleading. Of course, that is only a disadvantage if you genuinely believe we could face reality. I suspect most people in Britain, including the royal family, doubt that."[3]

The special relationship between the monarchy and the Britsh people has nevertheless defied the best intellectual efforts of Britons to liberate themselves from its emotional grip. They discuss it somewhat defensively with outsiders, half-acknowledging that their apparent need to cling to an archaic institution, which is founded on hereditary privilege, which takes at least £4 million annually from the national budget, and which draws most of its member from a tiny, élite, and unrepresentative land-owning class, is a sign that they do not quite belong to the modern world. Like Mosley, they wonder whether the monarchy is a metaphor for the state of modern Britain: its ceremonial splendour a conjuring trick performed with smoke and mirrors to disguise the annoying fact of being a small, old country. But what, they wonder, would we be without it?[4]

The funeral of the Duchess of Windsor provided a rare moment to look behind the dazzling images royalty has spun over the decade. It was one of the few public occasions in the 1980s when the royals were stripped of the larger-than-life roles manufactured by the gnomes of Buckingham Palace and the wizards of Fleet Street. As her body was borne by an honour guard out of the chapel, for burial beside her husband in the royal cemetery at Frogmore in Windsor, the attention of the crowds focused on the members of the royal family emerging in the brisk British sunshine. They stepped with pale, uncertain faces into waiting limousines. The Queen Mother, frail and elderly at 86, the Queen, Prince Charles and his wife Diana, Princess Margaret, the princes Andrew and Edward, Princess Anne — all of them characters in a brilliant real-life soap opera. That morning, like any family at the funeral of a relation for whom they held mixed emotions, they looked self-conscious and uncomfortably human. With the dazzle gone, at least momentarily, it was possible to marvel at the mixture of technique and faith that had lifted such ordinary people into the realm of national myth.

Many Britons are acutely aware that the "ancient" royal ceremonies that have enchanted the rest of the world are not ancient at all. From the coronation of the present Queen to the televised weddings of her children, they have been cobbled together over the past century from scraps of royal chronicles and fused by the romantic imagination of palace courtiers in order to save the throne. In the manner of all agnostics, the British re-invented their royals in succeeding epochs of their modern history to reflect the way they wanted to think about themselves. Today, the monarchy is more than ever a joint venture of crown and people, one of the few state enterprises Britons can take genuine pride in.

Queen Elizabeth II is the perfect example of how the process works. A shy, serious ten-year-old when her father was thrust onto the throne as a replacement for his wayward elder brother, she watched her parents compensate for the abdication crisis by turning themselves into paragons of morality, duty, and self-sacrifice. From the moment of her own coronation in 1953, she accepted the awesome responsibility of repairing a national psyche brusied by war and the loss of Empire. In the "second Elizabethan Age," as an advertisement in *Punch* magazine put it at the time, national recovery and rebirth had to happen in the Queen's name, if it was going to happen at all.

A palace aide in the 1960s used to tell his colleagues, "Remember, we're in the happiness game." The remark came at the conclusion of a long, intense battle between palace traditionalists and reformers over the role of the monarchy in modern Britain. The reformers noted that, although the monarchy had long since recovered the esteem it lost during the abdication crisis, it was in danger of becoming irrelevant. They argued that the palace needed to become more accessible, and they reasoned that a "relevant" monarchy would find its way much easier at a time when politicians and governments were coming into general disrepute. The first public evidence that the reformers had won came when the Queen agreed to participate in an unprecedented BBC television documentary that revealed her as an ordinary, if upper-class, country housewife. The program broke some of the barriers still separating the monarch from her subjects. From then on, the British monarchy, in a way that none of the other monarchies still scattered across the world could match, became the special property of its subjects. The royal family was not always convinced that it could successfully sell "happiness." As late at 1977, the Queen was doubtful about the celebrations planned across the country to celebrate 25 years of her reign. In a rare confession to one friendly journalist, she said it was an "enormous gamble." But the Jubilee was successful beyond anyone's hopes. When I visited London that year, there were 4,000 street parties in London alone. Even on my first trip to Britain, with only a passing interest in the affairs of the British throne, I became a captive of the royal mythology. As one writer described it at the time, the Jubilee "conjured up the old sense of community, and sometimes regenerated it." Conjured was the appropriate word.

The Queen's lack of real political power forged a powerful bond with the people. At a time of increasing bureaucracy and statism, she became the ultimate source of appeal in their battles with petty bureaucracy. The new Elizabethan monarchy remodelled itself to fit the postindustrial, bureaucratic character of modern Britain. In the 1960s and 1970s, the Queen became a buffer between the people and the government, a kind of super-ombudswoman to the welfare state. In the 1980s, the transformation of this private, aristocratic woman into the embodiment of her people's hopes of reversing an otherwise inevitable decline was the last, and possibly the most important, key to the British revolution explored in these pages.

During the 1980s, the monarch's appeal crossed party, political, and class boundaries. "We live in a time of political polarization, and politicians have lost the respect of the people they are trying to rule," maintained the Duke of Westminster. "This is true of other countries of course, but we are fortunate in Britain in that we have a non-political, non-controversial institution which people can look up to and respect. Everybody wants to respect something." Yet the closer the monarchy came to sharing the uncertainties of the 1980s, the more controversial it was destined to become. Even those most opposed on ideological grounds to the monarchy and the class system it appeared to represent found ways to exploit it. Ken Livingstone was not embarrassed to claim the Queen as an ally in his fight against abolition of metropolitan government, after she agreed to appear with him at the inauguration of the Thames flood control barrier in 1982.

The monarchy managed to be both a symbol of yuppiedom and social concern. Lord Colwyn once took his jazz band to the yacht club at Cowes to play for the up-and-coming rich of British society. Prominent among the guests was the royal family, unafraid to display their wealth and status. "At one point there were sixteen royals on the dance floor, dancing away — including relatives like former King Constantine of Greece," said Colwyn. "I thought that was a real accomplishment at the time." Yet pictures of the royal family and mementos of royal events also hang in the homes of the unemployed, and young blacks in the inner-city are only too pleased to welcome royal visitors. "They understand us," said a Rastafarian before a royal visit to his London housing estate, and he added cannily, "They also give us good publicity when they come." Sometimes, the Queen's subjects go to extraordinary lengths to see her. A young, unemployed man named Michael Fagin was so persuaded of the monarch's ability to solve his family problems that he climbed over the palace walls one night in 1982 and made his way undetected into the Queen's bedroom in order to tell her his story. The Queen, nonplussed, offered him a cigarette.

But it wasn't necessary to have Fagin's gymnastic abilities to visit the people's sovereign at her home. Thousands of ordinary Britons have come through the front door, in broad daylight, to receive one of the dozens of awards the Queen gives out for heroism, public service, or national achievement. Plumbers, soldiers, athletes, businessmen, policemen, pop singers, diplomats, and clerks have all at one time or another found themselves in the luxurious, quiet drawing rooms of Buckingham Palace, face to face with their sovereign. For a brief moment, as she pins an award on their chest and exchanges a few banal words, they have the undivided attention of the Queen of Great Britain, Wales, and Northern Ireland. Somehow, she seems to know each of them intimately.

The ceremony makes a vivid impression on anyone who witnesses it. "There is something almost maternal about the way in which she adjusts the ribbon or the pin, taking infinite care, tilting her head a little forward with a slight frown of concentration, then standing back, her face illuminated with a characteristically attentive, extraordinarily young look," according to one observer of the scene.[5] Presidents and prime ministers could not hope to match the special glow of the royal handshake. In fact, they have often succumbed themselves. Even President Ronald Reagan, a master in the art of public appeal, looked awestruck during a visit to Windsor Castle in 1982.

"Although bereft of actual power, the myth of kingship retains a potent and universal charge; and the British royal family have shown a kind of genius for making the most of it," wrote John Pearson in a 1986 book about the modern monarchy.[6] A visit to Buckingham Palace, the vast eighteenth-century mansion in southwest London used by the royal family both as home and office, goes a long way toward explaining the nature of that "charge."

Few buildings in the world have a similar impact on visitors. Although architecturally it is not as inspiring as England's great country mansions, walking up to the palace's imposing iron gates, past camera-toting tourists, fills a visitor with a sense of his importance.

A policeman in a sentry box inquires after the visitor's business in a gratifyingly polite whisper. Once properly vetted and allowed entry, the visitor follows the same path through the outer courtyard trod by ambassadors, heads of state, and visiting royalty, his feet crunching impressively on the gravel. As he passes red-coated sentries, a small door opens immediately from the inside, and a quietly polite man in a dark suit looks him over a second time. (Ever since Michael Fagin's visit, palace security is tight.) The visitor is shown deferentially to a small anteroom, slightly more elegant than a fashionable Harley Street doctor's waiting room, where there is a musty painting of King George III and King Alfonso of Spain reviewing the troops in Madrid in 1777, while he waits again for his appointment to be checked. In the guard's room across the way, he can observe two folded-up wheelchairs, a reminder of the eagerness of this palace to cater to all of its subjects.

A butler in tails and striped pants finally appears, leading the visitor down a long corridor covered in red brocade, lined with more paintings. In offices along the side, men in striped shirts, their jackets off, are talking urgently into telephones. Some offices glow with the unmistakable green light of computer screens. From the windows of the first-floor outer offices (located under the private apartments of the Royal Family) a visitor sees an astonishingly large park, whose dimensions would never be suspected from outside the computerized electric fence ringing the palace walls. A gently sloping green lawn, large enough to cater comfortably to garden tea parties for thousands during the summer completes the picture of a country estate bizarrely situated in the midst of London smog.

The palace's principal occupants display a similarly disconcerting mixture of pressurized salesmanship and leisured elegance. Many have served abroad as foreign service professionals. They have been heard to grumble sometimes that their gilded palace environment is too far from the real world. But in the next breath, they speak of themselves as employees in Britain's most successful international institution. At the palace, there is noticeably little evidence of the upper-class contempt for money and trade which are usually associated with Britain's establishment.

"After the riots of 1981, we had two *Time* magazine covers on Britain showing burning cities," said Michael Shea, the head of the palace's publicity machine. "Then came the [royal] wedding and the streets were thronged with Americans. The wedding brought in £200 million on its own!"

His remark also suggested how far the monarchy had come since the Windsor crisis. The institution, which had once been victimised by social scandal, now saw itself as an agent of social cohesion, and even social change. No one would think of measuring the "Palace Effect" in tourist dollars alone.

The list of Britons honoured with royal recognition widened to include the innovators and entrepreneurs working around the country during the 1980s. The palace seemed to make a special effort to hunt out those who represented an alternative solution to industrial problems. The Queen's Awards for achievements in exports or technological performance appeared in the tiny pre-fab boardrooms of some of the most advanced technological companies in Britain. The manager of an electronics plant in Scotland's Silicon Glen once showed me the distinctive bronze plaque just inside the entrance to his building. "It's quite something, isn't it?" he said. "I've given it pride of place, of course." The manger of a company whose working life was concentrated on the technology of the twenty-first century may be a surprising vessel for the traits of a nineteenth-century monarchist. But for him, the monarchy was identified with aspirations to excellence. In a mysterious and uniquely British way, the royal family — which privately likes to call itself The Firm — had joined the most important modernizing forces in the land.

Cyril Parkinson, famous for his discovery of Parkinson's Law, told an American journalist in 1987 that "the most efficient work unit in Britain isthe royal family."[7] A glance at the Court Circular of *The Times* every morning shows the truth of the remark. The section contains a dizzying round of appointments and appearances around the country, from the opening of children's play school to visiting a skills centre for the young unemployed. Each member of the family is expected to keep an exhausting schedule in direct proportion to his or her position on the "civil list," the register of "salaries" paid from the public purse to members of the working monarchy. Royals have been heard to say in private that they have a greater sense of the divisions and problems of the land than politicians or the news media. Many are openly contemptuous of the servility that used to characterize British subjects' approach to the throne. At a meeting with Fleet Street editors, the Queen called one newsman "pompous" for suggesting that Princess Diana should send a footman to do her shopping if she wanted to avoid intrusive photographers. Princess Diana was once heard to complain that a certain television interviewer "never looked me in the eye; I dislike people who will not look one in the eye."

The busiest member of The Firm is its chief executive. The Queen takes her job extremely seriously. A surprisingly short, somewhat stiff person when encountered in a public event, she is a relaxed and self-confident administrator in private. She starts work each morning she is in London at nine, sitting down at her Chippendale desk to work on appointments two years ahead. Few international executives could match her time in the air. Aside from her regular tours and duties around Britain, the Queen has travelled 711,646 miles since 1952, the equivalent of going 28 times around the world. Between 1980 and 1986, she took 21 trips to more than 40 countries.[8] Only one other public figure in the decade appeared to work as hard, or to be as driven.

Margaret Thatcher has a great deal in common with the forthright lady in Buckingham Palace. Both are intensely British, and both work feverishly to maintain their country's reputation and standing abroad. A Gallup survey in 1986 reflected remarkably similar public perceptions of the two women. Asked whom they valued most as the public figures shaping the country's future, 18 per cent of a representative sample of Britons answered the Queen. Seventeen per cent picked the Prime Minister.[9] The blurring of roles has occasionally made both women uneasy. The British author Anthony Sampson once triggered a minor controversy when a book he wrote contained a subtle hint of tension between the prime minister and the Queen. "The weekly meetings between the Queen and Mrs. Thatcher...are dreaded by at least one of them," Sampson wrote.[10] Sampson coyly refused to say which one; however, it was easy to imagine how the people's sovereign regarded the prime minister's imperious ways. One possibly apocryphal story making the rounds of London illustrated the difficulties of the relationship. Thatcher, invited to an event in which the Queen would also take part, asked an aide to inquire discreetly what the monarch would be wearing. She did not want to embarrass her sovereign by wearing an identical outfit. The reply came back from the palace with a certain haughty grace. Her Majesty, the aide was told, does not usually notice what other women wear.

The two women find themselves occasionally in overlapping roles. While Thatcher sometimes consciously evokes the glories of Britain's imperial past, the Queen — the country's sturdiest symbol of continuity and tradition — often promotes the advances in British technology desired so fervently by Thatcher to create the "new Britain." "You can take a Queen out of politics but you can't take politics out of a Queen," wrote Neal Ascherson, a columnist in the *Sunday Observer*. "The Palace is now becoming politicized by an irresistible process." Ascherson was writing a few months after the Wallis Simpson funeral, in the midst of an episode that brought all the tensions of the monarchy's relationship with British politics to a head.

The episode began when member states of the Commonwealth found themselves in open conflict with Thatcher over a proposal to tighten economic sanctions against South Africa. The British prime minister refused to go along with the Commonwealth majority, insisting that additional sanctions would cost jobs in Britain. Efforts to change her mind came to nothing. Finally, several countries announced they would boycott the annual Commonwealth Games in Edinburgh later that summer. It was even being suggested that there was no logical reason why Britain should continue to be regarded as the senior and most authoritative Commonwealth member. The possibility that Britain would be dealt an embarrassing snub by her former colonies rang alarm bells in the palace.

Most insiders knew that the Queen had long since expanded her ceremonial duties as head of the Commonwealth to play an important behind-the-scenes role in the organization. Sonny Ramphal, Commonwealth secretary-general and a frequent visitor to the palace, once told an interviewer that the Queen was crucial to its survival. "She has a way of knocking people's heads together without appearing to do so,"[11] he said. "The Queen was scheduled to open the Edinburgh Games, and the intensity of the quarrel over South Africa presented a potential conflict between her duties to the Commonwealth and her obligations to her own kingdom.

The conflict between throne and government had been building for years. As Britain began to reassess its foreign policies in line with its hopes of playing a world role more commensurate with its resources, the Queen's growing involvement in Commonwealth affairs inevitably opened a gulf between herself and her subjects — and sometimes her ministers. Britons are genuinely surprised when they are forced to acknowledge that, in Commonwealth terms, Britain is just one of 17 member countries to accept the Queen as head of state. Most Britons are inclined to treat the Commonwealth with a mixture of amused detachment and boredom, only rousing themselves when its member countries begin to appear ungrateful for the benefits bestowed by their former imperial masters. The Queen's emergence as an accomplished world stateswoman in the affairs of nearly one billion people in 48 countries has occurred beyond the immediate horizon of her subjects in Britain. "Nobody has occupied her position longer, which means that she has grown up alongside a number of other leaders, presidents, and prime ministers," Ramphal said. "I have known young prime ministers, meeting her for the first time, emerging amazed by the extent of her knowledge." Although the Queen has made the organization's care and nurturing a central element of her reign, Britons have had very little to do with it. Sometimes, they have not been slow to show their resentment at having "their" Queen co-opted by the "natives."

One of the monarch's annual Christmas broadcasts to the Commonwealth in the 1980s landed her in controversy. The broadcasts are usually scripted to be as inoffensive as possible, but on this occasion she expressed concern about world poverty and racial injustice. Her remarks were innocuous, but right-wing critics charged that they could be interpreted as support for a distinct (liberal) political view, and therefore violated the principle of the crown's impartiality. To add weight to their objections, the Queen's comments were welcomed in some quarters as a coded message of concern about the multicultural tensions in Britain's inner cities. The affair may have appeared to be a tempest in a teacup, but the politicization of the palace continued through the decade.

After the American invasion of Grenada in 1983, the Queen was said to be "furious" at Britain's allies for taking such a step without consultation with the island's head of state. Her anger was believed to have persuaded Thatcher to make one of her few open criticisms of American policy. Even more controversially, the palace challenged some key aspects of government economic policy as it applied to the Commonwealth. The Queen's aides were reported to have quietly registered, "in the right circles," her concern over decisions to reduce overseas student grants and to cut the budget of the BBC World Service. The row over South Africa was threatening to expand the palace role as enlightened foreign affairs lobby even further.

The rumours of palace interventions of course worried the government. Fearing the Commonwealth would use the Queen as a "fifth column" to influence its foreign policy, Thatcher fired what appeared to be a warning shot. Unidentified government sources were quoted in the press suggesting that the Queen's "emotional" stand in favour of her Commonwealth friends could plunge Britain into a constitutional crisis.

The palace fired back, or at least it appeared to. On July 20, 1986, a story appeared in the *Sunday Times* that caused a sensation even among seasoned palace-watchers. Under the headline, "The African Queen," the story claimed the Queen was not only disturbed by Thatcher's confrontation with the Commonwealth, but by the prime minister's policies over the decade.

She was said to be upset about the "lack of compassion" of the government. Palace advisers and "friends of the Queen," the *Sunday Times* wrote, had decided to go public with this attack because they believed it was in the "Queen's interest that Thatcher was curbed." The article went on to document the Queen's dismay over the miners' strike and the recent use of a British air base as a launching pad for an American attack on Libya. "Contrary to her public image, friends of the Queen say that, on a wide range of issues, her thinking is to the left of centre." Adding insult to injury, the *Sunday Times* asserted that "on social issues, at least, she has always been happier when dealing with Labour prime ministers."

With obvious echoes of the events of 50 years before, the newspaper issued an editorial warning to the Queen. "Her prime role," it advised sanctimoniously, "must be to remain above the political hurly-burly and on no account must she appear to take sides against her principal adviser, the British prime minister." The palace, however, quickly branded the report as false, and even broke its own rules by naming palace public relations head Michael Shea as the *Sunday Times'* source — in order to allow Shea the chance to say he was misquoted. But at this point, the story becomes murky. The issue was confused when the *Sunday Times* printed an involved explanation of its own role in the affair. A reporter had read the material to Shea on the telephone before publication — though not, as it turned out, some of the more provocative parts — and claimed he was given a green light. Whatever the palace was saying now, the paper maintained, it obviously had wanted its message out.

But why the palace would have chosen a newspaper that was unabashedly pro-Thatcher was never made clear. The *Sunday Times* even admitted that it had relayed the entire text of the story to a senior member of the government before publication. Nevertheless, when the story was published, the prime minister was said to be devastated.

The inconsistencies and gaps in the published accounts of the episode give rise to an alternative theory. The origin of the story might well have been at Number 10 Downing Street, rather than inside Buckingham Palace. The theory suggests that skilful political operators, anxious to bring the palace "opposition" into the open, set a clever trap. If the courtiers around the Queen could be lured into open hints of their disenchantment with the government of the day, they would provoke a resurgence of republicanism — conveniently assisted by the lingering after-effects of the

Wallis Simpson funeral. The effect was likely to be chastening on the palace.

Whether the theory was accurate or not, the results were the same. Almost without exception, letters to newspapers were bitterly critical of the palace. While they stopped short of a direct attack on the Queen, the letter-writers suggested that she was being badly served by her advisors. Thatcher gained the emotional edge with an image as the affronted, innocent party whose government was being suborned by pressure from the throne. The palace, according to the *Sunday Times* — this time citing no sources at all — was told that it must never happen again. As an even more useful political consequence, the attacks on the Commonwealth doubled in ferocity. The central issue — the British government's controversial policies toward South Africa — was lost in the shouting.

It was an affair worthy of any intrigue in Moscow or Peking, and the passions it aroused were soon covered with mandarin-like inscrutability. A year later, Thatcher was stoutly defending the royal family to an American TV audience. "We are very fortunate to have such a wonderful monarch and such a wonderful royal family," she said.

But one royal person would have observed the entire Commonwealth affair with a certain amount of foreboding. The royal family's limited ability to put its social concerns on the national agenda had been on the mind of Charles, Prince of Wales, for a long time. "A Prince of Wales has to do what he can by influence, not by power," he said before his marriage in 1981. "There isn't any power. The influence is in direct ratio to the respect people have for you." But how, he might have added, do you win respect, if not by using your influence to help shape the political debate that was changing the lives of your future subjects?

The prince, a vaguely good-looking and self-effacing young man whose image in Britain and abroad until his marriage had been confined to his efforts to excel in the most dangerous sports, was the member of the royal family most obviously transformed by the decade. Nothing in his education or training had prepared him for a realm rocked in the 1980s by growing unemployment and urban violence. As he began to read and think about the issues, he came to conclusions that were astonishingly similar to those reached by many other new Britons.

"I feel that we have concentrated too much in the last ten or twenty years on the economy of scale," he said in a fascinating interview with an American journalist in London. "Surely the reason, I think, for our existence on earth [is] to try and make the most of our human qualities and our human adaptability." Such remarks made people like social innovator Nicholas Albery claim the prince as one of their own. "I've got a lot of sympathy for Prince Charles," Albery said. "He seems quite a socially inventive fellow, with lots of green ideas and spiritual ideas. He's tremendous. There's no harm in having a monarchy, really, with people like him."

Charles's public musing about the future of postindustrial society parallelled his mother's sense of concern about the Commonwealth. But he displayed at the same time a marked restlessness and uncertainty about his own future. What does an intelligent young man do while waiting for the job he had been trained to fill?

It is, of course, the same dilemma that faced the last Prince of Wales. The parallels between the two men are obvious and immensely disturbing to the British Establishment. As the Depression deepened around the country in the 1930s, Edward had told starving miners in South Wales that "something must be done" about unemployment. The much-quoted phrase came to haunt him. Leading MPs accused Edward of meddling in political affairs, and ever since, British historians and politicians have used the prince's inpromptu remarks as an example of royals who have not learned their place. When his affair with Mrs. Simpson became public, it was not surprising that contemporary politicians seized the chance to get rid of a public figure whose views may have seriously threatened British parliamentary democracy. It was only after Edward died, in 1972, that people felt able to praise some of his intentions. "In all he did, he sought to make the monarchy less remote and more in tune with the aspirations of the time," said Prime Minister Edward Heath at the time.[12]

Charles, like his mother, was trying to do no less. But he was operating in an already highly politically charged environment. The Prince's Trust, a charity set up in the 1970s, became his principal vehicle for translating some of his concerns into action. Ideas of community development picked up from thinkers like E.F. Schumacher (being a prince, he not only read Schumacher's book, but had the flattered author over to lunch) were turned into projects in Britain's inner cities.

While there was nothing inherently controversial in such activities, the prince's involvement lent extra weight to alternatives that ran against the Thatcherian grain — even though Charles himself occasionally seemed to echo the prime minister's rhetoric. "Somehow we have to create some wealth," he mused in a 1985 interview. "Not everyone can go into the service industries. At the same time we need more people prepared to take risks to start up new enterprise; to support British inventiveness and innovatory genius before our foreign competitors develop them first." It could be argued that he was merely following in the footsteps of his father, who had carved out a role for himself as a gadfly to stagnant British industry ("Pull the finger out," Philip once advised businessmen). But Charles seemed eager to take on the system itself.

In a fierce public denunciation of modern utilitarian architecture, he led a successful campaign to halt a planned expansion of the National Gallery in Trafalgar Square. To the undisguised alarm of the architectural establishment, he openly sided with younger, more radical people who wanted to see more money spent on small-scale renovation and redevelopment schemes. Similarly, he challenged the medical establishment by announcing he was interested in holistic and preventive medicine. The prince has participated in a Royal Society of Medicine committee involved in linking "normal medicine with complementary medicine." Lord Colwyn, another member of the group, says the prince often comes to meetings. "His interest has helped legitimize what we are trying to do." Colwyn discreetly avoided saying what Charles's role on the committee was — but the prince could not always count on such discretion.

Thanks to one architect with whom the prince became associated, the first concrete indication of his disenchantment with the politics of the day filtered into the public domain. According to the architect, Charles worried that he would inherit a kingdom divided between "haves" and "have-nots" and suggested that Britain was in danger of becoming a "fourth-rate country." Not surprisingly, the palace press office immediately put out the message that Charles had been misinterpreted, but it was hard to avoid the conclusion, given the prince's earlier hints in public, that he had known exactly what he was saying. "There is a deep-seated frustration in Charles and some other royals," one of his friends told me. "They are individuals with their own minds and beliefs, and it's frustrating to be shackled by a nonpolitical role. That's why this frustration has on occasion boiled into the public eye."

The prospect of an increasingly dissident prince filled the guardians of parliamentary tradition with dismay. "He thinks he is the prince of all knowledge," complained Tory MP Anthony Beaumont-Dark after the "fourth-rate country" remark. "It would be useful if the prince, instead of thinking that just making speeches solves the problems, realized they can even make it more difficult." It was a gratuitous comment, but it clearly suggested harsher criticism would be on the way unless the prince held his tongue.

He didn't, of course. Through 1986 and 1987, the prince found himself increasingly on the front-lines of contemporary social problems. In disguise, he went to bug-ridden flophouses and shared stale coffee with vagrants and the young unemployed homeless living under the arches by the Thames. Other of the prince's activities were carried out in the full glare of publicity. With reporters in tow, he visited a sweatshop in London's East End, where Asian garment workers toiled in nineteenth century conditions. He emerged to say the experience had left him "absolutely appalled." In comments that made politicians bristle, he went on to say, "Too many people's lives are being wasted through…intolerable inertia to allow [the problem] to continue." He was known to be even more devastating in private about the poverty and wretchedness he had seen on his travels through the kingdom. His friend told me that Charles holds dinners regularly for people he meets or hears about on his forays and regards as "interesting" — architects, community workers, enlightened businessmen. They provide some of the most fascinating political conversations in the land, he said.

Characteristically, the prince has often seemed to help critics who portrayed him as a dilettante with no real experience of life. "I would dearly love to be able to get involved, you know, in the detail of things, or in the actual paperwork," he told a British journalist in one of his infrequent interviews. The journalist, Andrew Stephen, left a poignant record of the encounter. "Charles, Prince of Wales and heir to the throne of the United Kingdom, had exuded a sense that he had to justify himself, even to his interviewer, that he was a worthwhile person who understood and cared about life's problems," Stephen wrote. "He had referred constantly to 'people' as though they were an alien and distant race whom he would like to get to know better."[13]

The prince was not impervious to the gathering comparisons between himself and his great-uncle, and the inconsistencies of his own position. "I don't know if anybody listens to me or not," Prince Charles said to his American interviewer. As Charles heads into his forties and concentrates on his growing family, his activism and strong views may fade from public view. But the danger of a politicized royal family is not likely to pass. The British themselves will have tro decide whether the special sense of continuity and stability provided by the throne is worth the challenge that enlightened, activist royals present to democratic institutions.

For the moment at least, the end of the decade finds the British monarchy in as strong a position as it has ever been. A poll published in the *Mail on Sunday* in 1986 found that 89 per cent thought the monarchy should continue. The poll also made clear how successfully the monarchy had been identified with the British revival of the 1980s. Some 58 per cent agreed that without the Queen, Britain would have less influence on world affairs.[14]

EPILOGUE

*"Are you in pain, dear mother?" "I think there's
a pain somewhere in the room," said Mrs.
Gradgrind, "but I couldn't positively say that
I've got it."*

— *Charles Dickens,* Hard Times, *1854.*

Professor Charles Handy used to take visitors from abroad to the chapel at Eton public school to show them a war memorial listing the names of Etonians who had died in the First World War. "It runs the whole side of the courtyard outside the chapel," said Handy. "There are a thousand names there — the total output of that school in the four years of war." Similar memorials exist in every town and village of Britain. The professor used the grim excursion to try to explain to outsiders what had gone wrong with his country. "One of the reasons we have been reluctant to change for so long was that we had depleted the entrepreneurial gene stock between the world wars," he said. "We very nearly knocked out on one day in 1916 the future leadership and entrepreneurial talent of Britain. It happened not only at Eton, but at all the country's elite establishments. And those who survived — we killed their sons 30 years later. Those were the people who would have led us into a new world."

The economic and social upheavals Britain experienced during the Eighties again taxed British stamina. Whether they saw themselves as riding a lumbering "old trolley," in Simon Callow's phrase, or sailing on Harold Macmillan's "great sinking ship," Britons were forced to confront profound structural and psychological problems that had been festering for nearly a century. By the late 1980s, they were still a long way from solving those problems, but the energy and creativity they summoned gave cause for optimism.

On July 23, 1986, British attention focused on another royal wedding.

Prince Andrew and Sarah Ferguson, a large, bouncy redhead whose father had been Prince Charles's polo coach, were married at Westminster Abbey before a worldwide television audience estimated at 500 million. "A royal marriage of pure theatre," said the august *Times* in a headline that stretched across its front page. The screens filled once again with glistening swords, glass coaches, and other Cinderella images of royal romance. From early dawn, when the cameras showed the troops of the household cavalry moving across the courtyard of Buckingham Palace to the moment when the prince, wearing his Falklands medal, slipped the ring on his bride's finger, the royal glamour wove its magic. "Her hair is down! Her hair is down!" said one breathless television announcer as we caught our first glimpse of the new Duchess of York.

The royal hype — for weeks, newspapers had been speaking of nothing else but The Wedding — inspired inevitable comparisons with the wedding of 1981. Many British people were privately aghast. "The wedding was disgraceful." Craig Brown, a young Eton-educated journalist gave me his opinion as we chatted in his Notting Hill apartment in London. "They're such a ludicrous couple, lacking in glamour. Yet we fell for it. It must tell you that things haven't really moved on." Jonathan Miller, brooding in Regents Park, watched the wedding and wondered whether his country would ever grow up. A visiting American columnist thought he detected an undercurrent of apathy toward the latest royal spectacular. He wondered whether Britain was beginning to outgrow its monarchy. The wedding had a "morbid air," he wrote, "as if something important were coming to an end, without anyone being willing to admit it."

It was true that something had come to an end. Anyone who lived through the 1980s in Britain could not help noticing that an older order had disappeared. Whatever their politics, most Britons would find little to disagree with in Margaret Thatcher's triumphant claim to a Conservative Party conference in October, 1987: "The old Britain of the 1970s, with its strikes, poor productivity, low investment, winters of discontent, above all its gloom, its pessimism, its sheer defeatism — that Britain is gone."

But what had risen in its place? Britain seemed more fragmented than ever before. The young men earning astronomical salaries in the reformed, computerized City of London lived in a different world from that of the Linda Echlins and Dennis Turners. The images Britain projected in the 1980s blurred the issue. Was the Falklands War proof of a national revival or merely a sign of self-defeating chauvinism? Did Margaret Thatcher's revolution force the country into a bracing new discipline or did it tear Britain apart? The nation was still bogged down by institutional inertia, ideological conflict and, above all, by the burden of its past. The persistent agony of Northern Ireland, and an elitist educational system that has failed to prepare young people for life in a high technology society were only the most obvious of the problems to threaten British domestic peace in the 1990s. While some Britons had begun to operate on the frontiers of a changing industrial structure and to search for a redefinition of work, many others were condemned to a life of poverty, powerlessness, and joblessness that put them squarely in what the Bishop of Durham called the "Fifth World."

Yet even those who regarded the Thatcherian culture with particular distaste could see an important bridge had been crossed. "There is a sense of overcoming the fate of history," said Joan Ruddock. "Something happened," admitted John Gahagan in Silicon Glen. As the end of the decade neared, it was clear that Britain had avoided the fate even the country's friends had feared. The question of survival was settled.

If the second royal wedding was not as therapeutic as the first, perhaps it was because such therapy was no longer necessary. Britain was grittier and even more polarized than in 1981, yet it was arguably much stronger than it had been in the previous decade. The British had a right to feel a sense of accomplishment. They had survived industrial crisis, war, social turmoil, and a political revolution and had come up with some innovative answers to the technological and philosophical problems of late twentieth-century civilization.

Perhaps that was why the world still continued to watch events on this tiny, foggy island with extraordinary attention. "Britain is ahead," said Simon Loftus. "I don't mean qualitatively ahead, but on a time scale, it's ahead of most other industrial societies. We had the industrial revolution earlier, we went through the postindustrial agonies earlier, we are now going through the sort of post–postindustrial readjustments which I'm quite sure most advanced Western societies will follow."

Roger Scruton, who admits to a fascination with the order and rationality of preindustrial eighteenth-century Britain, summed up one of the decade's lessons with typical British archness. "We've seen unemployment on a scale most people thought could never be accommodated — and it's become a fact of life. It certainly doesn't trouble my students, many of whom are unemployed. They're quite happy, in fact, with the opportunities it's presented to them."

Here was an odd clue to the reason for Britain's curious position at the top of the world's "happiness league." I put the question of British "happiness" to Jonathan Porritt, a leader of Britain's ecology movement and one of the foremost of the "new Britons." "It's most peculiar," he agreed. "Britain doesn't actually want to be a hyper-successful industrial nation on the Japanese model. When people say we are lazier than continentals, there's a grain of truth in that. You won't see your average British citizen keeping his shop open from six in the morning till eight in the evening. It just wouldn't occur to him or her that was a rational way to behave. They make less money, but who, at the end of the day, has the better quality of life? There is a strongly ingrained contempt for people who say that life is all about work and money. Whether that can be directed into the creative acceptance of a society geared to self-reliance, decentralization, I don't know. We don't want to be a great empire again, so maybe we really can make something of this new humility."

Creative laziness. Energetic humility. This was the other dimension to the recovery of Britain's strength. It was as significant as Thatcherism to the future of the country. Perhaps more so. And as Western industrial culture began to wrestle with the problems of decline, it provided some interesting pointers to our future. "I like the laziness of British society," said journalist Craig Brown, "I like the fact that there are enough people around who aren't always wondering, God, what will I do today? It means there are always people whom you can have lunch with." Smiling, he leaned toward me across his kitchen table. "Do you want a glass of wine?"

NOTES

INTRODUCTION.
THE "DEAR OLD TROLLEY."

1. "Nine out of ten Britons told the pollsters they were content with their lives." *Economist*, Dec. 21, 1985.
2. Macmillan's words have often been misquoted. What he said was this: "Let's be frank about it. Most of our people have never had it so good. Go round the country, go to the industrial towns, go to the farms, and you will see a state of prosperity such as we have never had in my lifetime — nor indeed ever in the history of this country."
3. Peter Riddell, *The Thatcher Government*, p. 74; William Keegan, *Mrs. Thatcher's Economic Experiment*, p. 196.
4. Henry James, *English Hours*, p. 152.
5. Martin Wiener, *English Culture and the Decline of the Industrial Spirit*, p. 160.
6. Quoted in James Bellini, *Rule Britannia?*, p. 9.
7. Wiener, op. cit., p. 48.
8. Ibid., p. 160.
9. *Guardian*, Sept. 15, 1986.
10. Gorbachev visited the United Kingdom in 1984, less than a year before he became general secretary, and he had several private sessions with the British prime minister. They evidently respected each other. Gorbachev was "someone we can do business with," marvelled Thatcher. Gorbachev,

according to some independent observers in the Soviet Union, felt he had a lot in common with the Iron Lady. They were both trying to shake up sluggish societies.
11. *Guardian*, Jan. 25, 1985.
12. Quoted in *The Times*, June 10, 1985.
13. Quoted in Wiener, op. cit., p. 114.
14. Paolo Filo della Torre, *Viva Britannia*, p. 95.
15. Anthony Sampson, *The Changing Anatomy of Britain* (1982 ed.), p. xviii.
16. John Eatwell, *Whatever Happened to Britain?*, 1982, p. 12.
17. I am grateful to Sandra Gwyn, a Canadian writer living in London, for this phrase.

CHAPTER 1.
THATCHERIZED BRITAIN.

1. Quoted in Wiener, op. cit., p. 88.
2. Wiener, op. cit., p. 155. I have liberally borrowed other quotes and interpretations from the same source.
3. Most of the biographical material on Thatcher in this chapter, unless otherwise noted, comes from Nicholas Wapshott and George Brock, *Thatcher*.
4. Macmillan told Anthony Sampson in 1958, the year Thatcher was chosen to represent the Finchley Tories, that he was "rather depressed" by Britain's growing suburbanization. "To think," he said, "that within twenty miles of this

room there are eight million people living suburban lives" (Sampson, op. cit., p. 37).

5. Ibid., p. 43.

6. della Torre, op. cit., p. 56.

7. Quoted in Whitehead, op. cit., p. 27.

8. Wapshott and Brock, op. cit., p. 241.

9. Whitehead, op. cit., p. 281.

10. Margaret Drabble, *The Ice Age*, pp. 62–63.

11. Ian Bradley, *The English Middle Class Are Alive and Kicking*, pp. 160–161.

12. Quoted in Whitehead, op. cit., p. 216.

13. From Thatcher's 1968 speech to the Blackpool Conservative Party Conference. Quoted in Wapshott and Brock, op.cit., p.275.

14. Quoted in Whitehead, op. cit., p. 323.

15. Quoted in Riddell, op. cit., p. 232.

16. Quoted in Whitehead, op. cit., pp. 188–189.

17. Riddell, op. cit., p. 7.

18. Quoted in Whitehead, op. cit., p. 380.

19. Quoted in Keegan, op. cit.

20. *Crossbow* [magazine of the Tory Bow (reform) group], Autumn 1985, p. 6.

21. *New Statesman*, Dec. 13, 1985.

22. The number of millionaires in Britain tripled to 20,000 between the mid-1960s and mid-1980s, and a substantial percentage of them came from the working class *(Sunday Times,* Jan. 23, 1986).

23. *New Society*, Oct. 25, 1985.

24. *News of the World*, Feb. 9, 1986.

25. Riddell, op. cit., p. 165.

26. *Independent*, Jan. 22, 1987.

27. Bradley, op. cit., p. 228.

CHAPTER 2.
IRON IN THE SOUL.

1. Statistics on Britain's decline and failure to invest cited here and on subsequent pages found in Correlli Barnett, *The Audit of War*, p. 69, 92–93, 111; *New Society*, Oct. 4, 1984; and *News of the World*, Dec. 1, 1985. The Wolverhampton figures mentioned later come from *New Statesman*, April 25, 1986.

2. Barnett, op. cit., p. 97.

3. Peter Pagnamenta and Richard Overy, *All Our Working Lives*, p. 100.

4. Whitehead, op. cit., p. 374.

5. A number of sources have suggested that Britain's economic downturn was, if not exactly planned, permitted to happen. But it's a controversial point. Wapshott and Brock, op. cit., pp. 200–201, discuss the report of the Swiss monetarist. Riddell, op. cit., pp. 49–50, is the source of the Hoskyns quote, and mentions further a senior Treasury official who marvelled that "fear and anxiety" had done more for the economy than conciliation ever did (p. 78). Keegan, op. cit., p. 112, is the source of the comment from hard-right cabinet ministers (and others) about teaching Britain a lesson. Other writers, however, lean toward the conclusion that the crisis of 1979–81 was the result of incompetence and inexperience rather than design.

6. *Guardian*, Dec. 12, 1984.

7. In late 1987, a fatal fire in the King's Cross Station established just how deadly some of the London Underground's problems were.

8. The figures are cited in *The Times*, Jan. 24, 1987. Some other relevant facts: Less than 5 per cent of British telephones are connected to advanced digital exchanges, compared to about 50 per cent in France. Computer data can be transmitted in Britain over ordinary

telephones at 1,200 bits a second. In the U.S., it is "routinely" transmitted at 9,600 bits per second. *The Times* notes that Britain's telephone system is "firmly rooted in obsolete technology. ...Even when investment belatedly became available, there were delays in modernizing the network." *The Times* categorizes the service provided to ordinary customers in a word: "miserable." From my own experience as a British Telecom subscriber, I cannot help but concur.

9. The survey on food habits was reported in *The Listener*, Nov. 29, 1984.

10. Quote and all Bradford statistics from *District Trends*, City of Bradford Metropolitan Council, 1984.

11. *Wall Street Journal* (Europe), Nov. 11, 1986.

12. George Michael, the son of Greek Cypriot immigrants in North London, (real name Georgios Panayotou) and his partner, Andrew Ridgeley, constituted the astonishingly successful Wham! The two were unemployed 17-year-olds when the decade began, and like many other 1980s rock groups, they began writing songs and practising music under the "protection" of unemployment insurance.

13. *The Times*, Oct. 29, 1985.

14. *Observer*, Dec. 1, 1985. Ironically, Thatcher herself had used similar words to describe what it had cost her in her early political career to come to terms with the British establishment. When she dealt for the first time with the bureaucracy and problems at the Ministry of Education, she told a reporter, "Iron entered my soul" (Wapshott and Brock, op. cit., p. 105).

CHAPTER 3.
LOOK BACK WITHOUT ANGER.

1. della Torre, op. cit., p. 97.

2. Quoted in Whitehead, op. cit., p. 400.

3. *Spectator*, Feb. 22, 1986.

4. *Economist*, June 21, 1986.

5. *Spectator*, op. cit., Feb. 22, 1986.

6. *Sunday Express Magazine*, June 8, 1985.

7. Ann Barr and Peter York, *The Official Sloane Ranger Handbook*, p. 7.

8. Quoted in the *Observer*, June 22, 1986.

9. Quoted in the *Herald Tribune*, Jan. 17, 1986. David Puttnam led a group of advertising producers and video filmmakers into commercial film, helping to start a renaissance in the British film industry. The list of international film and television successes produced by Puttnam and his peers during the decade reads like a documentary of the 1980s: *Gandhi, The Killing Fields, A Room with a View, Brideshead Revisited.* Thirteen of Puttnam's seventeen films made money, and they earned four Academy Awards. Puttnam and his fellow commercial-minded producers sometimes had to overcome negative attitudes in their own industry. "A lot of my colleagues enjoy seeing a queue outside a cinema, but the idea of their film having been tailored for that queue is an ugly one to them," he said.

10. Much of the material in this section dealing with Britain's "angry" period is based on Brian Masters, *The Swinging Sixties*, and John Elsom, *Post-War British Theatre.*

11. Quoted in *City Limits*, June 5, 1986.

12. Quoted in the *Daily Mail*, June 19, 1986. The revived version of *The Entertainer* closed after a few performances. It seemed to illustrate the angry young

men's irrelevance to the 1980s world.
Osborne grumbled in another interview:
"Who would have thought the country
would have been taken over by the
worst of the lower-middle classes?"
13. Miller was in fact one of the first to
come to the defence of the word when a
pop musician uttered it blissfully on TV
in the 1960s.
14. I paid a personal visit to *Coronation
Street* in 1983. The actors and writers on
the show were immensely proud of their
contribution to modern British myth-
making. "The show reveals a Britain
that people would like to have again,
a place where people talk to each other
and are nosey about each other's
lives," said John Stevenson, a young
Manchester native who was then one
of the series' 10 scriptwriters. "People
would like their own streets to be
like this."
15. Richard Hoggart, *The Uses of
Literacy*, p. 338.

**CHAPTER 4.
LOVE ME DO.**

1. Many of the quotes and information
in this chapter are culled from newspaper reports and my notes taken at the
time. Thatcher's "shopkeeper" remark is
quoted in Whitehead, op. cit., p. 386.
2. This anecdote was told to thousands
of Conservatives attending their annual
party conference in October 1981 by
Freela Flather, a party delegate. The
crowd listened in incredulous silence,
and then gave her a spontaneous burst
of applause for her bravery in bringing it
up.
3. Powell's 1968 speech and the reaction
to it are recounted in Whitehead, op.
cit., pp. 35–36.
4. For Thatcher's speech and reaction,

see Whitehead, op. cit., p. 235.
5. *Youth Unemployment and the New
Poverty,* pamphlet summarizing Local
Authority Review and Framework for
Policy Development on Youth and
Youth Unemployment, Wolverhampton
Youth Review, June, 1985.
6. *The Times*, Sept. 1–3, 1986.
7. Quoted in the *Daily Telegraph*, June
17, 1986.
8. The "fear of crime" report was quoted
in the *Toronto Star*, Mar. 28, 1982. The
report, called "Self-Help in the Inner
City," was prepared by Barry Knight
and Ruth Hayes. Scotland Yard statistics
showed that violent crime increased
34 per cent between 1981 and 1982, but
in fact this was an increase from a
comfortably low base. And the only
categories of crime that actually showed
an increase were street robberies that
involved no violent assault, such as theft
from parked cars. Crimes in more violent categories — such as homicide,
rape, and fraud — were down. Subsequent studies over the years showed
little change. The only real increase in
British violence detected by one team of
researchers quoted by *The Economist* on
March 1, 1986, was in connection with
sport and leisure. (See later in this chapter.) The magazine noted that the
number of violent street disorders had
dropped this century, despite a population increase of 45 per cent between 1900
and 1975. "People are just less tolerant
of street violence than they used to be,"
The Economist suggested. The University of Reading professor is quoted in
The Times, May 9, 1986.
9. *Observer*, July 27, 1986.
10. Chesshyre article reprinted in the
Toronto *Globe and Mail* (courtesy
Observer Syndicate), Oct. 24, 1985.
11. Jeremy Seabrook comment,
Guardian, Sept. 23, 1985.

12. Quoted in the *Guardian*, July 1, 1986.

13. Quoted in *The Times*, Jan. 13, 1986.

14. For an excellent description of young Britons during the early days of the Victorian empire, see the first book of James (now Jan) Morris' trilogy, *Heaven's Command*.

15. *New Statesman*, Dec. 14, 1984.

CHAPTER 5.
JOHN BULL AND THE ARGIES.

1. Sources for the Commons debate, and most of the quoted material in this chapter, unless otherwise noted, come from my own file of newspaper clippings and my records and interviews from the period.

2. Anthony Barnett, *Iron Britannia*, p. 46.

3. James Morris, op. cit., p. 10.

4. Nott discussed the Falklands War and its relationship to Suez in an op-ed article in *The Times*, Nov. 6, 1986.

5. *London Evening Standard*, Apr. 6, 1982.

6. Quoted by Paolo Filo della Torre, op. cit., p. 95.

7. Max Hastings and Simon Jenkins, *The Battle for the Falklands*, pp. 388–389.

8. The complete text of Thatcher's "Falklands Factor" speech can be found in Barnett, op. cit., pp. 149–153.

CHAPTER 6.
THE WAR OF JENKINS' MOUTH.

1. Quoted in Asa Briggs, *A Social History of England*, p. 104. For a good account of the break with Rome and the rise of the English Reformation, see J.R.H. Moorman, *A History of the Church in England*, pp. 161–179. Moor-

man cites an earlier writer [F.M. Powicke, *The Reformation in England* (1941), pp. 1, 34] who suggested that the English Reformation, at least in its early stages, was a 'parliamentary transaction,' or an 'act of state,' more than a religious revolution.

2. *The Times*, Oct. 5, 1984. In 1960, more than two million Britons celebrated Anglican communion on Christmas Day. In 1982, the figure was less than 1.6 million, a drop made all the more noticeable by the increase in the general population.

3. Commercial buildings in London alone produced £20 million in 1985. The figures are quoted in *The Times*, Jan. 15, 1985, and Dec. 12, 1985.

4. *The Economist*, Apr. 2, 1983.

5. James Bellini, op. cit., p. 173.

6. The issue of ordination of women priests was still threatening to divide the church in 1986 and 1987. The apparent suicide of an Anglican cleric who had written a blistering critique of liberalism and the Archbishop's policies in late 1987 threw the war inside the Church into more painful relief.

7. Shortly before John Paul II became the first Roman Catholic pontiff to step on British soil, a public opinion poll indicated that nearly 50 per cent of Britons either disapproved of his mission or were suspicious of its purpose. The dangers of the visit could not escape any Briton reared in that country's tangled religious history.

8. *The Times*, Sept. 25, 1984.

9. Peter Wilsher, Donald Macintyre, Michael Jones, and the *Sunday Times* Insight team, in *Strike*, provide one of the better overall accounts of the miners' dispute and the leadup to it. They cite one 1983 postelection anecdote suggesting Thatcher knew what she would be up against. She called into her office

Peter Walker, then Agriculture minister and told him he was getting a new job. "I want you to go to Energy," she said. "We are going to have a miners' strike." 10. Mrs. Thatcher rewarded MacGregor with a knighthood in 1986.
11. The strike was never formally ended. Miners began trickling back to work in early 1984. The trickle became a flood by the spring, and the government could claim victory. The miners argue that they only returned to work to save their families further misery, while their refusal to sign a contract signified they had not buckled under to the Coal Board. In any case, it was effectively the end of an era in Britain. Trade union power never recovered from the shock. A new generation of union leaders was already looking for alternatives to mass industrial action. The 358-day struggle had cost the country more than the Falklands War: an estimated £7 billion. It also led to a major realignment of political power and started the first new thinking among unions for decades. The results of that re-examination were not obvious until years later, and they will be covered in Part IV.
12. MacGregor seemed the only one unmoved by the suggestion that he was too old and cranky to keep working. "My wife tells me the same thing," he wisecracked.
13. "The War of Jenkins' Mouth" was the creation of a witty, but unfortunately anonymous, headline writer in *Observer*, Apr. 14, 1985. It was a takeoff on the War of Jenkins' Ear (1739-1748), in which Britain went to war with Spain over the alleged maltreatment of a British seaman.
14. General Synod of the Church of England, Report of the Archbishop of Canterbury's Commission on Urban Priority Areas, *Faith in the City* (Church

House Publishing), 1985. The 398-page report is (along with the Scarman Report) one of the landmark social documents in postwar British history. It took two years to prepare and was produced by an 18-person commission drawn from trade unions, schools, parish churches, social work institutes, and universities. The commission was headed by Sir Richard O'Brien, a former chairman of the British Manpower Services Commission. The authors are unqualified in their attack on the abuses of a "free market economy" but they are no less scathing in their charge that Britons should take "collective responsibility" for the poverty in their midst — a comment pointedly overlooked by government critics.

CHAPTER 7.
THE COALBROOKDALE LEGACY.

1. The quotation from *Through the Looking-Glass* is cited by Geoffrey Beattie, *Survivors of Steel City*, (1986) p. 157. Although he uses it in a different context, his book, which centres on how a group of people in Sheffield survived the British depression of the 1980s, is a fascinating illustration of the concepts raised by many of the people in this chapter.
2. The "New Britons" study was reported by the *Guardian*, Feb. 7, 1986.
3. The steel workers went from 255,000 in 1970 to 166,000 in 1980. In 1983 it was chopped to 70,000. The origins of the term "Black Country" are unclear. Most people agree that it was popularized by Charles Dickens. The area had a stunning impact on all those who saw it. From Samuel Sidney in 1851 comes this morbid description: "In the Black Country...a perpetual twilight reigns during

the day, and during the night…the dark landscape [is lit] with a fiery glow. The pleasant green of pastures is almost unknown; the streams, in which no fishes swim, are black and unwholesome. …No buds are to be seen."

4. The duke politely refused to discuss how much he was worth. The estimate of the Grosvenor value I have used was made in 1981 by Simon Winchester, *Their Noble Lordships*, p. 256.

5. John Carvel, *Citizen Ken*, preface.

6. *The Times*, July 23, 1985.

7. *The Economist*, July 7, 1986.

8. *Observer*, Sept. 15, 1985.

9. Ranulph Fiennes quotes the British attaché in his own account of the Transglobe expedition, *To the Ends of the Earth*, p. 204.

10. *Journal of the Institute of Social Inventions*, 24 Abercorn Place, London NW8, various issues, 1986.

CHAPTER 8.
GOODBYE TO NANNY.

1. This figure includes middle-class recipients of child benefits and education grants, as well as the needy. A 1985 study of public employment in Western nations written by Professor Richard Rose, Director of the Centre for the Study of Public Policy at Strathclyde University, estimated that some 14 million Britons relied on pensions, unemployment assistance and other benefits alone. Yet despite such a high level of state-funded assistance, social workers and academics alike agreed that many people who were eligible did not even claim it. *Guardian*, Oct. 14, 1985.

2. An impressively strong case for the delusions under which the welfare state was created was made by Correlli Barnett, a Cambridge historian and author, in a provocative book, *The Audit of War: The Illusion and Reality of Britain as a Great Nation* (1986). I owe to his research much of the discussion in this chapter about the early years of the Beveridge report and its aftermath, including Churchill's initial opposition to it.

3. Barnett, op, cit., p. 304.

4. The *Britain 1987 Official Handbook* from the Central Office of Information, London (p. 133), lists planned social welfare spending as follows for 1986-87: health, £18.7 billion, social security, £43 billion, and additional personal social services spending, £3.2 billion.

5. *Financial Times*, March 26, 1987.

6. *Financial Times*, Nov. 5, 1986.

7. Ibid.

8. *New Society*, May 23, 1986.

9. Riddell, op. cit., p. 70. Riddell quotes OECD figures showing public spending in Britain rose less in real terms in 1981 and 1982 than in any of the other seven industrialized countries. Leaving out programs like defence and law and order, spending declined by nearly four per cent. On housing and environment, it was 16 per cent lower in real terms than in 1978-79. Riddell points out that these programs had been growing steadily in the 1960s and 1970s (p. 117).

10. David Howell, *Blind Victory*, p. 168.

11. Ibid., pp. 148, 185.

12. Ibid., p. 185.

13. Ibid., p. 67.

14. *The Economist*, Schools Brief, October 5, 1985.

15. *The Economist*, December 21, 1985.

16. *Privatization Worldwide*, Adam Smith Institute, 1986, p. 11.

17. Quoted in *International Herald Tribune*, March 27, 1985.

18. James Robertson, *Future Work*, p. 116.

19. Michael Ignatieff, *The Needs of Strangers*, p. 11.

CHAPTER 9.
ELECTRONIC CAPITALISTS.

1. Quoted in Sampson, op. cit., p. 364.
2. *International Herald Tribune*, Nov. 14, 1985.
3. From Sir James Goldsmith, *Gentrification or Growth: Cultural Causes of Economic Failure*, p. 3.
4. Segal Quince Wicksteed, *The Cambridge Phenomenon*, 1985, provides the statistical and analytical background for a study of the mushrooming of high-tech in the area around one of the world's oldest universities. Quote on p. 92.
5. Figures on the growth of Silicon Glen were provided by the Scottish Development Agency.
6. Tann was interviewed before the stock market collapse of October 1987. The subsequent financial problems have had their effect. High salaries have levelled off and there are fears for jobs. Still, most insiders in the City believe that the new environment created by the Big Bang will not be permanently affected.
7. Tom Lloyd, *Dinosaur and Co.*, p. 33.
8. Ibid., pp. 33-34.

CHAPTER 10.
A JOB IS A JOB.

1. *Guardian*, Dec. 12, 1984. Unless otherwise noted, figures and examples quoted in this chapter are gleaned from personal interviews and the British press over a four-year period, 1981-1985.
2. Additional figures in employment tell the story of a significant transformation in British working life. By 1985, white collar workers outnumbered blue-collar workers for the first time in Britain, and it happened in less than 10 years. In 1973, about 43 per cent of British workers were in non-manual jobs. In

1983, 52 per cent were. *New Society*, Nov. 8 1985.
3. From author's interview, 1984.
4. *Sunday Times*, Dec. 29, 1985.
5. *Sunday Times*, Jan. 12, 1986.

CHAPTER 11.
GREEN AND PLEASANT LAND.

1. *Guardian*, Jan. 9, 1986.
2. Figures quoted for 1985 in *The Times*, Feb. 4, 1986, from HMG Annual Review of Agriculture.
3. *Financial Times*, Feb. 8, 1986.
4. *Manchester Guardian Weekly*, July 19, 1987.
5. Shoard, *Theft of the Countryside*, 1980, quoted in Whitehead, *op. cit.*, p. 251.

CHAPTER 12.
DISTURBERS OF THE PEACE

1. Anthony Trollpe, *Can You Forgive Her?*, (1982 paperback edition), pp. 36-37.
2. The problem of secrecy in Britain would require a separate chapter. In 1987, the obsession of the Whitehall establishment with keeping its secrets extended to trying to prohibit the publication of an unauthorized book by a former British secret agent living in Australia. In the event, the attempt was unsuccessful, as British newspapers defied the courts to print excerpts.

Unofficial censorship is even more insidious. Civil servants have been prosecuted for leaking details of political debates, even though the government has regularly used the leak and the parliamentary lobby to relay information its wants made public. The controversial lobby system, in which a select group of reporters is given information on a non-attributable basis, was actually unmentionable in the press until recently.

The media, having long considered itself an arm of the Establishment, reflected a culture that assumed information was safer out of the hands of the "lower classes." For an excellent account by a journalist of the relationship between the British press and the political "disturbers" of the decade, see Mark Hollingsworth, *The Press and Political Dissent: A Question of Censorship*, 1986.

3. *Guardian*, Oct. 9, 1984.

4. The 1979 election represented the third consecutive election in which Labour's share of the vote fell below 40 per cent. Political analysts pointed out that the Conservatives had not so much won the election as Labour had lost it. In 1951, Labour had achieved more than 48 per cent. See David Butler and Dennis Kavanagh, *The British General Election of 1979*, 1980, pp. 338-340. For a comparison of election results in the 1980s, see below.

5. In 1974, 55 per cent of trade union members voted Labour. By 1987, only 42 per cent did.

6. Quoted in Whitehead, *op cit.*, p. 349.

7. *Ibid*, p. 49.

8. *Ibid*, p. 357.

9. For a fuller analysis of the early years of the SDP and its roots, see Ian Bradley, *Breaking the Mould? The Birth and Prospects of the Social Democratic Party*, 1981. I have also borrowed interviews with SDP leaders in this section from Anthony Sampson's *Changing Anatomy of Britain* and Phillip Whitehead.

10. The Dimbleby Lecture, Nov. 29, 1979, cited by Sampson, *op. cit.*, p. 35.

11. Superficially it was often hard to tell the two parties' supporters apart. I attended an SDP-Liberal ball one Christmas in an elegant hotel overlooking Hyde Park, with several close friends who were staunch Liberals. It might have been a meeting of Democrats in the United States or of Liberals in Canada. The guests chatting easily in their off-the-rack tuxedoes and evening dresses had an air of relaxed urbanity and classlessness I had rarely seen in other British political gatherings.

12. A study published by the *British Journal of Political Science* in 1987 finally demolished the charge that the "Falkland Factor" played the swing role in Thatcher's second victory. Cited in the *Independent*, June 12, 1987.

13. Having once compared the House of Commons to a "factory," Kinnock was not a strong favourite among his parliamentary colleagues. Most observers of the 1983 conference agree with Kinnock's own judgement that, were it not for the new electoral college, he would never have had a chance. See Robert Harris, *The Making of Neil Kinnock*.

14. Before I came to London in 1981, an expert on Europe from the Harvard University faculty told me, "The man you really want to meet is Neil Kinnock. No one knows him now, but he's going to be prime minister of Britain some day."

15. The worst crisis in Thatcher's first two terms came in 1986. Revelations of government efforts to intervene in the sale of Westland, a small Somerset-based helicopter manufacturer, produced the resignations of two ministers. Opinion polls at the height of the Westland Affair registered an astonishing 43 per cent who thought Thatcher should resign.

16. The political history of the decade could be summed up in a set of figures. Below are the results and voting percentages of the elections of 1979, 1983, and 1987:

Number of Seats/Share of Vote		
1979	**1983**	**1987**
Conservative 339/43.9%	397/43.5%	375/43.3%
Labour 268/37.0	209/28.3	229/31.5
Liberal 11/13.8	—	—
Alliance —	23/26.0	22/23.1

(Sources: Butler and Kavanagh, *op. cit.*, and *The Financial Times*, June 13, 1987.)

17. *Economist*, Dec. 21, 1985.

CHAPTER 13.
SMOKE AND MIRRORS.

1. From a mock advertisement entitled, "New History of Britain, Chapter XII, New Renaissance 1953-2000," and quoted in John Pearson, *The Selling of the Royal Family*, p. 70.

2. The poll on abolition of the monarchy has been cited many times in numerous places. The latest reference I have found for it is in the *New Statesman*, Oct. 25, 1985.

3. Talk for Channel 4 "Opinions" program reproduced in *New Society*, Aug. 2, 1985.

4. In 1986, the amount paid directly by the state for the upkeep of the "Queen's Household" was £3,976,200, roughly equivalent to what it was the year before. This does not include the cost of special items such as the royal yacht, airplanes of the Queen's Flight, or upkeep of the royal palaces, which are met by individual government departments. (Sources: *Britain 1986 Handbook*, prepared by the Central Office Information, and *The Daily Express*, April 20, 1986.)

As a matter of additional interest, the Queen is one of the richest, if not indeed the richest, women in the world. Her private wealth, including property around the world, art treasures, and homes, is said to be £4.5 billion, and her investments earn an estimated £700,000 a day. She pays no taxes.

5. *Daily Telegraph*, April 20, 1986.

6. *Pearson, op. cit.*, p. 264.

7. *International Herald Tribune*, Sept. 26, 1987.

8. Queen's travel statistics cited in *The Mail on Sunday*, April 20, 1986.

9. Poll cited in *The Times*, July 24, 1986.

10. Sampson, *op. cit.*, p. 7.

11. Ramphal interview in *The Times*, April 16, 1986.

12. Edward's comments may not have been completely innocent. Despite his personal remoteness, the prince was anxious to create an activist monarchy. There were rumours that a "king's party" had formed around the prince to take over the government if it proved too weak to withstand the pressures of economic crisis. Whether he encouraged such rumours or not, Edward certainly made no secret of his radical ideas. He had a vague concept of a populist throne with less overt ties to the religious hierarchy. Under his guidance, the House of Windsor might well have come to resemble the "bicycle-riding" monarchs of Scandinavia or might even have developed on the Spanish model, in which the monarch acted as a sort of governor-general between warring political camps. Years later, he admitted to a friend that he was even prepared to become "president" if Britain had abolished the monarchy. (For more information, see Frances Donaldson, *Edward*

VIII. The prince's desire to be president
is cited in a report on a book scheduled
for publication in 1987, Patrick
Howarth, *George VI – A Biography,*
quoted in a Reuters report, Oct. 9,
1987.)
13. *The Sunday Times,* Aug. 18, 1985.
14. A decade earlier, 86 per cent thought
the monarchy should continue. *The
Mail on Sunday,* March 23, 1986.

BIBLIOGRAPHY

Artley, Alexandra and John Martin Robinson. *The Official Georgian Handbook: A First Look at the Conservation Way of Life.* London: Ebury Press, 1985.

Barnett, Correlli. *The Audit of War: The Illusion and Reality of Britain as a Great Nation.* London: Macmillan, 1986.

Beattie, Geoffrey. *Survivors of Steel City: A Portrait of Sheffield.* London: Chatto and Windus, 1986.

Beer, Max. *A History of British Socialism.* Nottingham: Spokesman, 1984.

Bellini, James. *Rule Britannia? Who Rules Modern Britain: A Progress Report for Domesday 1986.* London: Sphere Books, 1981.

Blue Guide, England. London: Ernest Benn Ltd., 1980.

Blue Guide, London. London: Ernest Benn Ltd., 1978.

Bradley, Ian. *Breaking the Mould?: Birth and Prospects of the Social Democratic Party.* Oxford: Martin Robertson, 1981.

_____ . *The English Middle Classes are Alive and Kicking.* London: Collins, 1982.

Briggs, Asa. *Iron Bridge to Crystal Palace, Impact and Images of the Industrial Revolution.* London: Thames and Hudson (in collaboration with the Ironbridge Gorge Museum Trust), 1979.

_____ . *A Social History of England.* London: Weidenfeld & Nicholson, 1983.

Chapple, Frank. *Sparks Fly: A Trade Union Life.* London: Michael Joseph, 1984.

Cook, Chris and John Stevenson. *The Longman Handbook of Modern British History, 1714-1980.* London: Longman, 1983.

Dahrendorf, Ralf. *On Britain.* London: BBC, 1982.

Donaldson, Frances. *Edward VIII.* London: Weidenfeld & Nicholson, 1986.

Drabble, Margaret. *The Ice Age.* Harmondsworth: Penguin, 1985.

Eatwell, John. *Whatever Happened to Britain? The Economics of Decline.* London: Duckworth/BBC, 1982.

Elsom, John. *Post-War British Theatre.* Revised edition. London: Routledge and Kegan Paul, 1976.

Faith in the City — A Call for Action by Church and Nation: The Report of The Archbishop of Canterbury's commission on Urban Priority Areas. London: Church House Publishing, 1985.

Galbraith, John Kenneth. *The New Industrial State.* Harmondsworth: Penguin, 1985.

Handy, Charles. *The Future of Work: A Guide to a Changing Society.* Oxford: Basil Blackwell, 1984.

Harris, Robert. *The Making of Neil Kinnock.* London: Faber & Faber, 1984.

Hastings, Max and Simon Jenkins. *The Battle for the Falklands.* London: Michael Joseph, 1983.

Hoggart, Richard. *The Uses of Literacy.* London: Penguin, 1984. First published in 1957 by Chatto & Windus.

Hollingsworth, Mark. *The Press and Political Dissent: A Question of Censorship.* London: Pluto Press, 1986.

Howell, David. *Blind Victory: A Study in Income, Wealth and Power.* London: Hamish Hamilton, 1986.

Ignatieff, Michael. *The Needs of Strangers.* London: Chatto & Windus, 1984.

James, Henry. *English Hours.* Oxford: Oxford University Press, 1981.

Keegan, William. *Mrs. Thatcher's Economic Experiment.* Revised edition. Harmondsworth: Penguin, 1984.

Lacey, Robert. *Aristocrats.* London: Hutchison/BBC, 1983.

BIBLIOGRAPHY

Lambert, Angela. *Unquiet Souls: Indian Summer of the British Aristocracy*. London: Macmillan, 1984.

Lloyd, Tom. *Dinosaur and Co.: Studies in Corporate Evolution*. London: Penguin, 1986.

Masters, Brian. *The Swinging Sixties*. London: Constable, 1985.

Monson, Nicholas and Debra Scott. *The Nouveaux Pauvres, A Guide to Downward Mobility*. London: Quartet Books, 1984.

Pagnamenta, Peter and Richard Overy. *All Our Working Lives*. London: BBC, 1984.

Pearson, John. *The Selling of the Royal Family, The Mystique of the British Monarchy*. New York: Simon & Schuster, 1986.

Pym, Francis. *The Politics of Consent*. Revised edition. London: Sphere Books, 1985.

Riddell, P. *The Thatcher Government*. Oxford: Martin Robertson, 1983.

Robertson, James. *Future Work: Jobs, Self-employment and Leisure After the Industrial Age*. Aldershot: M.T. Smith, 1985.

Sampson, Anthony. *The Changing Anatomy of Britain*. London: Hodder & Stoughton, 1983.

Strike: 358 Days That Shook the Nation. Sunday Times Insight Team. London: Hodder and Stoughton, 1985.

Thatcher, Carol. *Diary of an Election*. London: Sidgwick & Jackson, 1983.

Torre, Paolo Filo Della. *Viva Britannia: Mrs. Thatcher's Britain*. London: Sidgwick & Jackson, 1985.

Townsend, Sue. *The Growing Pains of Adrian Mole*. London: Methuen, 1984.

Trollope, Anthony. *Can You Forgive Her?*. Oxford: Oxford University Press, 1982. First published in 1864.

Wapshott, Nicholas; Brock, George. *Thatcher*. London: Futura, 1983.

Whitehead, Philip. *The Writing on the Wall, Britain in the Seventies*. London: Michael Joseph, 1985.

Wiener, Martin J. *English Culture and the Decline of the Industrial Spirit 1850-1980*. London: Penguin, 1985.

Winchester, Simon. *Their Noble Lordships: The Hereditary Peerage Today*. London: Faber & Faber, 1981.

York, Peter and Ann Barr. *"Harpers and Queen" Official Sloane Ranger Handbook*. London: Ebury Press, 1982.

INDEX

INDEX